A History of Alternative
Dispute Resolution

Jerome T. Barrett,
with Joseph P. Barrett

A History of Alternative Dispute Resolution

The Story of a Political, Cultural, and Social Movement

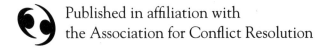

Published in affiliation with
the Association for Conflict Resolution

JOSSEY-BASS
A Wiley Imprint
www.josseybass.com

Published by Jossey-Bass
A Wiley Imprint
989 Market Street, San Francisco, CA 94103-1741   www.josseybass.com

Jossey-Bass books and products are available through most bookstores. To contact Jossey-Bass directly call our Customer Care Department within the U.S. at 800-956-7739, outside the U.S. at 317-572-3986, or fax 317-572-4002.

Jossey-Bass also publishes its books in a variety of electronic formats. Some content that appears in print may not be available in electronic books.

Library of Congress Cataloging-in-Publication Data

Barrett, Jerome T.
  A history of alternative dispute resolution : the story of a political, cultural, and social movement / Jerome T. Barrett, Joseph P. Barrett ; foreword by William J. Usery.— 1st ed.
     p. cm.
  Includes bibliographical references and index.
  ISBN 0-7879-6796-3 (alk. paper)
  1. Dispute resolution (Law)—United States—History. 2. Dispute resolution (Law)—History. I. Barrett, Joseph P. II. Title.
  KF9084.B37 2004
  347.73'9—dc22
                                    2004003238

Printed in the United States of America
FIRST EDITION
HB Printing   10 9 8 7 6 5 4 3 2 1

Contents

Foreword

I am pleased to have the opportunity to write this Foreword for Jerry Barrett's much-needed book on the history of alternative dispute resolution (ADR).

I met Jerry Barrett over thirty years ago, when I served as President Nixon's assistant secretary of labor. At that time, Jerry headed a new office providing advice to state and local governments and their unions on establishing procedures for resolving disputes. When I became national director of the Federal Mediation and Conciliation Service (FMCS) in 1973, I asked him to leave the Department of Labor and head the newly created Office of Technical Assistance at FMCS. In that capacity, he managed mediator training, preventive mediation, and the start of FMCS work outside the labor-management field.

Jerry has outstanding credentials to present this history of ADR. Having worked as mediator, arbitrator, and trainer—often on the cutting edge of new approaches to conflict resolution—he knows the field as a practitioner. On the scholarly side, he has armed himself with several degrees and displayed a curiosity about the past by writing extensively as historian of FMCS and its predecessor organization, the U.S. Conciliation Service, and the Society of Professionals in Dispute Resolution.

It is actually surprising that an ADR history book of this kind was not written much earlier, given the growth of ADR in the past twenty years and the extraordinary growth in the number of ADR practitioners and users in the United States and elsewhere. This publication is long overdue.

Having spent all of my adult life as a negotiator, mediator, and arbitrator, I found this book most informative and useful, because it presents the centuries-long ADR history that I have been a part of without knowing it. In that respect, I am sure I am no different from many other ADR practitioners in lacking knowledge of the origins of the profession in which we justifiably take great pride. While much has been written in the past twenty years describing and explaining ADR, no other book has connected the ADR work of the twenty-first century with that of previous centuries.

Readers can try to link their current ADR practice to that of ancient practitioners, such as an ancient Phoenician negotiating an agreement in the eastern Mediterranean in 700 B.C., or a Chinese mediator practicing his art in the Western Zhou Dynasty 2,000 years ago, or a Panch (arbitrator) making binding arbitration awards 2,500 years ago in India. This book presents numerous other examples displaying the rich history with which today's ADR practitioners and users are linked.

Readers will enjoy ADR examples from early American history: Thomas Jefferson mediating the relocation of the nation's capital to the Potomac River, George Washington including an arbitration clause in his will, and Lewis and Clark's ironic horse negotiations with Native Americans.

Some ADR practitioners may believe ADR history began the day they discovered it, others mark its beginning as the 1976 Pound Conference, when lawyers turned their attention to ADR as legal reform. Still others see the start in the civil-rights protests of the 1960s. As former director of FMCS and former secretary of labor, I know that labor-management negotiations, mediation, and arbitration can trace their roots at least as far back as the creation of the U.S. Conciliation Service (USCS) during the Wilson administration.

This book identifies much deeper roots. By researching and identifying the precursors of ADR, the author traces ADR roots over two thousand years.

Playing up the human-interest side of the ADR story, the book identifies ADR's unsung heroes—Benjamin Franklin, the Great

Compromiser Henry Clay, Howard University founder General Oliver Howard, presidential assistants Colonel Edward House and Dr. John Steelman, and others.

With war, terrorism, and violence currently dominating media attention, this book provides an important reminder that peaceful ways of resolving conflict have existed throughout human history. From the Kalahari Bushmen and Hawaiian Polynesians to the formation of the United Nations, both traditional and developed societies have fashioned peaceful practices for resolving their conflicts.

The wealth of information in this very readable book provides useful references for making a speech on ADR or offering cogent illustrations in the midst of a dispute. It is a valuable addition to the library of all ADR practitioners and users.

I strongly recommend this enlightening history of ADR to both practitioners and scholars of the field, and anyone with an interest in finding new and better ways to work out our differences.

William J. Usery
Secretary of Labor, 1976–1977

This book is dedicated to the unsung heroes of ADR who have expanded our options for achieving a more peaceful and just future.

Preface

From the beginning of time, there have been those who sought to exploit their advantages—physical, financial, familial, technological—to dominate others. Kings and dictators, robber barons, and Enron executives all have benefited from a rigged system that allowed them to ignore the good of others.

But there have also always been those who have appealed to higher ideals—fairness, common interests, the greater good, a sense of community—to put aside power and try to work out differences without resorting to fighting. From the Kalahari Bushmen, who emphasize group harmony over discord, to the ancient Athenians, who appointed all men during their sixtieth year as "arbitrators," and on to the "win-win" negotiators of today, there is a long history of those who have attempted to resolve disputes peacefully and to the benefit of all.

This book is about all of these unsung heroes who have struggled to find a level playing field that allows the weak and strong to address their differences based on rights and interests. The book describes alternative paradigms for how disputes can be resolved, paradigms largely ignored and even denigrated, by the powerful who focused exclusively on their own rights and interests.

The subject of this book is the history of alternative dispute resolution (ADR), a movement born of the social unrest—and progress—of the 1960s. Many authors trace ADR's roots to the tumult of that period and stop there. I strongly argue that the movement's roots are much deeper and go back much further.

❖

I have been a practitioner of ADR for more than forty years. I have seen ADR work in labor-management, civil rights, and community disputes, and I have helped spread it to a dozen countries. Starting with the 1960s, some of this history is my own. But I have also long been fascinated by the history of the processes that came before ADR flowered in the 1960s, beginning with some writing I have done on the history of the Federal Mediation and Conciliation Service and its predecessor, the U.S. Conciliation Service. This book seeks to capture even earlier history. It looks for the roots of the ADR processes as it traces the parallel histories of what I call ADR precursors: negotiation, arbitration, and mediation. Before we can understand how ADR came about, we must first understand what came before it. Before we can understand where to take ADR from here, we must first understand the obstacles faced by those who came before us.

In some ways, ADR is defined by what it is not. It is an alternative to solving problems by power, the courts, violence, or any other forum in which one party's inherent advantages rule out a fair settlement. It can be applied to any problem between individuals, groups, or nations, from labor strife to trade issues to marital discord. In its purest form, it seeks to get beyond the cloud of the present difficulties and resolve matters in a way that does not just stop the fighting but allows the participants to build a better relationship for the future.

The social and political environment in any given period provides both the need and opportunity for ADR. Here are five illustrations:

• On the islands of ancient Greece, disputes between city-states over property or money could quickly boil over into warfare. For this reason, smaller islands often appealed to more powerful city-states to arbitrate their disputes. Often these decisions would be "published" by inscribing them on the walls and pillars of the famous temples of Delphi and elsewhere, placing ADR at the very foundation of Western civilization.

- With their own courts outlawed by Rome and later the Christian-dominated Middle Ages, Jews developed a system resembling arbitration to handle disputes within their community. In Jewish tradition and law, the concept of compromise and dispute resolution was highly valued, a further encouragement of negotiations and mediation.

- As the railroads grew in importance to the U.S. economy in the late 1800s, Congress passed a number of laws dealing with employment issues exclusively in that industry. When those laws failed to provide a process to resolve disputes on a continuing basis, railroad unions and management developed their own bill and persuaded Congress to pass the Railway Labor Act of 1926. Working together, labor and management were able to create their own level playing field, with a professional staff at their service, greatly reducing strife in this vital industry.

- The Great Depression and high unemployment of the 1930s resulted in great hardship, protests, and riots. In response, Congress passed the National Labor Relations Act, guaranteeing the rights of workers and providing conflict resolution processes. The number of conciliators already available in the Department of Labor was greatly expanded to deal with the increased number of unions attempting to negotiate collective bargaining agreements.

- The conflicts caused by the civil rights movement, the Vietnam War protests, and the cultural revolution of the 1960s nudged both private sector and governmental action to encourage peaceful conflict revolution. The Civil Rights Act of 1964 created the Community Relations Service with full-time conciliators to provide services in community conflicts. The Ford Foundation funded the National Center for Dispute Settlement in Washington, D.C., and the Center for Mediation and Conflict Resolution in New York. Both centers experimented with using the labor-management dispute settlement process of mediation and arbitration in community conflicts.

A strong component of the ADR story, especially in the United States, is expansion of rights to more and more groups. Up to the nineteenth century, rights were essentially limited to white male property owners. Gradually, this changed as workers, women, and blacks and eventually other minorities won increased recognition. Although the story of ADR begins with efforts at resolving conflicts between the powerful—businesses, governments, and the like—ADR would truly flourish when it was applied to disputes affecting the groups that had been traditionally excluded from processes that allowed them to get a fair hearing.

This book examines these developments in the history of ADR and identifies the movement's unsung heroes and the conditions favorable to ADR. The story begins with the roots of ADR from prehistoric times to the era of the European law merchant. Next, Chapter Two traces the history of ADR in diplomacy. Then we turn to ADR in early America in Chapter Three. Chapter Four discusses how the Civil War shows the limits and the promise of ADR. Chapter Five traces the history of ADR in business settings. The rest of the book explores the history of ADR in the United States in the twentieth century, from the early struggles for worker rights that first opened up the possibility of ADR use, through expansion of ADR to other disputes, including the civil rights movement, and on to the flowering of ADR in the 1980s and 1990s. The final chapter focuses on ADR in the twenty-first century—both the challenges it faces and its vast potential.

This may seem like a bad time to talk about solving problems peacefully. The United States has adopted an our-way-or-the-highway foreign policy. Large companies use the continuing threat of competition as a club to beat back employee gains at the bargaining table. The greed of corporate executives has been exposed in a series of scandals. But there are also strong signs of hope. Schools across the country are teaching students how to resolve their differences amicably. ADR practitioners are spreading their message and working through problems on the job site, in city governments, and even in the home.

No matter how thorny the dispute, how dark the clouds of international conflict, this book demonstrates that ADR has worked and can work even better in the future.

Acknowledgments

For a number of years, I thought about writing a book on alternative dispute resolution in labor-management disputes focused on the Federal Mediation and Conciliation Service and the U.S. Conciliation Service. Unable to find an interested publisher, I wrote a number of papers and articles on the subject. As labor-management disputes declined in number and impact and ADR continued to expand in other arenas, the prospects for the book that I wanted to write declined further. I explained my dilemma to Bill Breslin, managing editor of the *Negotiation Journal*. He suggested that I contact Alan Rinzler of Jossey-Bass, and the rest is history.

Writing this book was an amazing experience: challenging, discouraging, exhilarating, overwhelming, exhausting, satisfying, all-consuming, and more. Given the nature of this book—covering the broad field that ADR has become in the past forty years and the historic precursors of ADR—help was crucial. Some of those listed below offered their help and were aware they were helping. Others helped by just talking with me or exchanging e-mails with me, maybe unaware they were helping. The valuable writings of others are listed in the bibliography. To each, I offer my sincere appreciation and gratitude. I could not have done it without their help:

Peter S. Adler
Elham Atashi
Margery Baker
Lori M. Barrett
Robert C. Barrett

Juliana E. Birkhoff
Frank Blechman
J. William Breslin
Thomas R. Colosi
Gerald W. Cormick

John T. Dunlop
Thomas Dunn
Nick Fidandis
Connie Gunkel
Hank Guzda
Jack Hanna
Phil Harter
Doug Henning
Kevin Jessar
William Kimme
Deborah S. Laufer
Fran Leonard
Peter R. Maida
Louis J. Manchise
Bruce Meyerson
Linda S. Neighborgall

Richard Peloquin
Charles Pou, Jr.
James F. Power
Joseph Reres
Mary Roe
Donald T. Saposnek
Dennis L. Sharp
Ibrahim Sharqieh
Margaret L. Shaw
Mike Snider
David F. Snyder
John Stepp
Rose Stoller
John Truesdale
Wallace Warfield
Arnold M. Zack

While expressing my thanks for their help, I also want to relieve them of any responsibility for errors, omissions, or misstatements. I accept responsibility for any such shortcomings.

I especially appreciated the financial assistance of the Friends of FMCS History and the Hewlett Foundation, since their support paid the rent on the USCS/FMCS Archive, which I established in Falls Church, Virginia, and for some research assistance. Thanks to my sons Tom and Steve, who have been the two most generous contributors to the Friends of FMCS History.

A very special thanks to Rose, my wife and partner, who has always supported my undertakings, large and small, wise and otherwise, from our first meeting more than fifty-five years ago. I promise, Rose, that we will catch up on the movies we missed while I frowned at the computer screen and scowled at my notes on a napkin written when I should have been listening.

Other family members sacrificed for this book also. My son John helped me at a crucial time after I broke my arm in February 2003. John flew from his home in Salt Lake City and helped for ten days by substituting for my single-finger, broken-arm typing. More important, he gave me much-needed encouragement when a deadline was looming, and I was feeling the need for a fresh start on the early chapters. He helped me through that period before returning to Salt Lake.

John's sixteen-year-old son, Nick, upon seeing a rough draft of an early chapter, remarked to his dad, "Grandpa has a lot of work to do." His dad and grandpa both agreed. My son Joe's help made finishing the book by the deadline possible, and it produced a much better book than I could have done alone. Joe devoted so much time in the past few months from his busy schedule of work, family, and a dog that his six-year-old son Henry complained about "Grandpa's dumb book," which kept his dad at the computer rather than playing with him.

Joe is a tenacious researcher and great writer. He can convert an awkward sentence or paragraph without losing facts or intent, and he can find where I buried my lead five paragraphs into a chapter. He can find obscure facts that eluded me.

The most polite editor I have ever encountered, Joe assured me he wasn't just helping out his old dad; he was enjoying the experience of our working together. That matches my experience in working with him. For me, it was the part-time writer getting to see up close how a pro puts a story together. It also involved the added satisfaction of having known the pro before he was a story. He told his mom that kismet best described our partnership, bringing together his journalistic and academic work with my experience.

A word of thanks is due to my son Bob, whose long-time devotion to minority rights has helped me focus on the significance of expanding rights to the growth of ADR.

Thanks also to my long-time friend Hugh D. Jascourt, with whom I have collaborated on other projects. Hugh helped with his dogged determination in tracking down needed facts, sources, and other data.

I dedicate this book to ADR's unsung heroes, who, in both ancient and modern times, appealed to better human inclinations

with fair and balanced processes, eschewing the powerful entice-
ments of war, aggression, and power-based advantage taking.
Although their likeness is not displayed heroically on horseback in
a Washington, D.C., traffic circle, they have shown us a better way,
and they deserve high honor and our lasting appreciation.

Jerome T. Barrett
Falls Church, Virginia

List of Acronyms

AAA	American Arbitration Association
ABA	American Bar Association
ABA/CEELI	American Bar Association/Central and Eastern European Legal Initiative
ACR	Association of Conflict Resolution
ACUS	Administrative Conference of the United States
ADR	Alternative dispute resolution
ADRA	Administrative Dispute Resolution Act
AFL	American Federation of Labor
AFL-CIO	American Federation of Labor–Congress of Industrial Organizations
AFM	Academy of Family Mediation
AIM	American Indian Movement
ALMA	Association of Labor Mediation Agencies
ALRA	Association of Labor Relations Agencies
BIA	Bureau of Indian Affairs
BOI	Board of inquiry
CC	Consensus Councils
CJRA	Civil Justice Reform Act
CMCR	Center for Mediation and Conflict Resolution
CPR	Center for Public Resources
CREnet	Conflict Resolution Education Network
CRNC	Conflict Resolution Network Canada
CRS	Community Relations Service
CPRED	Consortium for Peace Research, Education and Development
EEOC	Equal Employment Opportunity Commission

ENA	Experimental negotiating agreement
EPA	Environmental Protection Agency
FAA	Federal Aviation Administration
FAN	Federal ADR Network
FMCS	Federal Mediation and Conciliation Service
ICAR	Institute for Conflict Analysis and Resolution
IDEA	Individuals with Disabilities Education Act
IDRS	Indian Dispute Resolution Service
JAMS	Judicial Arbitration and Mediation Service
MED-ARB	Mediation-arbitration
NAA	National Academy of Arbitrators
NAFCM	National Association for Community Mediation
NAHB	National Association of Home Builders
NCDS	National Center for Dispute Settlement
NCPCR	National Conference on Peacemaking and Conflict Resolution
NIDR	National Institute of Dispute Resolution
NLRA	National Labor Relations Act
NLRB	National Labor Relations Board
NMB	National Mediation Board
OD	Organizational development
ODR	Online Dispute Resolution
OFPR	Office of Federal Procurement Policy
P.A.S.T.	Principles, Assumptions, Steps and Techniques
PATCO	Professional Air Traffic Controllers Organization
PAU	Pan American Union
PCP	Public Conversation Project
PIC	Partners in Change
PON	Program on Negotiation
RegNeg	Regulatory Negotiations (also called negotiated rulemaking)
SCG	Search for Common Ground
SLC	Southern Law Center
SPIDR	Society of Professionals in Dispute Resolution
TAGS	Technology Assisted Group Solutions

TRC	Truth and Reconciliation Commission
UCOA	University and College Ombuds Association
UMA	Uniform Mediation Act
USAID	United States Agency for International Development
USAO	United States Association of Ombudsmen
USCS	U.S. Conciliation Service
VOMA	Victim Offender Mediation Association
WLB	War Labor Board

ADR Timeline

1800 B.C.	Mari Kingdom (in modern Syria) uses mediation and arbitration in dispute with other kingdoms.
1400 B.C.	Ancient Egyptian Amarna system of international relations uses diplomacy.
1200–900 B.C.	Phoenicians (in the eastern Mediterranean) practice entrepreneurship and negotiations.
960 B.C.	Israel's King Solomon arbitrates dispute over baby by threatening to split the child.
700 B.C.	Rhodian Sea Law codifies traditional rules for determining liability for ship cargo losses and dispute resolution.
500 B.C.	Arbitration, called *Panchayat*, used in India.
400 B.C.	Greeks use public arbitrator in city-states. Arbitration decisions between city-state "published" on temple columns.
300 B.C.	Aristotle praises arbitration over courts.
100 B.C.	Western Zhou Dynasty establishes post of mediator.
452 A.D.	As Attila the Hun destroyed city after city in his sweep across Europe, Pope Leo the Great successfully negotiates to spare the city of Ravenna, Rome's western capital.
1000	European law merchant used in marketplaces.
1263	King Alfonso the Wise of Spain directs the use of binding arbitration with the publication of *Siete Partides*.

1400	Venice establishes first overseas diplomatic offices.
1632	Irish Arbitration Law provides statutory basis for arbitration.
1648	Count Maximilian mediates an end to the Thirty Years War for the Holy Roman Empire, establishing contours of Europe for a century.
1624–1664	During Dutch colonial period, commercial arbitration in wide use in New York City.
1664–1776	In British colonial period, commercial arbitration use continues.
1750s	Benjamin Franklin, as Pennsylvania's Indian commissioner, reports learning persuasion, compromise, and consensus building from Native Americans. He also prints some of their peace documents.
1770	George Washington places arbitration clause in his will.
1776–1785	Benjamin Franklin, John Adams, and Thomas Jefferson negotiate in Europe on behalf of the weak United States, establishing a diplomatic history for the young nation.
1775–1860	From the Continental Congress to Lincoln's inaugural, repeated negotiations and compromises reach temporary solutions to the slavery issue.
1790	Thomas Jefferson mediates between Treasury Secretary Alexander Hamilton and Congressman James Madison, establishing the U.S. capital at Washington, D.C., and creating the national debt.
1865	Generals Lee and Grant negotiate the terms of the South's surrender, ending the Civil War.
1866	General Howard institutes arbitration in employment agreements between former slaves and former owners.

1888	Arbitration Act passed. Probably the first ADR statute in the United States providing voluntary arbitration and ad hoc commissions to investigate the cause of specific railway labor disputes.
1902	President Teddy Roosevelt mediates a long anthracite coal strike.
1906	Teddy Roosevelt mediates peace agreement ending the Russo-Japanese War, earning him the Nobel Peace Prize.
1913	Department of Labor created and mediates first labor dispute; mediates thirty-three disputes in its first year.
1914–1918	World War I uses ADR process to resolve labor disputes and establish labor agreements to aid war effort. Unions experience substantial growth. All wartime arrangements end with the peace in Europe.
1917	U.S. Conciliation Service created with permanent staff to mediate labor disputes.
1920	New York state passes first modern arbitration law; within five years, fifteen other states would follow.
1920s	Aggressive employer tactics and a compliant government reduce collective bargaining and union membership.
1926	American Arbitration Association created from merger of an arbitration foundation and society.
1926	Railway Labor Act is passed after labor and management create a draft that both can support.
1932	Norris-La Guardia Act limits injunctions stopping union activities.
1935	National Labor Relations Act creates employee and union rights and prohibits antiunion practices of employers.
1942	War Labor Board created; uses ADR.
1945–1946	Most strikes ever in a single year.

1947	Taft-Hartley Act creates Federal Mediation and Conciliation Service, prohibits some union activities, and establishes ADR for national emergency disputes.
1962	President Kennedy's Executive Order 10988 required federal agencies to engage in collective bargaining with unionized employees, starting a movement toward public employment unionization at all levels of government.
1962	Steel Trilogy: U.S. Supreme Court recognizes labor arbitrators' expertise as final authority.
1965	Civil Rights Act protects minority rights and creates Community Relations Service to conciliate civil rights disputes.
1968	National Advisory Commission on Civil Disorder (Kerner Commission) reports the need for major social and legal changes to avoid a dangerous split in U.S. society.
1968	Ford Foundation creates National Center for Dispute Settlement and Center for Mediation and Conflict Resolution to apply labor-management ADR to civil rights, campus, and community disputes.
1969	President Nixon's Executive Order 11491 expands Kennedy's executive order on federal employment relations.
1972	Society of Professionals in Dispute Resolution (SPIDR) created as membership organization for all ADR practitioners. It would merge to become the Association of Conflict Resolution in the late 1990s.
1973	First environmental mediation: Snoqualmie River Dam project in Washington State.
1973	Prisoner grievance procedure in New York and California begins with nonbinding arbitration.

1974	Federal Mediation and Conciliation Service expands mission statement beyond labor-management.
1975	Collective bargaining honored with first-class postage stamp, first ADR process so honored.
1975	American Arbitration Association commits to new areas of ADR by moving experimental programs handled by the National Center for Dispute Settlement into AAA proper.
1976	Pound Conference promotes legal reform by encouraging ADR processes, including the multidoor courthouse.
1978	Camp David Accords result in Israeli-Palestinian agreement, with President Carter using single text negotiation process.
1979	Judicial Arbitration and Mediation Service established.
1981	*Getting to Yes* published, popularizing interest-based negotiations.
1981	Institute of Conflict Analysis and Resolution established at George Mason University.
1981	Air traffic controller strikers replaced by the government, subsequently labeled the beginning of the decline of the labor movement and collective bargaining.
1982	Academy of Family Mediators founded.
1982	Former President Carter establishes the Carter Center in Atlanta to, among other things, use ADR in international disputes.
1983	Program on Negotiation officially established at Harvard University.
1983	National Institute for Dispute Resolution established to encourage ADR with foundation funds.

1983	Federal Aviation Administration becomes first federal agency to use negotiations to establish rules (RegNeg).
1984	Hewlett Foundation begins major funding for ADR.
1985	National Institute of Dispute Resolution funds pilot programs to encourage state governments to use ADR.
1987	Administrative Conference of the United States sponsors the Colloquium on Improving Dispute Resolution: Options for the Federal Government, and issues the *Sourcebook: Federal Agency Use of Alternative Means of Dispute Resolution*.
1989	Public Conversation Project begins, followed shortly by the Consensus Councils, which use comprehensive consensus processes to address public issues.
1990	Negotiated Rulemaking Act directs federal regulatory agencies to use consensus building and negotiation to create administrative rules.
1990	Administrative Dispute Resolution Act directs federal agencies to expand use of ADR.
1990	Civil Justice Reform Act initiates experiments to reform the federal courts with focus on ADR use.
1993	President Clinton issues Executive Order 12871 promoting partnership between federal agencies and their unionized employees, and the use of interest-based negotiations between them.
1995	Martindale-Hubble publishes the *Dispute Resolution Directory*, a comprehensive directory on ADR.
2000–2001	*U.S.* v. *Microsoft* antitrust case mediation effort.

A History of Alternative
Dispute Resolution

Chapter One

The Roots of ADR

The Deciding Stone to the European Law Merchant

Two men glare at each other. Long-haired and bearded, their fur garments oily from use, they hold gnarled clubs loosely at their sides. Emotions have been building since the rainy season started and the river overflowed. Who will be forced to brave the swollen river to hunt, and who will hunt near their village? Today it will be decided. With war cries, the disputants raise their clubs and begin to circle. Suddenly an old man appears, shouting: "Behold, the Deciding Stone!" The two men stop in midstride. The old man says, "Ush, the smooth side is yours; Ore, the rough side is yours." The pair hesitate, looking angrily at each other and at the old man, and finally they nod in agreement. With all his might, the old man throws the stone into the air. Their heads turn to the sky as they watch the stone turn over and over.

This imagined story of prehistoric times illustrates that while humans have always had the tendency to solve their differences by fighting, they also have recognized the benefits of settling matters peacefully by flipping a coin or some other way. This search for alternatives to violence gave birth to the precursors of alternative dispute resolution (ADR).

The most basic form of ADR is negotiation: at its core, two people simply talk about a problem and attempt to reach a resolution both can accept. It follows that mediation started when two negotiators, realizing they needed help in this process, accepted the intervention of a third person. If the third party was asked to make a decision or placed the decision in the hands of some arbitrary mechanism, the process was arbitration. Other methods followed:

When the third party undertook an investigation that helped bring the matter to closure, this was fact finding. If the matter is brought before the community and all members had to be satisfied with the outcome, we today call that process consensus building.

ADR is often thought of as a new way of resolving disputes. In fact, its roots run deep in human history, and they have long played a crucial role in cultures across the globe.

ADR in Traditional Societies

To trace the roots of ADR, we can turn to anthropological and sociological studies of traditional societies for a glimpse of some of the ways early humans may have resolved disputes without the use of fists, clubs, or poison arrows. Many of these ways of resolving conflicts are starkly alien to our Western way of looking at the world. Nevertheless, they have much to teach us about the utility of conflict in airing the disagreements of everyday life and how to use them as opportunities to deepen relationships and achieve lasting harmony.

The Bushmen of Kalahari

William Ury and others have written extensively about the Bushmen of the Kalahari, a traditional people whose sophisticated system for resolving disputes in many ways puts modern society to shame. The Bushmen are hunter-gatherers living in a large, arid plain in Namibia and Botswana. Despite the encroachment of agrarian people, the Bushmen have largely stuck to their traditional ways of life, including a way of settling disputes that avoids fighting and the courts.

The Bushmen are far from a passive people. Rivalries over mates, food, and land are common. But when a dispute arises, they are slow to fight and quick to find others who will intercede. When two people have a problem, they bring others around to hear out both sides. If things get testy, some members of the tribe are appointed to hide the hunters' poison arrows—an early form of gun control. If small-scale intervention fails, the whole group is brought into the process. "When a serious problem comes up," writes Ury (2002), "everyone sits down—all the men, all the women—and they talk, and they talk and they talk. Each person has a chance to have his or her say. It may take two or three days. This open and inclusive process continues until the dispute is literally talked out" (p. 40). The processes involved here include mediation and consensus building.

Hawaiian Islanders

Hawaiian islanders of Polynesian ancestry use their own traditional system for resolving disputes amicably. The practice, known as ho'oponopono, involves a family's coming together to discuss interpersonal problems under the guidance of a leader. The common translation of the term is to "set things right" on both a spiritual and interpersonal level. The leader of the session is someone both sides look to with respect. He or she leads the session and acts as mediator. To avoid hard feelings, all discussion is directed toward the leader rather than directly between the disputing parties. The leader opens the session with a prayer, asks questions of the participants, and at times will call for a moment of silence when tempers are running hot or one side is refusing to listen to the other (Boggs and Chun, 1990). After hearing out both sides and attempting to get at the heart of the dispute, the leader works to bring about reconciliation.

The Kpelle of Central Liberia

The Kpelle people of central Liberia have evolved a moot court to resolve family disputes that are too small or intimate for the traditional courts. The sessions, attended by a group of neighbors and family members, are presided over by someone with a kinship tie to the participants and usually political standing in the group. In one typical dispute, a man named Wama Nya had one wife but inherited a second when his brother died. He accused this second wife of cheating on him, staying out late, and denying him some of the food she brought in from the fields. The assembled group listened to the complaints of the man and the first and second wives, offering their opinions as the principals spoke and in side conferences. The process in some ways was therapeutic: it allowed everyone to be heard and to feel that their complaints were legitimate enough for others to take the time to listen to and consider seriously. In the end, the group decided that the husband was mostly at fault. He was ordered to bring rum, beer, and food for the entire group and thus reintegrate himself and his family into the community (Gibbs, 1963).

The Abkhazian of the Caucasus Mountains

In the Caucasus Mountains of Georgia in the former Soviet Union, the Abkhazian people have long practiced mediation by elders to resolve disputes within their group and among the tribes in the surrounding areas. The mediators are generally respected elders, usually male but sometimes female. The disputing sides tend to call in mediation after a cycle of revenge has allowed each side to feel that it has exacted equal retribution but before any reconciliation has been achieved. In one case, a drunken argument between members of different families had led to violence. The mediators essentially shamed the two sides into a reconciliation, which was followed up by a joint feast. This feast of reconciliation, according to participants, cements family bonds and is considered more sacred than any court document (Garb, 1996).

Interestingly, Abkhazian reconciliation before World War II had often involved either intermarriage between groups or the adoption of a child from one family into the other, thus creating an extended family link. The bond was dramatized by the new mother's taking the adopted child to her breast—either literally or symbolically. At times, an adult male seeking to end a dispute would steal into the home of the rival family and attach himself to the breast of his adversary's wife or mother. Sometimes this method would have the desired effect of ending the dispute. Sometimes (perhaps understandably) it would not.

The Yoruba of Nigeria

In Nigeria, the Yoruba live in modern cities but cling to traditional ways of resolving disputes. When a matter between Yoruba ends up in court, it is generally considered a mark of shame on the disputants: they are viewed as not good people who favor reconciliation. This is not to say that the people do not feel conflict has a place in life. An old Yoruba saying makes this clear: "The tongue and teeth often come in conflict. To quarrel and get reconciled is a mark of responsibility" (Albert, Awe, Herault, and Omitoogun, 1995, p. 9).

Disputes at the family level, such as an argument between co-wives or between parents and a youth who has run away, are generally brought before the *mogaji*, the lineage head, and the *baale*, an elderly head of the district. After the two sides state their case, the elders ask questions and then try to work toward a compromise in which both sides accept some of the blame. The elders have an arsenal of techniques for reaching a settlement: proverbs, persuasion, subtle blackmail, precedent, and even magic. The only real power behind the elders' decisions is cultural: they can threaten social excommunication or use emotional blackmail.

Some disputes transcend the family. One unique venue for resolving such disputes is a television program known as *So Da Bee*, which acts as an informal arbitrator. Land disputes are a common topic. In one case, broadcast in 1995, a blind woman had given a piece of land to a man for farming some twenty years earlier. After the old woman and the farmer died, their heirs, each assuming they held ownership, sold the land to different parties. Through a fact-finding process, the program's arbitrators determined that the agreement between the old woman and the farmer had related only to farming, not full possession of the land. The farmer's heirs were forced to rescind their sale.

The traditional head of the Yoruba, known as the Olubadan, also acts as an arbitrator in many disputes. In a 1983 case, two men each sought the title of *mogaji* of the Sodun family. All internal efforts to resolve the dispute had failed, so the matter was brought before the Olubadan, who sat in council with his most powerful chiefs. After both sides presented their case and were questioned by the council, the situation still could not be resolved, so the Olubadan ruled that the family would have two *mogaji*.

Mediation in China

China, where the traditional view of dispute resolution has its origin in Confucian ethics, adopted mediation early. Confucius (551–479 B.C.) taught that natural harmony should not be disrupted, and adversarial proceedings were the antithesis of harmony. Since the Western Zhou Dynasty two thousand years ago, the post of mediator has been included in all governmental administrations. Today in China, it is estimated that there are 950,000 mediation committees with 6 million mediators—in fact, there are more mediators per 100 citizens in China than lawyers per 100 people in the United States (Jia, 2002).

Given the emphasis on harmony, Chinese mediators have long played a far-reaching role: "Chinese mediation aims not only to respond to a conflict when it breaks out, but also to prevent it from happening. . . . [It] is a continuous process of being vigilant against any potential threats to harmony, even after the harmony has been built" (Jia, 2002, p. 289). Chinese mediators thus do more than try to settle a dispute and move on: they also instruct the participants in how to have a better relationship for the long term. It would be many, many years before Western practitioners of ADR would catch up to these ideas.

Ancient Greek Roots of Arbitration

In the Western World, the story of ADR can be traced back to the ancient Greeks. One famous story of arbitration comes down through mythology. The goddesses Juno, Athena, and Aphrodite were squabbling over who was the most beautiful and called on Paris, the royal shepherd, to decide. Paris, it seems, was not above accepting a bribe from Aphrodite, who thus won the contest. But Juno, wife and sister of Jupiter, was not one to forgive and forget. She was so furious at Paris that she unleashed a host of plagues on Aenaes, his fellow Trojan, as the great hero strove to found the new Troy. Thus, one of the classics of Western literature, Virgil's *The Aeneid,* can be read as a long meditation on the evils wrought by an arbitration gone awry.

Arbitration was not simply a matter of mythology to the ancient Greeks. As Athenian courts became crowded, the city-state instituted the position of public arbitrator some time around 400 B.C. (Harrell, 1936). According to Aristotle, all men served this function during their sixtieth year, hearing all manner of civil cases in which the disputants did not feel the need to go before the more formal, and slow, court system. The decision to take a case before an arbitrator was voluntary, but the choice of being an arbitrator was not. Unless he happened to be holding another office or traveling abroad, any eligible man selected to serve as an arbitrator was required to do so; if he refused, he would lose his civil rights (Harrell, 1936).

The procedures set up by the Greeks were surprisingly formal. The arbitrator for a given case was chosen by lottery. His first duty was to attempt to resolve the matter amicably. This failing, he would call witnesses and require the submission of evidence in writing. The parties often engaged in elaborate schemes to postpone rulings or challenge the arbitrator's decision. An appeal would be brought before the College of Arbitrators, which could refer the matter to the traditional courts. In one such appeal process, Demosthenes had alleged that one Midias had used disrespectful language toward Demosthenes and his family. Midias took legal steps to put off the decision by the arbitrator, Straton, including failing to show up on the day the final decision was to be rendered, but Straton ruled against him. Although the official record is incomplete, Midias successfully appealed the decision before the College of Arbitrators, and Straton was expelled from the board. This outcome may seem a setback for arbitration at a very early stage, but it can also be read as an example of a strong self-policing mechanism. A traditional judge later upheld the board's censure of the arbitrator. The system, it seemed, had worked.

Both Aristotle (384–322 B.C.) and Cicero (106–43 B.C.) commented favorably on arbitration in words that certainly could be used to describe modern arbitration. They made clear that arbitration was an alternative to the courts. Aristotle said arbitration was introduced to "give equity its due weight, making possible a larger assessment of fairness" (Aristotle). Cicero said a trial is "exact, clear-cut, and explicit, whereas arbitration is mild and moderate" (Cicero). He added that a person going to court expects to win or lose; a person going to arbitration expects not to get everything but not to lose everything either.

Other Early Uses of Arbitration

The ancient Greeks were not alone in using arbitration at an early date. Other examples around the world include the following.

- India used a system of arbitration, *Panchayat*, beginning twenty-five hundred years ago. The arbitrator, called a *Panch*, was given such high status that his decisions were irreversible. All types of cases could be subject to arbitration, including criminal matters. This practice of arbitration was so strong that it continued even during the eight hundred years of Muslim rule in India.

- Arbitration was also a feature of the Old Irish Brehon Law system, a body of indigenous law that existed in Ireland from the Celtic settlement before Christ. In early Irish law, a *brithem*, who had trained in law but had not been appointed by the king as the official judge, could work as an arbitrator. The law established the arbitrator's pay at one-twelfth of the sum at issue.

- The Spanish king Alfonso the Wise directed the use of arbitration and allowed lawyers to practice with the publication

of *Siete Partides* in 1263. This arbitration was binding;
however, the arbitrators maintained a spirit of conciliation
by attempting to make decisions harmonious with cultural
norms.

- The early Yi Dynasty in Korea (1392–1910) is remarkable for
its longevity and its extensive use of arbitration. Because of its
isolation, the regime did not employ arbitration in international disputes, but it was widely practiced in a variety of
commercial and civil disputes between citizens.

Religious Roots of ADR

The three main monotheistic strains of Judaism, Christianity, and
Islam played significant roles in conflict resolution among their followers. These early religion-sponsored precursors to ADR practices
included negotiation, mediation, and arbitration, as well as ecclesiastical courts. The courts, with their strong interest in establishing peaceful relations within the religious group, strongly
encouraged disputants to use negotiation, mediation, and arbitration prior to or in place of a court case.

The Wisdom of Solomon

Solomon was king of Israel around 960 B.C. Although he was
essentially the law of the land, his improvisational form of jurispru-
dence in many ways makes him more akin to an arbitrator than a
judge. One famous case holds lessons for all who seek to understand
the true nature of justice.

Two prostitutes came before the king, according to the story.
The first woman said that the second woman had rolled over in the
night and crushed her infant, who was only a few days old. This
second woman then took the living baby of the first woman and
replaced it with her dead child. When it was her turn to speak, the
second woman accused the first of having carried out much the

same scheme. Both babies were about the same age, and no one else could tell them apart.

Solomon dramatically called for his sword, saying he would cut the living child in two so that each woman could have her half. One woman agreed. The other said that he should award the baby to her accuser so that the child's life would be spared. Solomon awarded the child to the woman who was willing to give it away.

The case has been endlessly parsed by lawyers and child welfare advocates. Why couldn't Solomon have worked out joint custody? How would he know which mother would be a better one in the long run? In reality, the king's wisdom shone through, and arbitrators got an excellent early role model.

Jewish Bitzua and P'Sharah

Jewish tradition, based on the Torah and Talmud, provided a judicial setting called Beth Din in which disputants argued their case before three rabbinical judges. The disputants first had to agree to be bound by the judges' decision. Prior to appearing before the judges, the disputants were strongly urged to resolve their differences informally in *bitzua* (mediation) or *p'sharah* (arbitration). In Jewish tradition and law, the concept of compromise in dispute resolution was highly valued, a further encouragement of negotiations and mediation.

While the Romans occupied the Holy Land (63 B.C. to 66 A.D.) and Hebrew courts were abolished, the Hebrews created their own informal system resembling arbitration. This continuing Jewish tradition made it possible for Jews to avoid Christian courts during the Middle Ages, when they objected to testifying under an oath identifying Jesus Christ.

Jewish courts were later established wherever the growing Diaspora landed: from cities across the Middle East, throughout Europe, and in Asia. In the United States, the modern Jewish Arbitration Court, originally located on the Lower East Side of New York City, heard a variety of disputes between Jews involving everything from questions of paternity to proper burials, business disputes to purely family matters. The board offered a formal forum for the airing of disputes large and small, many of which would seem quite out of place in a traditional court.

In one case, a man in the fur trade complained that he had not received his full wages after being promised that he would receive his regular salary even in the slow season. The employer responded by saying that the payment was based on the worker's staying with the firm after the end of the slow times. Instead, the worker had quit. The arbitration board ordered the firm to pay the worker one-third of the full wages (Goldstein, 1981).

In a more touching case, a couple who had been married for fifty years came before the board to ask its permission to separate. In the middle of the wife's complaints about her husband, the arbitration judge asked why, after such a long marriage, the couple wanted to split up now. The wife responded that after raising the children and watching the grandchildren grow up, "I have time to think of my own problems. So I want a separation." After the couple were allowed to air their grievances, the board persuaded them to give their marriage another try.

Christian Peacemaking

The Christian tradition of conflict resolution relies on a number of biblical references, including one on arbitration in 1 Corinthians that suggests very early knowledge of ADR as an alternative to war: "In the obscurity of older time a desire would arise to replace armed combat by arbitration." Matthew 18 speaks of forgiveness and peaceful reconciliation. In numerous other places, the Bible speaks of peacefully working with others to avoid using the court or violence for resolving disputes.

The parish or village priest often served as mediator and arbitrator on an array of issues involving his parishioners. The issues handled by the parish priest went well beyond the realm of the spiritual and involved him in matters appropriate to a state court. In the fourth century, when the Roman Empire adopted Christianity as its official state religion, the state courts assumed some of the role previously played by the parish priest. However, by then, ecclesiastical courts operating under the jurisdiction of each bishop were well established and were used wherever Catholic majorities prevailed.

The Catholic church used councils, which were gatherings of local or regional bishops, to resolve issues on doctrine and practices. These councils primarily involved negotiation, with the pope's representatives playing a heavy mediation role.

The popes themselves often stepped into negotiations, sometimes on their own behalf and sometimes on behalf of others. In perhaps the most famous case, Pope Leo the Great, in spectacular and mysterious fashion, persuaded Attila the Hun to spare the city of Ravenna, the western capital of the Roman empire, in a meeting on the banks of the Mincio River in the summer of 452.

The incident, which inspired at least one artistic masterpiece, is heavily shrouded in papal image building. The concrete facts are few. Attila had swept across Europe, sacking city after city. He had so thoroughly destroyed Aquilieia, on the northern edge of the Adriatic Sea, that it was many hundreds of years before any trace of it could even be found. With Ravenna's fall seemingly assured and thus Attila's path clear for a direct assault on Rome, Pope Leo and two senators, Trigetius, the prefect of Rome, and Gennadius Avienus, a rich and successful politician, set off on a mission to dissuade him.

Attila is said to have received the delegation while reclining in his tent. By the later papal account, the meeting took place on horseback—with the pope's two senatorial companions replaced by St. Peter and St. Paul. This is how Raphael of Urbino depicted the scene in a fresco in the Vatican Palace and is doubtless how it was pictured in the mind's eye of generations of Italians. Some accounts emphasize that Pope Leo impressed Attila with his bearing and his shimmering robes. Others say the apparition of the two saints frightened the fearsome warrior. A substantial payment may also have been involved. Or it may simply have been that it was late in the year, and Attila was ready to head home to Hungary for the winter. For whatever reason, Attila turned his army back, and the pope's reputation as a powerful peacemaker was born (Howarth, 2001).

Muslim Tahkim

From the earliest days of Islam, Muhammad (570?–632) encouraged and practiced *tahkim*, or arbitration, to resolve a variety of disputes. Muhammad's role as arbitrator is sanctioned by revelation. Once Islam became dominant in a community, local law was amended to include arbitration (Moussalli, 1997).

In one of Muhammad's most significant cases, he helped avert a war over the reconstruction of the Kaaba, the small stone building in the court of the Great Mosque at Mecca. The building houses the sacred black stone that is the goal of Islamic pilgrimage and the point toward which Muslims turn in their daily prayers. After the rebuilding, the leaders of the local clans fought over who would have the honor of replacing the sacred stone. For five days, the clans argued. On the brink of war, Muhammad was called in to arbitrate. He placed the stone on a small cloth, telling the head of each clan to carry a corner to its designated area. Muhammad himself then set it in its final resting place (Moussalli, 1997).

Tahkim has a long tradition in the Arab world. One of the most famous wars of the pre-Islamic period, the war of al-Basus, began with the death of a camel that had been allowed to graze on another man's land. The dispute escalated into a long-running cycle of revenge and counter-revenge and was settled only through the process of *tahkim* and payment of blood money. Another famous and long-lasting quarrel began over which of two horses, Dahis and Ghabra, had won a race. This violent cycle too was eventually resolved through arbitration.

The Islamic tradition and culture focuses more on the group or community than on the individual. Originating in ancient Middle Eastern tribes and villages were the dispute resolution practices of

Sulh (settlement) and *Musalaha* (reconciliation). The two together, often referred to simply as *Sulh*, have been used to control conflict and maintain harmony within and between tightly knit social groups. The ritual practices involve conversations, information sharing, and exchanging promises about the future.

Conflicts of many types, even those involving a criminal act, used *Sulh*. For example, if the person who committed the criminal act was known, *Sulh* would be used to achieve restorative justice and diminish revenge that one group or family might use against another. Thus, the Islamic tradition supported the use of all three original forms of ADR.

From the Middle Ages to the Age of Discovery

A few examples from this extended period of time will illuminate the collective experiences that colonists brought with them to the British colonies in North America.

Medieval Practices

After the fall of the Roman Empire, fighting between nobles to resolve disputes in medieval Europe was the rule rather than the exception. Nevertheless, forms of ADR did exist, though some aspects of them were truly medieval.

Probably the best-documented instances of ADR in the Middle Ages were matters brought for judgment before a king. Pippin the First (who ruled Aquitaine from 819 to 838) heard numerous property disputes. In 861, a group of sixty-one peasants, including women and children, brought a different sort of case before Charles the Bald. The records of the king's court details their claim: "That they ought to be treated as free coloni [citizens] by birth, like the other coloni of St. Denis, and that Deodadus the monk wanted unjustly to bend them down into an inferior service by force, and to afflict them" (Davies and Fouracre, 1986, p. 51). After a preliminary hearing, a review of the documents, and further testimony, the king ruled in favor of the monk. What is perhaps remarkable is that the serfs felt they had a strong enough case to bring before the king.

ADR is essentially a nonviolent process, but in its early stages, this was a matter of degree. In some ways, the ritualized violence of the duel can be seen as an early form of ADR. To the participants, a duel, or trial by combat, was not viewed as a matter of might makes right; it was a way of divining the judgment of God. A text from Carolingian West Francia dating back to 816 explains how, in a dispute over property rights, the matter can best be resolved: "If a party suspects the witnesses brought against him, he can put forward other, better, witnesses against them. But if the two groups of witnesses cannot agree, let one man be chosen from each group to fight it out with shields and spears. Whoever loses is a perjurer, and must lose his right hand" (p. 47). Of interest here is the notion that the common violence was slowly being channeled into a process. The result was still a fight, but only under certain circumstances and to resolve a specific issue.

In the year 1037, a nobleman named Bernat Orger and the Abby of Saint Cugat had a disagreement over a piece of land on Spain's Mediterranean coast. Unable to resolve the dispute, they took the matter before the court of the count of Barcelona. A distinguished group was assembled to hear the case, including the Countess Ermessende and the bishop of Barcelona. But when it came time for the disputants to place themselves under the law and be sworn in, Bernat refused. Rather than let the panel decide, he asked for trial by water. In this procedure, a child from each side is plunged in cold water. The matter was won according to which child survived the ordeal. If the trial ended in a tie, the land would be split in half. In the end, the results were indeed inconclusive, and the land was divided equally (Salrach, 2001). Other forms of the trial included placing a burning iron in the hands of a disputant. If the wound healed properly after three days, he won. If it became infected, he lost. Another involved reaching into a boiling cauldron and attempting to pull out a tiny ring (Bartlett, 1986). Although these practices sound barbaric by today's standards, they in fact represented a step up from knocking the other fellow over the head before he knocked you over yours. All of these trials were thought to put the resolution of the matter in God's hands, the most impartial arbitrator of all.

A similarly rough form of justice prevailed in the Languedoc region on the French Riviera about this time. Dueling had been a favored means of settling disputes, though it was falling out of favor by the end of the eleventh century, and war remained popular, but there were some new methods coming to the fore: arbitration by a panel of fellow nobles, or mediation by the nobility or the church. In 1143, after the defeat of Alfonse Jourdain, count of Toulouse, by Vice Count Roger the First, a treaty was reached with the help of Bernard, count of Comminges, Raimond Trencavel, brother of the vice count, and Sicard de Laurac. What is significant here is that none of the mediators imposed their will on the negotiators. They helped them reach a settlement that brought peace (Debax, 2001).

European Law Merchant

During the tenth and eleventh centuries, commercial arbitration became widely used in many European cities under a practice referred to as the law merchant, although no governmental law was involved. This ADR predecessor was voluntarily developed, adjudicated, and enforced by merchants. The legitimacy of the process was founded on an understanding of fairness, mutual benefits, and reciprocity of rights.

In urban centers, markets, and trade fairs, merchants made available these informal judges, drawn from the merchant ranks, to resolve disputes using rules and laws evolved through years of experience. The voluntary and participatory nature of the process contributed to its acceptability to the vast majority of merchants. Those who refused to accept a judge's decision faced ostracism by other merchants. One reason the law merchant was allowed to operate separate from the traditional courts was the specialized nature of the cases. A case from 1278 makes the point. One William

Dunstable of Winchester brought a matter against Robert le Balancer of Winchester. William had bought 103 sacks of good-quality wool from Robert at two prices. He opened four sacks of each lot and accepted them as to quality. But when he went to deliver the wool to another party, 68 of the sacks were found to be "vile and useless." William claimed the turn of events put his life in danger and cost him 100 pounds sterling. The law merchant affirmed William's account and the long-standing practice of sales by sample. Robert was ordered to make amends (Hall, 1930).

By the late Middle Ages, state courts had taken over some work of the law merchant. These courts, however, lacked the technical expertise of the merchant judges, who were more akin to arbitrators with their extensive knowledge of travel and commerce.

In 1698, Ireland enacted the first arbitration law, and it remained unchanged for 250 years. It used these words to authorize arbitration:

> It may be lawful for all merchants, traders and others desiring to end by arbitration any controversy, sute or quarrels—for which there is no other remedy but by personal action or sute in equity, to agree that their submission of the matter to the award or umpirage of any person or persons should be made a rule of any of his Majesty's courts of record, which the parties shall chuse (Dublin International Arbitration Centre, 2004).

The law established several important principles that continue in arbitration today: the parties were allowed to choose their own arbitrator, arbitration awards were recorded in a state court, and the court was likely involved in enforcing the awards.

Age of Discovery

By the seventeenth century, the coastal nations of Western Europe were engaged in significant commercial trade and maritime pursuits. That commercial activity and the growth of diplomacy spawned by a greater sense of nationhood and competition advanced the need for and use of ADR. Although war remained the dispute resolution technique of last resort, a developing middle class, with an interest in peaceful resolution of commercial disputes, and a developing diplomatic class, with an interest in resolving international disputes, fostered negotiation, mediation, and arbitration as alternatives to battle.

Chapter Two

Diplomatic ADR

Akhenaton to Woodrow Wilson

Throughout history, relations between peoples and nations have spawned disputes over trade, tariffs, conquests, and boundaries. Diplomacy developed as the practice of peacefully managing these conflicts. Often, diplomats have called on the ADR precursors of negotiation and mediation, and less frequently, arbitration, to promote coexistence and to assure that war remains a tactic of last resort.

Preliminary Efforts

The first evidence of an extensive system of diplomacy dates back thirty-five hundred years to the Bronze Age in the region between the Mediterranean Sea and the Persian Gulf.

Earliest Diplomacy

In 1887, archaeologists discovered 350 letters written on clay tablets at Tell el Amarna, Egypt, and from this cache of documents, they pieced together what they labeled the Amarna system of international relations beginning in 1400 B.C. This system was developed and used by the great kings of the region to communicate on trade, war, peace, and their relationships.

Some of the most mundane letters tell the most about the system. Gift giving was a huge concern of the powers as they sought to maintain or deepen their relationships. A constant flow of messengers brought valued trade and also kept open channels of communication. When the usual protocol was not followed, it was taken as a serious sign of trouble. In one letter, Burnaburiash, Kassite king of Babylonia, strongly reprimands the pharaoh: "From the time of Karaindish, since the messengers of your ancestors came regularly to my ancestors, up to the present time, they have been friends. Now, although both you and I are friends, three times have your messengers come here but you did not send me one single beautiful gift and therefore I did not send you one beautiful gift" (Cohen and Westbrook, 2000, p. 149).

At other times, the communications were more urgent. Rib-Hadda, ruler of Gubla and vassal of the Egyptian pharaoh Akhenaton, began a letter to Akhenaton plaintively: "Rib-Hadda says to his lord, king of all countries, Great King, King of Battle: May the Lady of Gubla grant power to the king, my lord. I fall at the feet of my lord, my Sun, 7 times and 7 times" (Moran, 1992, pp. 147–150). The situation was dire: Rib-Hadda was rapidly losing control of his small empire. Abdi-Ashirta, the ruler of Amurru and another vassal of the Egyptians, had taken control of most of his territory, turned his people against him, and left him isolated in his last stronghold. Declaring his undying allegiance to the pharaoh, he sought the help he felt he was due under this relationship.

The Amarna system reveals many early aspects of diplomacy, including protection of diplomatic envoys, systems of agreements with means of enforcement, a trained diplomatic corps, and relative flexibility in handling disputes. But another group of letters would provide even greater insight into the development of ADR.

Arbitration and Mediation in the Kingdom of Mari

In the 1930s, French archaeologists found an even older trove of documents from the ancient kingdom of Mari, a land on the Euphrates River in modern Syria. Most of these documents, dating to about the nineteenth century B.C., are addressed to the Mari kings. They are fragmentary in nature, but several contain references to the use of arbitration and mediation in international affairs.

In one dispute, Zimri-Lim, the Mari king, intervened in a dispute that occurred around 1800 B.C. between Hammurabi of Yamhad and Amut-pi-il of Qatanum (Munn-Rankin, 1956). All three leaders were strong kings, and each had fifteen to twenty lesser kings pledging allegiance to him. Thus, the dispute between Hammurabi and Amut-pi-il, the nature of which is not clear from the records, would have been a matter of considerable concern to regional peace. Zimri-Lim, who may have been the strongest of the three, stepped in to help establish a treaty.

Zimri-Lim also often stepped in to settle disputes between his vassals. When Arriwaz invaded the land of Asqur-Adad of Karana, Zimri-Lim was firm in his orders: "Asqur-Adad of Karana is residing with me . . . you have raided his country. Everything you took, gather it together and return it" (Munn-Rankin, 1956, p. 95). The Greeks would make even more extensive use of these early forms of ADR.

The Greeks and Arbitration

Beyond their classical beauty, ancient Greek temples also contain fascinating glimpses of the early history of ADR. Beginning in the late fourth century B.C. or even earlier, the Greeks made extensive use of arbitration and mediation in their interstate affairs. Usually two smaller city-states would appeal to a larger and more powerful one to intervene in their disputes. The decisions in such matters were generally "published" by being inscribed on stele, carved stone slabs, or directly on the columns themselves in ancient temples (Ager, 1996).

Most of these disputes were over territories, but they also involved issues of debt or the possession of certain prized temples. In a typical dispute, Melos and Kimolos were arguing over the possession of three even smaller islets and appealed to the League of Corinth for help. The league appointed Argos as an arbitrator, and he imposed a settlement on the two (Ager, 1996).

As we saw in Chapter One, the Athenians relied on arbitration to help unclog their busy court system. In international affairs, their attachment to the process can be seen through the inclusion of arbitration clauses in many treaties. In a treaty between Miletos and Herakleia, for example, the arbitrator in any future disputes was to be "a free and democratic city" (Ager, 1996, p. 8).

The Greeks were highly sophisticated in their use of arbitration. At times, they would choose a democratic process—the appointment of a large number of arbitrators chosen by lot from the arbitrating city-state—and at other times would seek arbitrators with expertise in the matter at hand—usually just one or two citizens chosen for their wisdom or specialized knowledge. In all cases, there was a sense that the greater the prestige of the arbitrator, the greater power the settlement would have over the disputants. Alexander the Great was thus a frequent early arbitrator in Greek affairs. The powerful city-states of the mainland were also called on. As Rome grew in influence in the Mediterranean world, the Greeks often turned to its officials for help (Ager, 1996).

Papal Peacemakers

The popes were frequent diplomats. Initially the papal legates focused on spiritual and administrative matters within the Catholic church. But as political leaders began to meddle in church issues, and vice versa, legates' assignments expanded to dealing with larger issues, gathering information, seeking political allies, and negotiating agreements.

With no army of its own, the papacy at times turned to diplomacy as a matter of survival. In 753, Stephen II, bishop and patriarch of Rome, was in trouble. Since the fall of the Roman Empire, his predecessors had ruled the former capital under the nominal protection of the Byzantine Empire. Now the Lombards of modern-day northern Italy were demanding Stephen's allegiance and monetary tribute.

Just before the winter snows of that year, Stephen set off on a perilous six-week journey to meet with Pippin the Third, king of Francia. A good negotiator, Stephen brought something to offer: in return for the protection of Pippin, Stephen granted the precious commodity of legitimacy. Drawing on the aura of the fallen empire and the burgeoning power of Christianity, Stephen granted his blessing on the Frankish king. Pippin, in turn, sent his men in a series of raids to control the Lombard insurgency.

Stephen II, after essentially severing his ties to Constantinople and securing the help of his new-found protector, would shortly extend his reach over Christendom. The reign of the popes had begun. As for the Franks, Pippin's son, Charles, whom the king sent to meet Stephen when he entered the Frankish domain, was perhaps inspired by the expansive ambitions of the undertaking. He would be known as Charlemagne (Davies, 1997).

In the nineteenth century, Pope Leo XIII played a less self-interested role in settling a dispute between Germany and Spain over the Carolines, a chain of about five hundred small coral islands in the Pacific Ocean some twelve hundred miles east of the Philippines. Spain had discovered the islands in the sixteenth century but had done little more than claim them for the Crown. Germany, Europe's preeminent power by the nineteenth century, controlled trade in the Carolines and wanted to establish a permanent refueling station and naval base.

In early August 1885, Bismarck announced his intention to annex the islands. Spain immediately dispatched two warships, the *San Quentin* and the *Manila,* to raise the flag there and declare the territory for the Spanish crown. The Germans dispatched the *Itlis* to claim any islands not claimed by the Spaniards. In the race to Yap, the largest island, the Spanish arrived first, but the Germans were more efficient. The Spanish had taken a few days to survey the island and had plans for a flag-raising ceremony. As they dallied, the Germans sailed into the harbor on the morning of the planned Spanish ceremony and raised the German colors within half an hour of arriving (Hezel, 1995).

The two sides engaged in such Keystone Kops adventures for days until word reached Europe of the exploits. The Spanish populace was outraged. Mobs threatened the German embassy in

Madrid, and rumors of war began to fly. Bismarck, taken aback by the Spanish reaction, quickly regained the upper hand by proposing that the matter be placed in arbitration, suggesting the pope as the perfect intermediary. The heavily Catholic Spanish could hardly refuse.

The resulting compromise was masterful and face-saving for all sides. Although the pope is believed to have done a creditable job in handling the negotiations, Bismarck, some believe, orchestrated much of the negotiations. Spain retained possession of the islands, but Germany was guaranteed its right to the sea lanes, as well as the coal stations and naval bases it had wanted in the first place. Still, the incident enhanced the papal role as a trustworthy neutral in international disputes.

First Diplomatic Corps

Initially, European kings recalled their diplomats after they had relayed a specific message. But by the fifteenth century, Venice had established a network of permanent embassies abroad, and the papal nunciatures and other Italian states soon followed suit. By 1500, monarchs began to see establishing foreign embassies as a sign of their status. A permanent diplomatic corps also kept information flowing and aided trade.

War and diplomacy have always been closely linked. With diplomats, the violence is at least not so overt. In 1661 at the Hague, groups of Spanish and French ambassadors, locked in a long rivalry, reached an impasse when they crossed paths at a narrow road. The diplomats are said to have remained deadlocked in a contest of protocol for an entire day. The city finally removed railings on the side of the road that allowed the parties to pass with neither side yielding ground (Davies, 1997).

Although Europe would remain wracked by warfare for hundreds of years, continuing efforts at diplomacy would become a key feature of the international landscape.

Peace of Westphalia

The Peace of Westphalia, which brought to an end the Thirty Years War, provided the first great triumph of the new diplomatic ideal. The war, which according to some historians actually lasted about forty-seven years (1601–1648), had cleaved Europe along religious, national, and ethnic lines and turned Germany into a desolate war zone in the process. Making the peace in 1648 would require patience, a willingness to compromise, and a conciliatory attitude. Count Maximilian von Trautmansdorff, the representative of the Holy Roman Emperor, possessed all of these qualities and is generally given much of the credit for helping to reach the peace, which essentially set the contours of Europe for the next century.

The peace granted something to all sides. Each of the great powers—France, Spain, and Sweden—gained territory. Calvinists, Catholics, and Lutherans were given equal status in Germany. Switzerland and the United Provinces received independence. And the various princes under the Holy Roman Empire were granted the right to make foreign treaties.

Only the pope, Innocent X, was left out in the cold—his dream of reuniting Christendom in shambles. He declared the treaty "null, void, invalid, iniquitous, unjust, damnable, reprobate, inane, and devoid of meaning for all time" (Davies, 1997, p. 564). The diplomats had granted the first glimmering of religious freedom, and they had given hope to those who longed for a peaceful Europe.

America's First Diplomacy

A weak player at best on the military stage, America from the beginning attempted to use negotiation to achieve peaceful resolution of disputes, avoid war, and further the nation's interests. A significant slice of early American history, much of it familiar to readers, illustrates how extensively diplomatic negotiations were used.

When the American colonies declared their independence in 1776, the new nation had one very experienced diplomat and two future presidents with legislative and legal experience who would prepare them for crucial diplomatic roles. These three founding fathers—Benjamin Franklin, Thomas Jefferson, and John Adams—will each be remembered for their history-book roles in helping to form the young nation. They also helped lay the groundwork for ADR.

Benjamin Franklin

Benjamin Franklin (1703–1790) was the most experienced of the three in diplomacy and the least formally educated. His extensive business experience, however, included numerous negotiations to establish his successful printing business, as well as acting as arbitrator when asked to resolve disputes between other businesses.

In his first overseas excursion, Franklin was forced to make the best of a poor hand. He spent 1757 to 1762 as a negotiator for his own Pennsylvania Colonial Assembly, as well as the colonial legislatures of Georgia, New Jersey, and Massachusetts. One of his biggest successes was persuading the British Crown to diminish the power that the Penn Proprietors held over the Pennsylvania Colonial Assembly (Franklin, 1964).

Although his entreaties often fell on deaf ears, Franklin was the ideal person to deal with the Europeans, who viewed Americans as rough frontiersmen lacking refinement. Before his arrival in London for the first time, Franklin was the most widely known American in Europe through his writings, scientific experiments, homespun philosophy, and support of Enlightenment ideals. During his extended stays in Europe, he became a popular participant in the social and intellectual life of London and Paris.

His second trip overseas was equally frustrating, as the American pursuit of self-determination and the British desire to maintain colonial rule pushed each side into a harder position. Over his ten-year mission from 1765 to 1775, he did not seek independence for the colonies but believed at that time in an Anglo-American empire. Later, he described his role as that of a mediator between the American colonies and England because his reputation assured him of an audience with opposing sides. But as a good negotiator and mediator, he knew when success was not possible. He returned home just as "the shot heard round the world" was fired at Concord, Massachusetts, starting the Revolutionary War.

Immediately after the Declaration of Independence, Franklin began his long pursuit of the French as an American ally. In 1777, when word reached Paris of the American victory over the British at Saratoga, New York, he used that battle to persuade the French to enter the war on the American side.

With French help, the war ended in 1783, at which point, Franklin joined John Jay and John Adams to negotiate a treaty with England. At age eighty, Franklin retained his negotiating skills. Although Jay and Adams did most of the work on the treaty, it fell to Franklin to report the results to the French, who were unhappy that they had been excluded from the negotiations.

As a still-weak nation thrust onto a diplomatic stage dominated by France, the lion of the Continent, and England, the shark of the Atlantic, America faced a complicated diplomatic task. Franklin's years of experience and nuanced view of diplomacy rose to the challenge. When Franklin showed the treaty details to Minister Vergennes at Versailles and asked for an additional loan, his long-time friend pointedly asked how he could assure his king that America and France were still allies. Franklin admitted that the treaty appeared to tilt American favor toward the English. But he carefully spun out an interpretation that was pleasing to the French. The English, he said, would assume that the United States had firmly turned away from the French. He assured Vergennes that this was not the case and, furthermore, that the British, sailing along on their own misapprehension, would one day "find themselves totally mistaken" (Srodes, 2002, p. 364). The French did provide another loan to the United States, although relations with the French would remain a source of frustration for administrations to the present day.

Meanwhile, the Jay Treaty would also create the first opportunity for the United States to employ arbitration in international disputes. The treaty established three commissions of arbitrators to settle unresolved questions between the United States and Great Britain left over from the Revolutionary War. As we shall soon see, the United States would turn repeatedly to arbitration in the nineteenth century to resolve other international disputes.

John Adams

John Adams (1735–1826) had a classical education from Harvard, read extensively in Greek and Latin, and became a practicing attorney and a political activist in the Massachusetts Colony. He served as an elected delegate to the First and Second Constitutional Conventions, where he played a leadership role, putting to use his skills as an orator and as a persuasive negotiator and mediator.

Beginning in 1778, Adams spent ten years overseas in his two stints as a U.S. representative to Europe. Frustration and impatience hounded Adams during most of his years in Europe. Given America's lack of power abroad, matters moved much too slowly for him. His diary and his almost daily letters to his wife expressed his frustrations (McCullough, 2001). Nevertheless, Adams displayed great persistence and thoroughness as a negotiator. His protracted work with Holland's complex government showed him at his best.

At a key juncture in the move toward independence, Adams negotiated recognition for himself as representative of the United States, secured a substantial loan, and signed a commercial treaty with the Dutch (McCullough, 2001).

Later, Adams would again call on his diplomatic skills to handle one of the most difficult issues of his presidency: French interference with U.S. shipping. Congress, editorialists, and popular opinion all leaned heavily toward declaring war with France.

France, still unstable following its own revolution, could easily have been tipped toward declaring war. In 1793, when Congress declared the French-American Treaties of 1778 null and void and began war preparation, Adams's own cabinet attempted to prevent him from sending representatives to seek a peaceful resolution. Always the negotiator, Adams took a peaceful conciliatory approach that ultimately achieved settlement, and thereby averted war. But the country was in no mood for peace with the French. Historians believe Adams's stance cost him the presidency in his reelection bid.

Thomas Jefferson

Thomas Jefferson (1743–1826) received a classical education at the College of William and Mary, practiced law, and became active in Virginia politics. He served in public office while very young as a magistrate, a vestryman, and in the House of Burgesses, where he displayed good drafting and committee skills but showed less interest in oratory.

As a member of the Continental Congress, he was asked to draft the Declaration of Independence, a classic statement—both well reasoned and rhetorically masterful—of the necessity to call off negotiations when one side is claiming all the power for itself. He also served in Virginia's legislature until elected governor in 1779.

Jefferson spent five years representing the United States in Paris, from 1784 to 1789. His initial assignment involved negotiating commercial treaties with other European nations, a task in which he had great success. He maintained a focus on America's need of markets for its agricultural products, a subject he knew well. His love of facts and strong writing skills enhanced his negotiating by ensuring that he began the process armed with extensive facts and notes analyzing the situation. In letters to friends and analytical papers, he critiqued his work and sought to improve (Adams, 1997). Although he lacked public speaking skill, he shined in small groups, where he showed great personal charm and persuasive communication skill. Speaking and writing French were other negotiating assets.

Later, as Franklin's replacement as minister to France, he continued the positive American presence in Paris that Franklin had established. His civil, solicitous presence during a time of great uncertainty in both nations and between them represented a form of preventive ADR—an effort to anticipate and resolve issues and questions before they became too difficult to manage.

American Successes and Failures

As the young nation struggled for legitimacy in the years following independence, a skillful, and flexible, cadre of leaders would help it navigate through the treacherous waters of international relations.

Diplomacy or War

Even after the United States won independence and ratified its Constitution, European governments did not view the new government under George Washington with the respect due a sovereign nation. There still would be the Undeclared War or Quasi-War with France, the Tripolitan War over piracy on the North African coast, the War of 1812, the impressment of American seamen, and other interference with U.S. shipping by the British and French.

Despite a still weak naval force and a small standing army, many U.S. editorialists and political leaders talked as if they believed victory in the Revolution was achieved by overpowering the British. In fact, the patience and shrewd tactics of General Washington with his ragtag army and the power of the French navy carried the day.

To maintain its independence, the United States needed skillful negotiators in the face of the hazards presented by the great powers of Europe with strong interests in North America's natural resources. The policy set out in Washington's farewell address (warning against "permanent alliances with any portion of the foreign world"), Jefferson's inaugural address ("peace, commerce, and honest friendship with all nations, entangling alliances with none"), and even the Monroe Doctrine (warning European nations to keep hands off the Americas) spelled out the contours of America's ambitions. The nation would continue to call on negotiators with a flexible outlook to deal with foreign aggression while the United States moved from a primarily agricultural nation to an economically strong trading and manufacturing nation.

Certainly diplomatic negotiations did not always provide the desired results in these early years. In 1794, President Washington sent Supreme Court Justice John Jay to negotiate a comprehensive treaty with England covering issues remaining from the Revolutionary War. Although Jay's Treaty had some favorable provisions—arbitration of prewar debtor claims and northern boundary disputes, for example—the treaty was denounced as too conciliatory on trade and shipping. Washington himself was criticized so much over the Jay Treaty that some historians believe it influenced his decision not to seek a third term.

War or the use of troops was not always avoided in favor of negotiations or mediation. President Washington sent troops to put down the Whiskey Rebellion by Pennsylvania farmers in 1794, believing that a show of force would discourage similar uprisings.

In 1797, President Adams sent two prominent representatives, John Marshall, future chief justice of the Supreme Court, and Elbridge Gerry, a future vice president, to negotiate an agreement to stop the French boarding of American ships and abusing of their crews. The French foreign minister refused to meet with the Americans. Instead, he sent three lowly representatives to demand a quarter-million-dollar bribe. In response, President Adams withdrew his negotiators, and an Undeclared or Quasi-War with France continued until 1800.

America's penchant for fighting, versus conciliatory approaches, created many war heroes but few, if any, negotiating heroes. Stephen Decatur in the Tripolitan War became a war hero by scuttling a U.S. ship, the *Philadelphia*, which had been captured by Tripolitan sailors, and by leading the bombardment of Tripoli. Although the War of 1812 had already ended without his knowledge, General Andrew Jackson's defense of New Orleans made him a popular hero, as did his 1818 unauthorized attack on the Spanish in Florida, even though it nearly jeopardized negotiation between the United States and Spain on acquiring Florida.

Jefferson's Louisiana Purchase

Thomas Jefferson entered the White House in 1801 having defeated John Adams, a vigorous supporter of a strong national government. Throughout his two-term presidency, Jefferson held to his belief that the national government's powers were limited and the states were primary. However, he did waver on his most important and successful decision, the Louisiana Purchase, and on his most unsuccessful decision, the Embargo Act of 1807.

Concerned about the free flow of U.S. trade through the mouth of the Mississippi River, Jefferson sought to purchase New Orleans from Napoleon, and he sent James Madison, his secretary of state, to Paris to negotiate the purchase. Expecting that Napoleon would refuse to sell, Jefferson directed Madison to proceed immediately from Paris to London to negotiate an alliance with England against France.

To the Americans' surprise, Napoleon agreed to the sale, not only of New Orleans, but all the land France claimed west of the Mississippi River. Madison returned home with a signed agreement for a $15 million purchase price. Jefferson, realizing the questionable constitutionality of the purchase, struggled for six months with his decision to ask Congress for its approval, as required by the Constitution. When he finally asked Congress to approve the purchase, the sale was readily approved in 1803. Had Jefferson delayed any longer, the question of Napoleon's authority for the sale might have deprived America of this windfall.

With the Louisiana Purchase, Jefferson allowed practicality and opportunity to overcome political philosophy, and by doing so, he more than doubled the size of the United States. More important for our purposes here, he demonstrated the ADR characteristics of flexibility and practicality to work matters out by negotiating.

Negotiations and the War of 1812

An examination of ADR and other peaceful strategies before and during the War of 1812 with England will show the many opportunities for ADR use—some of them successful and some not.

Toward the end of Jefferson's presidency, the long-standing competition between England and France at sea was causing extreme difficulties for American shipping. Given Jefferson's dislike of war, he sought to force both countries to negotiate an agreement respecting U.S. neutrality and right to the open sea. He hoped to force negotiation by suspending trade with them. For fifteen months, the Embargo Act of 1807 achieved the opposite of its desired effect: it reduced legitimate American exports to a trickle, with commercial New England merchants suffering significantly more than the embargo's targets. Jefferson's decision to enforce the embargo strictly with army troops violated the individual rights he held so dear. With his strategy a failure, Jefferson left office at the lowest point in his career. He abandoned the embargo and returned to Monticello four months before his term ended, leaving the problem for his successor, James Madison (Appleby, 2003).

The architect of Jefferson's failed embargo, Madison began his presidency still believing in it. He saw it as a contest between the evil, corrupt English who sought to suck every possible advantage from its trade with the United States, and the virtuous Americans willing to sacrifice for their freedom. With the failed embargo now abandoned and negotiation having been repeatedly rejected by the British, war seemed the only alternative for establishing America's right to the open sea.

But Madison, like Jefferson, did not favor war. In 1809, when David Erskine, the British representative in Washington, informed Madison that his government was prepared to respect U.S. shipping, the president was delighted. He immediately set a date to resume normal trade with England. Friend and foe alike praised the president, believing as he did that the recently ended embargo had influenced England's decision. However, several months later, when the British recalled Erskine to London in disgrace, it became clear that he had exceeded his authority. Madison was severely criticized for being duped (Wills, 2002).

Then Congress passed a bill authorizing exclusive trade with whichever country agreed first to respect U.S. shipping. When Napoleon jumped at the offer, the British were offended and continued to prey on U.S. ships. Halfway through his first term, Madison, in desperation, convinced Congress that British interference with U.S. shipping constituted an act of war.

As the War of 1812 began, Czar Alexander of Russia offered to act as mediator. Madison was so pleased with the opportunity to avoid war that he agreed to mediation and offered a concession even before he knew whether the British would agree to mediation. The British refused to be dragged to the bargaining table.

A year later, the British at last proposed direct negotiations for peace. The president sent John Quincy Adams and Henry Clay to Ghent, Belgium, in 1814 to negotiate with the British. Still angry with the United States, the British negotiators in Ghent rejected all American requests and demanded that the United States give up the Great Lakes and much of New York and Massachusetts. The Americans, seeing no room to negotiate, prepared to leave for home. Fortuitously for the United States, Napoleon had just been defeated, and British Foreign Minister Castlereagh stopped in Ghent en route to Vienna for negotiations on Europe.

Following two decades of fighting, Castlereagh felt that England was weary of war and wanted peace regardless of its anger with America. Thus, he softened the British negotiating stance, allowing negotiations to resume. Once the negotiators agreed that land boundaries would be restored to those before the war, a settlement was in sight.

Aroostook War

One other piece of business not addressed by the 1783 treaty ending the Revolutionary War was the boundary between what is today Maine and New Brunswick, Canada. This border became the subject of the bloodless Aroostook War. The controversy heated up when Maine became a state in 1820 and, without regard to British claims, granted land claims to settlers in the Aroostook River Valley. The Dutch king was asked to arbitrate the dispute. The British accepted the decision but the United States did not (Scott, 1992).

When British lumbermen entered the area in the winter of 1838–1839 and captured an American land agent, the situation began to look grim. Congress appropriated funds and readied a fighting force. General Winfield Scott, sent by President Martin Van Buren, reached an agreement with British forces to avert actual fighting.

Daniel Webster and the First Baron Ashburton eventually negotiated a compromise agreement that granted the British enough land to ensure year-round military communications by land with Montreal. The testy American side needed some persuading to accept the settlement: Webster employed a map marked with a red line by Benjamin Franklin in 1782. This was enough to win support for the treaty from Maine and Massachusetts.

More Confident American Diplomacy

As the United States approached the centennial of July 4, 1876, its industrial base was growing, and it was gaining the respect of other nations. The effect of the Monroe Doctrine of 1823, opposing any further colonization in the Americas by European powers, resulted in a U.S. sphere of influence in both North and South America. These developments encouraged the U.S. government to gradually begin exercising diplomatic influence beyond U.S. borders.

In 1871, President Grant won congressional approval for the Treaty of Washington establishing the principle of using arbitration to resolve disputes between nations. This triggered a movement to seek alternatives to war through arbitration and to codify international law in order to mitigate the attractiveness of war. This endorsement of arbitration became a crucial component of modern peacekeeping efforts that would eventually be the motivating principle behind the Hague Conventions, the League of Nations, the World Court, and the United Nations.

Twenty years after the Civil War, the United States had sufficient confidence in its standing and prestige to offer to mediate border disputes between its southern neighbors. In 1876, it mediated a dispute between Argentina and Paraguay; in 1880, between Colombia and Chile; in 1881, between Mexico and Guatemala, Argentina and Chile, and Peru and Chile. It also mediated a settlement of the War of the Pacific (1879–1884) between Chile and the alliance of Peru and Bolivia.

President Theodore Roosevelt (1901–1909), a very assertive internationalist, was not a consistent supporter of ADR in international matters. He promoted arbitration in disputes between other nations but preferred mediation when the United States was party to a dispute. But such negotiations were often accompanied by his "big stick"—a practice not known for mutual advantage to all participants, and pejoratively referred to as gunboat diplomacy. But Roosevelt proved a dogged supporter of peace in a matter seemingly far removed from American concerns. He won a Nobel Peace Prize in 1906 for his effort to settle the Russo-Japanese War.

The war began in 1904 when Japan attacked the leased Russian naval base at Port Arthur in China. Sensing a long, bloody struggle, Roosevelt immediately began offering his services as mediator. But Czar Nicholas instead dispatched his Baltic fleet to take care of the Japanese. The act of bravado cost him his entire fleet. Japan was successful in its other efforts in the war, but many of the victories came at a high price in lost lives and ships.

With Roosevelt continuing to keep lines of communication open to both parties—through telegraph, diplomatic channels, and a number of international intermediaries—they eventually agreed to meet in Portsmouth, New Hampshire, even as the fighting continued. Roosevelt played mediator and host.

A major sticking point arose over the question of reparations. Japanese newspapers were demanding major payment from the Russians and the handing over of the disputed Sakhalin Island. The Russians were willing to make serious concessions but not reparations for a war it had not started.

In the end, the Japanese won the war but lost the peace at home. By giving ground on the reparations issue, Japan won an end to the war, a claim over Port Arthur, greater influence over Korea, and a statement from the Russians that Japan was the supreme power in Asia. Roosevelt won international plaudits including his Peace Prize. Restive Japanese rioted in the streets (Esthus, 1988). Making peace can be extremely unpopular.

Negotiated Settlement of World War I

One of the most ambitious diplomatic endeavors by the United States was President Wilson's effort to create a lasting peace following World War I. It is discussed here to note the difficulties of reaching for all-encompassing agreements when the parties are not ready for them and also to contrast the skills of two Americans who led the effort.

Having saved the day for the European Allied forces, President Wilson wanted to play a major role in the armistice and the realignment of Europe. Wilson viewed the settlement of "the war to end all wars" as the key to future peace and international stability. A historian and former president of Princeton University, Wilson had only the best of idealistic intentions, and initially, his vision encouraged great hope and expectations in both the United States and Europe. Still, he faced daunting obstacles from continuing bitterness in Europe, fostered by centuries of war, to opposition in Congress at home.

In this diplomatic effort, the president had a large advantage in his chief aide, Colonel Edward House, a confidant whom the president often referred to as "my alter ego." Together, they had developed Wilson's Fourteen Points—a framework for resolving World War I that the president hoped would be a road map for a lasting peace—and worked on the concepts for the League of Nations. In treaty negotiations, House was at the president's elbow, and on occasion, he substituted for the president at the negotiating table.

As a politician, Wilson was a passionate, eloquent, and persuasive speaker. In small groups, he loved to use puns and limericks, and he excelled at telling folksy stories using Scottish or Irish accents. These are all good qualities in a negotiator. But for Wilson, who at heart had such a fierce belief in his own convictions that he could barely brook dissent, negotiating was a difficult task.

House, in contrast, was a natural at negotiating. He had the ability to convey a sense of intimacy, sympathy, and his own good intentions immediately. House was given the honorary title of colonel by a Texas governor whom he helped get elected. Independently wealthy, House had turned to politics in the late 1890s and advised Wilson on his presidential campaign. He had a soft and gentle voice and remained calm, reasonable, and cheerful regardless of the circumstances. He felt a conciliatory approach would provide a solution to any problem (MacMillan, 2001).

Wilson showed his inflexible streak even before he left for the Peace Conference. To ensure bipartisan support at home and in Congress, it was assumed he would appoint a high-ranking Republican to the team of negotiators. But Wilson did not trust the Republicans and put together an all-Democratic team. At the time, there were Republicans who supported his thinking on the treaty and even on the League of Nations. Later, when he needed that support, it was not available.

Wilson's stubbornness was revealed again when he returned to the peace conference after a short trip to the United States to deal with domestic matters. House, left behind in Europe to negotiate on the president's behalf, had compromised with France and England on border settlements and on the issue of German war reparations. For the first time in their long relationship, the president directed his considerable anger at his chief adviser, and their relationship was never the same.

Colonel House explained the president's stubbornness by describing the president's decision-making process. Before Wilson made any decision, he would listen to others with an open mind, but once he decided, he proceeded with absolute certainty, unwilling to revisit his decision.

Wilson died disappointed by both the European negotiations and the lack of congressional support for his long-range peace efforts. With Wilson's efforts largely unsuccessful in the negotiations to end the war, the harsh settlement that resulted, many believe, laid the groundwork for the next great war.

Chapter Three

ADR Comes to America

The Precolonial Period
to the Ten-Hour Day

The colonists who began arriving in America in the early 1600s were a diverse lot. In the South, many were loyalists, coming to the United States to earn their fortune and stake their claim for the British Crown. In New Amsterdam, they were mainly Dutch traders, establishing a commercial base for the seagoing nation. In New England were many religious protesters, chased from the Old World and bound for the New to set up their "city on a hill," in John Winthrop's famous phrase.

Still, the early colonists shared a common experience with some forms of early ADR. Most were familiar with negotiations, mediation, and arbitration. The challenge was to fashion ADR precursors to fit the new world they were building.

From Survival to Getting Along

The priority of the early colonial period was survival and establishing permanent settlements. As these basic issues were slowly taken care of and the rights of individuals expanded, ADR precursors gradually developed as well.

European Influences and Colonial Applications

Commercial arbitration was in widespread use throughout the Dutch colonial period (1624–1664) and the British colonial period (1664–1776) in New York City. Merchants in other colonies also had brought their commercial arbitration experience and skills to the New World.

Pilgrim colonists, convinced that lawyers threatened Christian harmony, scrupulously avoided lawyers and courts, preferring to use their own mediation process to deal with community conflicts. When a disagreement arose, two or three male community members would intervene with the disputants. Although they called their process mediation, that was a misnomer since the mediators could render a decision that would be enforced by the community. (Their process resembled a process that much later would be called mediation-arbitration, or med-arb.)

The Dutch colony of New Netherlands also developed a process for resolving community disputes. Although the colonists called it reconciliation, it was really arbitration followed by reconciliation. When a disagreement arose, a board of nine community leaders, all of them men, would seek to determine fault, assess damages, issue a decision, and then promote reconciliation between the disputants. The Swedish colony in Delaware used a similar process.

The Powerful Role of the Local Church

In Plymouth County, Massachusetts, there were three forums for resolving disputes between 1725 and 1825: the court, the town, and the church. Both the town and the court had serious limitations for day-to-day issues. The courts offered a formalized setting for resolving disputes, but at a high cost in money, inconvenience, and time. The town offered a forum for resolving matters, but often in a highly public setting that might bring embarrassment to the parties. Still, the towns quite often became the place where matters such as road routes were worked out. In Halifax, for instance, a town meeting essentially resolved a private matter by refusing to build a bridge "for the Convenience of William Holmes in going to meeting," in part because "a bridge there will prove Detrimental to Several persons who have petitioned against it" (Nelson, 1981, p. 15).

The church proved a versatile forum for resolving many disputes through a surprisingly sophisticated resolution process. Disputants were encouraged to resolve their disputes on their own before bringing the matter before the church. The First Church of

Rochester, for example, directed disputants to "follow the rule in 18 Mat 15:16 &c."—that is, to directly confront the alleged wrong-doer, then to do so with witnesses, and only then to involve the church (p. 38). These steps failing, the complaint would then usually be presented to the pastor in writing. Unlike the courts, the goal was not simply an abstract form of justice but a desire to encourage disputants "to lay aside Contention . . . forgive one another for [Christ's] sake," and "come to a mutual Agreemt respecting their old differences" (p. 39).

In bringing about such a resolution, the only power the church wielded was "censure, public confession, repentance, and restitution backed up by the ultimate sanction of excommunication" (p. 42). With harmony as the overriding goal, many disputes were resolved with no clear winner. In a case in Wareham, the church had thoroughly looked into one member's claim against the other and determined that the best method "for peace sake" was to "bury all." Therefore, the church resolved that the defendant's evidence was "satisfactory to clear him of ye charge laid in against him . . . & yt he ought be restored to our charity," and the plaintiff, too, should be "looked upon as clear from ye scandal of asserting falsehood" (p. 42).

These early methods of dispute resolution provide a valuable lesson for ADR today: the final outcome on the merits of a given dispute is not always as important as the method used in arriving at it and the spirit in which the process is undertaken.

Relations with American Natives

The long-term historical injustice of the settlers' dealings with Native Americans cannot be stressed enough, but in particular cases, it is clear that the white colonists were not always so much smarter than the "savages" as they thought they were.

Consider the purchase of Manhattan. It has long been told that a Walloon adventurer named Peter Minuit purchased Manhattan from the Lenape Indians in 1626 on behalf of the Dutch West India Company for various items, including axes and blankets worth the equivalent of about twenty-four dollars. Given the value of Manhattan today, some might be led to conclude that this was an example of exploitation. According to some sources, the Carnarsee band of the Lenape who agreed to the deal were just a passing hunting party; they actually lived on present-day Long Island. Besides the fact that their concept of landownership was much different from Minuit's, the swamp-infested island was not worth much to them anyway.

In some ways, too, the early colonists' contact with Native Americans provided an opportunity to observe their governance and dispute settlement processes. Benjamin Franklin, for example, learned about Indian governance as he printed documents from Indian assemblies and treaty negotiations. In the 1750s as Pennsylvania's Indian commissioner, Franklin said the Indians gave him an education in persuasion, compromise, and consensus building—skills that he put to good use later as ambassador to France and delegate to the Constitutional Convention (Franklin, 1964).

From his contacts with the League of Iroquois, Franklin learned of their constitution, called the Great Law of Peace, which had brought peace among the Oneida, Mohawk, Cayuga, Onondaga, Seneca, and Tuscarora tribes. The confederation of these tribes provided the discussion process for maintaining peace, an ADR precursor.

A tribal council handled internal conflict resolution in long discussions that used community values to make decisions. The words *caucus* and *pow wow* are Indian derivatives, underlining the Native American tradition of talking matters through. Indian governance and dispute resolution had been evolving for hundreds of years when the first European settlers arrived.

Lewis and Clark: Explorations in Negotiations

The adventures of Lewis and Clark, as they bribed and bluffed their way across the continent in pursuit of the Northwest Passage, also offer a complicated view of white-Indian negotiations. In the summer of 1805, the party had reached the foot of the Columbia Mountains, so close and yet so far from their ultimate destination, where the Columbia River emptied into the Pacific Ocean. Lewis entered into desperate—and sly—negotiations with the Shoshone Indians.

Time after time, Lewis used lies and half-truths to persuade Chief Cameahwait to help with the portage over the mountains and to trade for horses that would take the expedition on to its goal. He told the chief that he had persuaded his enemies not to attack him, and he promised guns and other aid to the chief in his constant battles with the rival tribes. Some three thousand miles by river from St. Louis, it was a promise he knew he would be hard-pressed to keep.

As always, Lewis could count on remarkable luck in his endeavor. Sacagawea, his guide and translator, turned out to be related to the Indians he was dealing with. Still, the lies flew, as Lewis repeatedly promised help, food, and reinforcements he could not deliver. When Lewis bought his first few horses from the Indians, the prices seemed good: on August 18, he purchased three good horses in exchange for a uniform coat, a pair of leggings, a few handkerchiefs, three knives, and some trinkets. He was optimistic that he would have a fine stable of horses when it came time to bargain for the bulk of the horses needed. But as the negotiations dragged on, the Indians, knowing that they had a desperate captive purchaser, raised their prices. By the time the deal was done, Lewis had paid premium prices for the dregs of the Indians' herd (Ambrose, 1996).

Famous Precursors to ADR

Some historic individuals and important events involved ADR precursors, thus demonstrating the variety of ADR used during this period.

George Washington's Will

George Washington included an arbitration clause in his last will and testament based on his personal experience as an arbitrator during the 1770s. Here are Washington's own words:

> But having endeavored to be plain, and explicit in all Devises—even at the expense of prolixity, perhaps of tautology, I hope, and trust, that no disputes will arise concerning them; but if, contrary to expectation, the case should be otherwise from the want of legal expression, or the usual technical terms, or because too much or too little has been said on any of the Devises to be consonant with law, My Will and direction expressly is, that all disputes (if unhappily any should arise) shall be decided by three impartial and intelligent men, known for their probity and good understanding; two to be chosen by the disputants—each having the choice of one—and the third by those two. Which three men thus chosen, shall, unfettered by Law, or legal constructions, declare their sense of the Testators intention; and such decision is, to all intents and purposes to be as binding on the Parties as if it had been given in the Supreme Court of the United States [Washington, 1799].

Declaration of Independence

In 1776, the Declaration of Independence labeled King George III an opponent of peaceful relations and expressed frustration with the Crown's refusal to negotiate its relationship with the colonies: "In every stage of these Oppressions, we have petitioned for Redress in the most humble terms; our repeated Petitions have been answered only by repeated injury. A Prince, whose character is thus marked by every act which may define a Tyrant, is unfit to be a ruler of a free people."

The fact that the colonies' requests for negotiations did not succeed in preventing a war is neither a failure of a process fully used nor the colonists' lack of skills. Rather, this failure highlights the key ingredients of successful negotiations: a joint interest in resolution, an acceptance of the other party's right to participate, and an attitude that allows the practical to prevail over the ideological.

Ultimately, negotiations did resolve the relationship with the British, but only after the Boston Massacre (1770), the Boston Tea Party (1773), Paul Revere's ride (1775), the "shot heard round the world" (1775), and a long Revolutionary War (1775–1783), illustrating that for some, peaceful alternatives to fighting are used only when fighting proves too difficult.

"The Star Spangled Banner"

Francis Scott Key, a Baltimore lawyer, was engaged in an ADR mission when he wrote the national anthem. In the War of 1812, the British became the first sovereign state to attack Washington, D.C., burning down the White House in the process. Just before leaving the capital in August 1814, the British army took captive one of Key's friends, Dr. William Beanes.

Key left for Baltimore to obtain the services of Colonel John Skinner, the government's prisoner of war exchange agent. Together they sailed down the bay on a truce ship and met the British fleet. After securing an agreement for Beanes's release, Key was required to remain behind the British lines until morning. During that confinement, while watching the British naval assault on Fort McHenry, Key wrote "The Star Spangled Banner."

ADR Precursors and Governance

The task of deciding on the form of governance and then operating the new government provided numerous opportunities for Americans to develop and refine their negotiating skills.

Negotiations at the Constitutional Convention

The delegates who assembled in Philadelphia beginning in 1774 were residents of colonies that had evolved early democratic institutions during the 150-year colonial period. The delegates knew from personal experience how colonial legislative bodies, government executives, and courts functioned to regulate conditions not determined by the British Crown. These institutions had given the delegates experience with negotiations and problem solving. They displayed those skills in Philadelphia as they negotiated, built consensus, and created coalitions in their work of declaring independence, raising an army, overseeing a scattered central government, and drafting a federal constitution.

Although the delegates had different interests on some issues based on the colonies they represented, they found common ground as much as possible and made it the basis of written agreements. The give-and-take of their debates, their fashioning of workable compromises, and their caucusing and coalition building all demonstrate a let's-work-it-out attitude that is crucial to ADR. It is accurate to think of the colonial institutions as experiential labs for the development of ADR skills and the attitudes that support ADR. The delegates demonstrated their adaptability when the shortcomings of their first efforts, the Articles of Confederation, became apparent; they resumed negotiations to fashion an even more elegant and balanced document. The intricate interplay of the executive, legislative, and judicial branches of the federal government remains a highly effective testament to the power of ADR principles.

ADR Within the New U.S. Government

In 1790, Thomas Jefferson acted as a mediator to resolve two vexing public issues, one financial, the other geographic. Alexander Hamilton, treasury secretary in George Washington's cabinet, confided to Jefferson, a fellow cabinet member as secretary of state, that he intended to resign in frustration. Hamilton's plan for the recovery of public credit had been tied up in Congress for six months by southern opposition. Since the opposition leader, Congressmen James Madison, was Jefferson's long-time colleague and fellow Virginia Democrat, Jefferson invited the two men to supper at his New York City residence, where, in his words, he would "conciliate their differences."

Over a congenial meal and drinks, Jefferson managed to focus the conversation with gentle questions. By the end of the evening, an agreement emerged in which Madison stopped opposing the national government's assumption of the states' public debt and allowing a congressional vote on the matter. To make that less painful to southern congressmen, Hamilton agreed to throw his Federalists' support behind establishing the U.S. capital on the Potomac River. Within a month of Jefferson's mediation, Congress approved both items (Ellis, 2000).

Jefferson's intervention was motivated by a concern that the young American government would be torn apart by these two vexing issues that had embroiled Congress in months of partisan and sectional impasse. Jefferson understood that the American experiment in self-governance required creative solutions to difficult issues and selfless compromises to bridge differences and discover common ground. His successful mediation began a pattern for legislators and government officials' behavior in political conflicts in a manner that would protect the Union. (The one great exception to this pattern is the Civil War, the subject of Chapter Four.) Under the U.S. Constitution with its three branches of government, ADR skills continued to be used and developed. The growth of the free press, the exercise of free speech, the development of political parties, and the growth of interest groups and lobbyists all contributed to further development of ADR precursors, particularly negotiations.

The new government also gained experience with arbitration. The Patent Act of 1790, for example, provided for arbitration of competing patent applications. An arbitration board, consisting of one member appointed by each patent applicant and one appointed by the secretary of state, would make the decision. If an applicant refused to use arbitration, the patent application of the other would be approved. One of the first cases handled under this law involved the steamboat applications of John Fitch and James

Rumsey. Fitch's patent application was granted when Rumsey refused to use arbitration.

All of this ADR in governance was in stark contrast with other nations, where such freedoms and institution did not exist and where the rare change in governments typically followed unrest and violent overthrow.

American public officials and others advanced the ADR art of negotiations and mediation, the art of working things out peacefully. An exception was the way workers and nonlandowners were dealt with since they lacked rights that would have provided access to ADR processes.

Rights and ADR Precursors

The subject matter of ADR processes involves disputes over conflicting rights. The interplay of rights between nations, between buyers and sellers, and between individuals and groups are potential areas of conflict that ADR processes can help resolve. In a society with broadly distributed rights, there is great opportunity for using ADR. As American society gradually—and often reluctantly—expanded rights, the potential use of ADR also expanded.

Human and Individual Rights

The Bill of Rights became part of the U.S. Constitution as an amendment in 1791. Before the amendment, rights were established in each colony by custom, common law, or statute, with gender, race, and landownership being major determinants of rights. Women had few rights: they could not buy, own, or sell property; vote; serve on a jury; or seek a divorce. Slaves had no rights, and freed slaves had difficulty asserting any rights.

Religion also influenced rights in the colonies. The early Massachusetts colonists had come to America to escape religious intolerance, and yet their own intolerance caused the Salem witch trials and forced liberal clergyman Roger Williams to leave the colony. Williams found greater tolerance for his views in the Rhode Island colony.

A positive influence on rights in early America was the availability of land. Only wealthy families owned land in Europe, so others used land at the forbearance of the owners. Colonists without wealth but with initiative could acquire land and the accompanying rights.

The growth of rights throughout American history is key to the growth of ADR since the application of rights often gives rise to disputes to which ADR could be applied.

Workers' Rights and the Lack of Access to ADR Precursors

During colonial times, most individuals without a profession worked as farmers or artisans. All employment practices were controlled by the employers, not by law. Ironically, indentured servants were an exception: they signed contracts committing themselves to a period of servitude with a bonus at its expiration, thus making them the only employees with legal standing in court. For most of American history, workers' wages, hours, and working conditions were at the discretion of the employer.

Colonial history is marked by infrequent and modest efforts by workers to resist or challenge the dominance of employers. In 1636, a group of Maine fishermen mutinied when their wages were withheld; in 1741, New York City bakers refused to bake bread without a wage increase; in 1677, licensed New York City street cleaners resisted a wage reduction; in 1778, printers in New York City joined together for wage improvements. These colonial worker groups dissolved or became dormant once their objective was achieved or, more typically, defeated, thus failing to create a continuing institution to negotiate their rights.

After the Declaration of Independence, workers were slightly more successful in enforcing some employment rights by striking, or what they referred to as "turn-outs" or "stand-outs." Wages were the typical issue in dispute, and a very primitive form of negotiation was used: workers would agree on the wage they were willing to work for, let the employer know, and go home until it was met, or, more frequently, if the employer did not agree within a few days, the employees returned to work under the initial conditions or looked for other jobs. Strikes by skilled workers who were difficult to replace had a greater likelihood of success.

The modest success of strikes was diminished further by a Philadelphia shoemakers' strike in 1806. The court found the strike leaders guilty of a criminal conspiracy to increase wages and do harm to the owners. Employers used this legal doctrine, known as the union conspiracy doctrine, to get the courts to stop strikes and in many cases destroy unions. Courts supported the conspiracy doctrine since it was consistent with the prevailing legal view that rights were based on property ownership (Rayback, 1959).

In 1832, building tradesmen in Boston, tired of working from sun-up to sundown, struck for a ten-hour day. A powerful alliance of masters, capitalists, and the press put down the strike. But in 1835, a general strike in Boston seeking the same goal was successful. In 1840, President Van Buren issued an executive order establishing a ten-hour day for federal employees (Brooks, 1971).

In 1835, in what was probably the first documented case in which a government official mediated in a labor dispute, Vice President Martin Van Buren mediated a strike at a New York shipyard. He did so without establishing any precedent for such government intervention. Given that Van Buren was the first documented labor dispute mediator, it is perhaps fitting that he was nicknamed the "little magician."

Economic slowdowns typically diminished the organizing of unions and the use of strikes. The extreme slowdown of 1837 wiped out most unions until the early 1850s. Strikes resumed with a vengeance, with four hundred occurring in 1854–1855. The number of wage workers changed significantly during the first half of the 1800s, from 10 percent of the workforce in 1800 to 32 percent fifty years later. By the 1830s, one-third to one-half of the labor force was under age sixteen.

While the type of work in America changed from early colonial times to the Civil War, neither groups of worker nor unions enjoyed much success in resolving conflicts with employers. Unsympathetic courts committed to the primacy of property rights, governments willing to use police or military intervention to control workers, and a press more inclined toward the wealthy combined to restrain workers and unions in gaining rights and access to negotiations.

A Foundation for ADR

By the mid-1800s, enough experience with ADR precursors—negotiation, mediation, and arbitration—existed in the United States to suggest strong potential for ADR's continuing development. ADR precursors also took hold during this period in diplomacy, as we saw in Chapter Two, and business disputes, which are addressed in Chapter Five. But efforts to resolve differences peacefully would be drastically put to the test over the issue of slavery.

Chapter Four

The Civil War

The Limits and the Promise of ADR

The Civil War is the great conflagration of American history. It killed more Americans than any other war before or since. It left the South paralyzed and stripped of the free labor that had been the foundation of its economic might. The North won the preservation of the Union, but at a horrible cost in lives and national trauma. Left unresolved for a century—or perhaps longer—was the status of the freed slaves.

From the perspective of this book, the Civil War provides an object lesson in both the limits and possibilities of ADR. Much effort and energy was poured into attempts to hold the Union together through negotiation and compromise without resorting to a bloody and destructive war. In their failure, these attempts point out an important lesson of ADR: for any ADR process to work, the parties, however divided on the issues, must bring a basic willingness to try to get along. That was not the case in a dispute that divided Americans politically, economically, racially, and morally. After the war, with the South utterly defeated, there was a much greater willingness to try to bring about a lasting peace.

The Challenge of Slavery

Slavery had been a bitterly divisive issue from the first days of the Republic. The Constitutional Convention and the First Congress made serious efforts to resolve the issue. When none of these efforts gained sufficient support to achieve a majority, the delegates decided to leave its resolution to another day. Seventy years later, that day had arrived.

Many people from both the North and South worked to avoid war through negotiation, but the task grew more difficult with each passing year. As the industrial North grew ever further from the need for slave labor, its moral repugnance at the idea multiplied. Meanwhile, in the South, the "peculiar institution" had become a way of life and an economic necessity.

Early Legislative Efforts to Accommodate Slavery

When the Declaration of Independence was written in 1776, slaves had been in America for 157 years, the first having arrived in Jamestown, Virginia, in 1619. With the demand for field hands to grow and pick tobacco and cotton, the number of slaves in 1790 was almost 700,000 out of a total population of nearly 4 million. Slaves were confined largely to the South since most northern colonies had passed laws prohibiting slavery. James Madison wrote that the question of slavery was the most difficult issue during the Constitutional Convention, and without the accommodations made to the South, there would have been no Union. For instance, the delegates agreed that for representational purposes in Congress, three-fifths of the slave population would be counted. They also decided that there would be no limitation on the importation of slaves until 1808.

Given the passions surrounding the issue, neither Congress nor the various occupants of the White House would touch the slavery question until the issue periodically bubbled to the surface. The new territories were the most likely flashpoints of conflict and negotiation.

Henry Clay and His Uneasy Compromises

The issue came to a head with Missouri's application for statehood in 1817. When Representative James Tallmadge of New York attempted to add an antislavery provision to the legislation in 1819, a controversy erupted. Thomas Jefferson said the sudden flare-up over slavery after years of dormancy was "like a firebell in the night." With the House mustering enough northern votes to support the antislavery issue and the Senate deadlocked by its even North-South divide, Congress adjourned without resolving the issue.

When Congress reconvened in December, it faced a new statehood application from Maine. Into the fray stepped an extraordinary, though in some ways unlikely, peacemaker, who for the next thirty years almost single-handedly would keep the Union together. Henry Clay (1777–1852) was born to a middle-class family in Virginia, studied law in Richmond, and set off to earn his way in the rough-and-tumble legal battlegrounds of Kentucky. He was a lover of strong drink and gambling, a participant in at least two duels, and a twice-failed presidential candidate.

For Clay, the slavery issue was a matter of personal experience and deep contradiction. As a southerner, he had grown up around slaves, and he owned them all his life. But as a champion of freedom, he sincerely deplored the institution. His personal solution, which he championed for years, was gradual emancipation followed by colonization of the freed blacks in Africa.

As a popular House Speaker and leader of the Whig party, he was able to reach out to both sides in the brewing controversy. His efforts to preserve the Union at its darkest hour are the stuff of congressional legend. At one key moment, he spoke for four straight hours. No record of his words exists; some speculate that this is because his audience was so transfixed by the performance. Clay was a master of the theatrical speech, raising and lowering his tones, shrugging, grimacing, and twisting "his features, & indeed his whole body in the most dreadful scowls & contortions," according to a contemporary (Remini, 1991, p. 183). He caucused with small groups, wheedling, coaxing, and using every variety of "outdoor politics" imaginable. At one point, he spoke with the Pennsylvania delegation, trying to win over the Quaker leader Thomas Forrest. Clay "wielded the powers of pathos in a manner so sublime and touching, that the old man himself became restless, and half the House were in tears," wrote the *New York Daily Advertiser* (Remini, 1991, p. 183).

Still, the controversy raged on for weeks. Ultimately, Clay engineered a plan to admit Missouri as a slave state and Maine as a free state, thus preserving the equal balance of the time. His Missouri Compromise also banned slavery in the rest of the Louisiana Purchase north of latitude 36°30'.

Clay resorted to masterful parliamentary trickery when Representative John Randolph of Virginia rose to try to unhinge all of Clay's hard work. When Randolph asked that the House reconsider the measure, Clay, as Speaker of the House, protested that the hour was late and adjourned. In secret, however, he sent the measure on to the Senate. The next day, he further stalled Randolph until the Senate reported back approval of the compromise.

This delicate balance—essentially cleaving the nation in two generally along the Mason-Dixon line—was not to hold. When the new Missouri legislature considered a plan to ban free slaves from the state, the North erupted in indignation. Clay, who had resigned as Speaker to attend to his personal finances, returned to the House to finish out his term as an ordinary representative. But he again was called to the center of the controversy. This time, his manner had changed significantly. He "assumed a new character," wrote Representative William Plumer of New Hampshire in a letter to his father. "All is mild, humble, & persuasive—he begs, entreats, adjures, supplicates, & beseeches" (Remini, 1991, p. 187). Clay twice called for small groups to get together to hash out compromises, cleverly reserving the power of appointment to each group himself. In the second group, which included members of both houses of Congress, Clay labored mightily for consensus in order to win over the entire bodies. He very nearly got it: this second Missouri compromise admitted Missouri but said that it could not adopt any measure that would infringe on the rights of any citizen of the United States. For a second time, he had kept the Union together without bloodshed.

Some thirty years later, the issue was again heading to a boil as the nation attempted to parcel out a vast new expanse of territory it annexed as a result of the Mexican War. In the North, sentiment strongly favored admitting Texas and California as free states; in the South, secession was slowly gaining a foothold as a viable idea. Clay felt strongly that compromise was critical to hold the Union together. In a series of legislative high-wire acts that he engineered, California was admitted as a free state and slavery was banned in Washington, D.C.

Troublingly, the Fugitive Slave Act also became law as a sop to the South. The new law required any citizens who came in contact with a runaway slave to attempt to return him to his master. While the compromise was good enough to win passage in Congress, it was a disaster for blacks trying to build a life in the North. Some twenty thousand fled to Canada over the next few years (Van Deusen, 1937). Meanwhile, abolitionists were even more determined to do something about slavery. Growing ill, Clay had pushed for the legislation over the summer of 1850, but he was resting in Newport, Rhode Island, when the legislation passed. He died in Washington two years later, on June 29, 1852, of tuberculosis.

Clay had labored long and hard for the principles of compromise and the preservation of the Union. He was a master of the techniques of ADR in pursuit of a losing cause. The issue of slavery was too explosive to be contained.

Within a few years, the first substantial white blood of the conflict would begin to spill in Kansas. Senator Stephen A. Douglas (1847–1861) of Illinois, a Vermont native who had helped Clay press through the Compromise of 1850, played a different role in the Kansas-Nebraska Act. Advocating the concept of "popular sovereignty," Douglas pressed for the citizens of Kansas and Nebraska to decide their own fate. The Kansas-Nebraska Act of 1854, regarded by some as the most important piece of legislation in the 1800s, had none of the delicate touches of the Clay-backed bills that preceded it. In fact, it explicitly repealed the Missouri Compromise and threw open each new state to a test of the popular will. The result was a bloodbath in the streets of Kansas as free and slave supporters fought to drive each other out of the territory.

Failed Negotiations to Avoid Civil War

James Buchanan, a Democrat from Pennsylvania, was president in 1857 when southern states began serious talk of secession. Buchanan was a skilled lawyer who had negotiated the first commercial agreement with Russia while serving as an ambassador. As secretary of state, he had negotiated the annexation of Texas and the boundary of the Oregon territory with the British. Having served twenty-five years in Congress, he had many friends, both northern and southern, and a strong sense of how the legislature operated. Although he believed that slavery was morally wrong, he felt as a lawyer that the Kansas-Nebraska Act, with its provision for state-by-state referenda on the issue, had settled the matter (Klein, 1962).

Buchanan believed that reasoning and a conciliatory attitude toward the South would save the Union. But as his presidency began in 1857, he faced an increasingly stacked deck. Two days after his inauguration, the Supreme Court issued its *Dred Scott* ruling that Congress lacked authority to exclude slavery in any state or territory, essentially placing the territories in the slave camp. The decision caused the South to rejoice, while northern abolitionists called for strong measures to restrict the spread of slavery.

With political rhetoric growing more heated in both the North and South, President Buchanan continued his attempts to reason with both sides. But even within his cabinet there were strong differences of opinion on the right of secession, as well as a war aimed at stopping a secessionist move. Abolitionist John Brown's attack at Harpers Ferry in October 1859 only added to Buchanan's difficulties. The episode encouraged southern secessionist talk, while Brown's execution turned him into a martyr celebrated in northern marching songs. With the House and Senate held by opposite parties and his own Democratic party badly split, Buchanan's last two years as president were a constant battle. In spite of his negotiating skills and his strong desire for a peaceful resolution, his presidency stumbled and lurched toward the dissolution of the seventy-year-old Union.

With the election of Abraham Lincoln on an antislavery platform, the South's secessionist impulses grew stronger. In his final report to Congress in December 1860, Buchanan underscored his dilemma while lecturing all sides about the North's "intemperate interference" with slavery. The election of the abolitionist-leaning Lincoln, he noted, was no cause for secession as many in the South believed. Indeed, secession was not even a right the states had under the Constitution.

Still, Buchanan's hope for a negotiated resolution was not completely unrealistic. When the Nashville Convention of southern states had met in June and November 1850 to discuss the slavery question, moderates succeeded in foiling talk of secession, at least for a time.

Even in the last days of Buchanan's administration, other negotiating efforts were attempted. The House and Senate each appointed well-regarded committees to look seriously at southern grievances. Ironically, on the day the Senate committee first met, December 21, 1860, news reached the Capitol that the day before, a South Carolina convention had unanimously adopted an "ordinance of secession." While this news may have discouraged the committee, the members moved quickly to discuss and vote on a comprehensive proposal by Senator John J. Crittenden of Kentucky, a highly respected elderly gentleman from a "union-loving border slave state." Crittenden envisioned six constitutional amendments that would essentially maintain the North-South divide over slavery all the way to the Pacific, although popular sovereignty would also play a role within individual territories. Although the plan might have proved acceptable to all states save South Carolina, Crittenden's plan was narrowly defeated in the Senate on March 2, 1861. Crittenden had introduced a resolution two months earlier calling for a national referendum on these proposals, but the Senate never acted on this resolution. By this time, northern senators were moving beyond the point of compromise (Rhodes, 1895).

Exhausted and nearly seventy years old, Buchanan spent his last months in office focused on holding the Union together until Lincoln's inauguration. Even that modest goal was denied Buchanan when seven southern states left the Union just prior to Lincoln's swearing in.

Former President Tyler of Virginia, at age seventy-one and out of political office for nearly twenty years, presided over a Peace Convention in Washington on February 4, 1861, with representatives from northern and a few southern states. On the same day, ironically, the seven seceding states met in Montgomery, Alabama; they adopted a temporary constitution and declared themselves a provisional congress.

Having spent his White House years as a Whig in continuing battles with both Democrats and Republicans, Tyler was an unlikely mediator. Nevertheless, his Peace Convention adopted the substance of the Crittenden proposal with some modifications more attractive to the South. When Congress rejected the proposal, Tyler, angry and disappointed, returned home and urged Virginia to leave the Union immediately. When Virginia did withdraw, Tyler offered to serve in the Confederate Congress but died before he could (Wise, 1881).

The failure of negotiations to avoid war is not surprising given the stark differences in the two sides' positions. The South, having lived with and benefited from slavery for so long, saw being without slavery as unthinkable. The North, having outlawed slavery years ago and recently electing an antislavery president, felt that tolerating slavery was equally unthinkable and immoral. These two absolute positions ultimately rendered any form of ADR unworkable. The parties' unshakable determination to resist any modification of their positions precluded a peaceful resolution. Thus, just thirty-eight days after Lincoln's inauguration, four years of civil war began on April 12, 1861.

Successful Negotiations to End Civil War

Two major surrender documents were negotiated at war's end, involving the two largest commands of southern forces. The first, and better known, at Appomattox, Virginia, involved Generals Grant and Lee, the commanders of the Union and Confederate armies, respectively.

Typical of most traditional negotiations, neither negotiator revealed his true concerns or desires. For example, when Grant sent his first appeal to Lee to surrender, the Confederates were surrounded, outnumbered, and starving. Yet Lee's response mentioned none of this. Instead, he said he had no intention of surrendering but did ask what terms Grant intended. Grant simply said "total capitulation with the promise of no punishment." He said nothing of how he and President Lincoln dreaded the thought of the war continuing even one more day. In fact, both generals had the same desires: to end the bloodshed, restore the Union, and begin to heal the nation's wounds.

What made this negotiation different was the complete respect and lack of rancor between the two negotiators. If Lee had expressed anger or resentment for his defeat or if Grant had gloated over his victory, the future of the United States might have been different. Certainly Lee had the option of dispersing his army into the Blue Ridge Mountains to continue the war as a guerrilla action. The longer the war lasted, the less likely was a peaceful ending. But with Grant's desire for fairness and Lee's acceptance of defeat with dignity, they preserved the Union and set an example for future generations (Winik, 2001).

As with most other successful negotiations, small things can set the tone and influence the outcome. The two generals greeted each other respectfully and initially talked about the April weather and having met as young officers during the 1846 war with Mexico. Grant was unarmed and did not ask for Lee's saber or handgun as a symbol of surrender. Lee was wearing his best dress uniform. Grant, wearing a field uniform dusty from riding, apologized for not being in dress uniform. Lee had heard earlier that his son had been killed. Having received a message from Union General Williams that morning that contradicted this bad news, Lee asked Grant if he might speak to Williams. Grant immediately sent for Williams, and when he arrived, Lee thanked him for his thoughtfulness in reporting on his son's safety.

Since the treaty required the return of all U.S. government property, Lee said that most horses were personal property. Grant immediately agreed, adding that the men would need them for farming. Before they finished the reading and signing of the treaty, they discussed how many Union prisoners Lee had and how many troops. Grant, knowing that Lee had virtually no remaining supplies, told General Sheridan to provide enough rations for both groups (Commager, 1982).

A second surrender negotiation, seventeen days after Lee's surrender, between Union General Sherman and Confederate General Johnston also could have gone much differently. In November and December of 1864, General Sherman's devastating and vicious march to the sea in Georgia cut a destructive path sixty miles wide and three hundred miles long, earning him a reputation as a punitive and violent warrior. General Johnson's army was in much better shape than Lee's had been. Also, Lincoln's recent assassination had removed the Great Emancipator's powerful support for a nonpunitive peace.

At the negotiating table near Durham Station, North Carolina, General Sherman was not the fierce warrior his reputation suggested. The pact he worked out with General Johnson displayed great compassion. The agreement provided for Confederate state governments to resume governing as soon as they swore allegiance to the United States, plus several other provisions favorable to the South. When the Sherman-Johnson surrender document reached Washington, General Grant and Secretary of War Stanton noted how much it differed from the Appomattox surrender. Their primary concern was the almost immediate resumption of state and local government authority.

In an emergency meeting, newly inaugurated President Johnson ordered Grant to tell Sherman to inform the Confederates that hostilities would resume in forty-eight hours unless the surrender matched that of Appomattox. General Grant rode immediately from Washington to North Carolina and returned with a document identical to the one signed by Lee. Sherman willingly admitted he exceeded his authority, but he thought his proposals would have speeded reconstruction (Castel, 1979).

ADR and Reconstruction, 1865–1877

Four presidential administrations were involved in Reconstruction: those of Lincoln, who had already set up military protectorships in some southern states before the end of the war, Johnson, Grant, and Hayes. Many northerners were angry and resentful and wanted to punish the South so secession would not happen again. Officials sent to administer reconstruction programs in the South, along with many private profiteers, were referred to pejoratively as carpetbaggers. Some officials were opportunistic and corrupt, adding greatly to southern resentment and bitterness (Current, 1988).

One lingering consequence was the negative impact on race relations. Once southern states were allowed self-government in 1870, whites created a thicket of laws, called Jim Crow laws, separating the races and significantly restricting the rights of former slaves. Blacks were granted limited access to public places such as hotels, restaurants, schools, and hospitals, and their employment and housing opportunities were also extremely restricted. Many of these restrictions and their enforcement would continue long into the twentieth century.

However, many northerners came South with the best of motives and worked hard to help rebuild the region. Many had served in the war, were well educated, and had much to offer. Some stayed, starting successful businesses or running for public office (Current, 1988). A few applied ADR precursors to the issues of Reconstruction.

Arbitration for Former Slaves

General Oliver Howard was an extraordinary man by any standard. He was born in Maine, graduated from West Point, and served in twenty important Civil War battles. At the Battle of Fair Oaks, he lost his right arm. He went on to found and serve as president of Howard University, to write four books, including two on Native Americans, and to serve as head of West Point. As the lead commissioner of the Bureau of Refugees, Freedmen and Abandoned Lands during Reconstruction from 1865 to 1874, he emerged as an unsung hero of ADR.

Following the Civil War, in 1866, the Freedman's Bureau under General Howard established an arbitration process to resolve disputes between former slaves and their former owners. Over 100,000 such disputes, most over the issue of pay, arose annually during Reconstruction. The bureau created a three-person arbitration board to resolve such cases. It appointed the chairman, the former owner appointed a member, and the former slave was to appoint a third. But since most former owners refused to deal with a former slave's appointed member, the bureau appointed a white person as the former slave's representative. While this process was used frequently, many former slaves felt it was not fair. Certainly on its face, it did not appear to be neutral. However, since blacks could not be witnesses in courts until 1886, the process provided the only dispute settlement process available to a freedman (Foner, 1988).

Other ADR After the War

After the war, the United States continued the march of settlement to the Pacific. Business interests dominated federal politics, and the courts backed a view of the law in which property was often the determining factor in disputes.

The wartime need for arms, equipment, ships, and other supplies resulted in a tremendous growth of manufacturing capacity. All of this was done with government encouragement and with virtually no restrictions on business practices. Following the war, business expanded even more, and with Republican government supporters, the absence of regulation continued. Not satisfied with the freedom provided by this laissez-faire environment, business and their Republican partners arranged generous government subsidies of free western land for railroads, logging, and mining rights. State and local governments, eager for growth and services, provided similar encouragement to business organizations.

The work of a brilliant biologist was used to define the prevailing view of capitalism and conflict resolution: social Darwinism. Under this view, only the strong have a right to survive; thus, the weak have little recourse to use the courts, let alone ADR processes, to address their grievances.

In the next chapter, we step back and look at the development of ADR in business negotiations, then return to the nineteenth century to see how the United States found its way through social Darwinism to a new expansion of rights and further use of ADR.

Chapter Five

Commercial and Business ADR

The Phoenicians to the American Arbitration Association

As we saw in Chapter One, the use of alternative dispute resolution in commerce and business goes at least as far back as the Middle Ages law that allowed merchants to resolve marketplace disputes. But the roots of business disputes go even deeper.

Business, Profits, and ADR

In a domain where time truly is money, parties to commercial disputes generally prefer to resolve their differences quickly so they can get back to the business of making a profit. That priority has generally encouraged them to seek out alternatives to the lengthy process of litigation. What is more, business arrangements, in the form of written or oral contracts, from which disputes often arise, are the results of negotiations, a precursor of ADR.

Thus, merchants and other businesses have traditionally been at the forefront of the development of ADR, including negotiations, mediation, and arbitration. It would take much longer for businesses to extend these practices to include dealings with their employees.

Phoenician Traders: Inventing Business Negotiations

The Phoenician traders were a remarkable group whose greatest influence lasted three hundred years (1200–900 B.C.). Initially, they dominated sea trade at the eastern end of the Mediterranean, and they eventually traded with colonies throughout the Mediterranean. These early adventuresome seamen, first to use the North Star to navigate, discovered the Atlantic Ocean and circumnavigated the African continent.

More important for our story, they introduced a new way of organizing economic activity and put the business entrepreneur at the center of society. For generations, the trading of goods was mostly a ceremonial activity involving gift giving and patronage between states or up and down the political chain of command. The Phoenicians were the first to load up their ships with goods and set off to sell those goods in exchange for silver and gold.

Herodotus (484–425? B.C.) tells a story of trade between the Libyans and the Carthaginians (Harden, 1963). The Carthaginians would leave goods on the beach and return to their ship, where they would send out a smoke signal. The Libyans would then leave a quantity of gold next to the goods. The Carthaginians would inspect the offer and return to their ships to raise another signal and so on, until they were satisfied with the offer.

The Phoenicians and other early traders greatly streamlined such transactions, introducing two critical features of business negotiations: ports of trade and entrepreneurial merchants (Aubet, 1993). Ports of trade were temporary settlements outside major cities—and thus beyond the control of the authorities, who would generally take a cut of any activity that fell inside their city walls. Classic examples include Tyre, founded by the Phoenicians in about 2000 B.C., Carthage, and Hong Kong.

These new ports and the developing trade system created a new class, dominated by wealthy merchants who had ties to royal families and their own purely commercial interests. These merchants were deeply engaged in marketplace negotiations. Early records indicate the signing of contracts and other evidence of sophisticated negotiations. Some have speculated that arbitration may have been employed to resolve the inevitable disputes—the practice was already in use in international affairs as we saw with the Greeks, Egyptians, and Maris in Chapter Two—but there is no written evidence of such a practice.

During centuries of seagoing trade, other maritime practices and customs experienced sufficient acceptability among those affected that documentation began to occur. The earliest may have been on the island of Rhodes, a flourishing pre-Christian mercantile center. The document called Rhodian Sea Law, which dates from around 700 B.C. but is based on much earlier tradition, set out to resolve one of the most common areas of conflict at sea: who is responsible when a cargo is lost to storm or piracy. The Rhodian principle apportioned any such loss equally among the shipowner, the owners of the cargo, and the passengers. This early form of insurance and conflict resolution was employed throughout the shipping industry through the twelfth century.

Pre-Revolutionary Practices

A few early American colonists arrived with an understanding of ADR precursors from their business experience in Europe. Merchants engaged in shipping in European ports were acquainted with the arbitration traditionally used to resolve disputes in that milieu. Gradually, these practices began to take root in colonial ports. A few colonial laws helped the process. In 1632, Massachusetts, and in 1705 Pennsylvania, gave legislative approval to arbitration.

Colonial courts provided an obvious place for business organizations to seek resolution of their disputes. But ADR precursors were also developing outside courts, often in private settings. Businesses using ADR precursors preferred this privacy because it avoided undesirable negative attention. But the private nature of the process also limited the growth of precursors because it kept other businesses from learning about these alternatives to court.

Colonial lawyers were an unexpected group at the forefront of dispute resolution outside a court setting. A number of scholars point out that colonial lawyers were often viewed as dealmakers and problem solvers rather than court lawyers. Thus, they played a crucial role in helping farmers, merchants, and businesses work matters out by using the ADR precursors of negotiation, mediation, and arbitration. By 1760, when John Adams began practicing law, lawyers were more focused on the courts, which had grown more complex. Adams reported losing his first trial by failing to include several words in a writ.

Early U.S. Arbitration

By the end of the eighteenth century, New York had become a busy arbitration center, with a strong focus on the shipping industry. The earliest arbitration records of the New York Chamber of Commerce open a window onto the kinds of disputes that prevailed between 1779 and 1792. Many of the cases highlight the perils of the seagoing trade of the time. Several involve seamen seeking promised wages. One involves a cargo of rum that was unloaded from a ship that had sunk in a storm at Sandy Hook, just at the mouth of New York Harbor.

In one somewhat convoluted case, dated October 6, 1779, the New York City police brought a matter before the board involving a dispute between Peter Campbell, on the one hand, and John Walker and William Heath, on the other. Campbell had agreed to purchase a one-third share of a brigantine named the *Success* from the other two. Together, the owners had loaded the ship with apples and salt bound for Halifax. With the ship moored awaiting a pilot to take it out to sea, Heath prevented Campbell from returning to the *Success*. In his efforts to get back to the ship, he was eventually arrested and detained for three days by the master pilot. While he was detained, the *Success*'s cargo was unloaded and the ship resold, without Campbell receiving any of the proceeds. Campbell was out a considerable sum of money. Walker and Heath responded that Campbell did not have sufficient crew to handle the voyage. The arbitration panel disagreed, ordering Heath and Walker to repay Campbell in full, plus legal expenses, under a payment plan of 22 pounds a month (Chamber of Commerce of the State of New York, 1913).

After independence, the two nascent political parties lined up on opposite sides regarding the use of arbitration in business disputes. Federalist lawyers and courts in Massachusetts were so devoted to English common law that they resisted the use of arbitration as much as possible. Massachusetts did pass an arbitration law in 1786, for example, but it was seldom put to use because of this antipathy.

The anti-Federalists of Thomas Jefferson believed that arbitration offered a better approach to conflict resolution than the courts. It was quicker, simpler, and less expensive. Although Jefferson and many of his closest associates were lawyers, they were critical of lawyers and courts because of the expense, delay, and complexity they added to resolving disputes. They saw the Federalists' promotion of the courts over arbitration as retarding their young nation's capacity to grow commercially and financially. A Boston newspaper editorial made the Jefferson argument in 1804: "Continuances, appeals, demurrers, defaults and appeals therefrom, are chiefly all the work of the Attorneys: from motives of interests. By these means, the honest creditor is either delayed, forced to a sacrifice, or utterly deterred from seeking that justice of which our laws have become only a pretense" (Independent Chronicle, 1804).

Competition between courts and arbitration would play out for many years since this issue involved more than just the question of which forum would resolve a specific dispute. It also included the importance of court enforcement when there is an agreement between the parties to use arbitration in the first place, as well as the court enforcement when a losing party refused to abide by an award. If an individual court was disinclined toward arbitration, it could refuse to use its enforcement power and thus weaken the arbitration process by denying its finality.

Mississippi was the last state to abandon this type of court resistance to arbitration. Until 1998, Mississippi courts had reasoned that if a party had a legal right to bring an issue to court, the existence of a private agreement to arbitrate that issue could not keep the court from exercising its jurisdiction. Based on that reasoning,

Mississippi courts refused to order a reluctant party into arbitration even if that party had signed an agreement requiring it. The courts also refused to enforce arbitration awards. Courts in all other states had dropped this reasoning years earlier, and began enforcing arbitration awards and directing parties to use arbitration if they had an agreement to arbitrate their future disputes.

Nineteenth-Century Precursors to ADR in Business Disputes

During the nineteenth century, precursors to ADR continued to develop in commercial disputes as business activities and the population grew. On a number of fronts, ADR precursors gradually gained supporters, but it was largely limited to ad hoc use.

Mediation in the South and Southwest

Dispute resolution in the territory from Florida through Texas to California was strongly influenced by Spain in the first half of the 1800s. Spanish dispute resolution favored mediation, in contrast with the Anglo-American preference for courts and some arbitration. The Spanish community practice of electing *alcaldes* was prevalent in the South and Southwest.

An *alcalde*, or mayor, was a community leader with legislative and judicial roles. In their judicial role, *alcaldes* encouraged the use of mediation and required it before a lawsuit could be filed. With his broad discretion, an *alcalde* could encourage flexibility and creative options for resolving a dispute. Since *alcaldes* were not required to base their decision on formal law, they often took community values as a starting point (Simmons, 1968). By the mid-1800s, with the decline of Spanish influence in the region, *alcaldes* were being replaced by more formal judicial arrangements. However, the use of mediation remained popular for resolving business and other disputes.

Written Arbitration Opinions

In 1826, during the Greek War of Independence, a highly publicized dispute between a New York shipbuilder and the exiled government of Greece went before three arbitrators over a million dollar claim. Two American merchants, Le Roy, Bayard & Co. and G. G. & S. Howland, had contracted to build and outfit two frigates, the *Hope* and *Liberator*, which the exiled government planned to use to help rid their country of four hundred years of occupation by the Ottoman Empire. When the government could not continue to pay the shipbuilder during construction of the two ships, the disputants agreed to arbitrate the matter.

The arbitrators, one appointed by each party and the third by the other two, were asked to determine the actual cost of construction and outfitting, plus the disposition of the ships. They determined the merchant's cost was $894,908.62, and the outfitting cost was $34,246.44. The arbitrators directed that the *Liberator* be sold at auction to pay the builder. (The United States was the successful bidder.) Once the builder was paid all costs due, including a profit, the arbitrators directed that the *Hope* be turned over to the exiled government, along with any money remaining from the sale of the *Liberator*.

It was the practice at the time for arbitrators not to explain their reasoning, even in such a large arbitration award. As late as 1947, written guidance from the American Arbitration Association did not require a written explanation: "The Arbitrator, unless the submission provided otherwise, is not required to state the reasons for the conclusions reached but may do so if he sees fit. In labor arbitration, it has become a general practice to write an opinion to accompany the award, so as to promote a better understanding of the collective bargaining agreement and the human relations involved" (Kellor, 1948, p. 241).

But in the exiled government–shipbuilding case, the arbitrators issued a seventy-two-page document explaining their reasoning for their award (Zubrod, 2001). In a document titled, "Report of the Evidence and Reasons of the Award," the arbitrators wrote in part, "The prominent facts relating to the enterprise have gained publicity; and in a form grossly caricatured and incorrect. The Arbitrators feel constrained by a respect for public opinion, and a just regard for their own character, to make an exposition of the subjects of controversy submitted to them, with the grounds of their award" (p. 2).

The practice of arbitration has always been an evolving one, modifying as necessary to accommodate the desires and interests of the parties and the public.

Courts and Writers

After seven years of traveling and writing in Europe, James Fenimore Cooper returned in 1833 to a nation much changed by Andrew Jackson's election in 1829. Cooper's prolific writing in Europe showed him more comfortable with the gentlemanly upperclass politics of Jackson's predecessors. Having enjoyed years of success as an American writer, he now faced serious criticism from newspapers and journals accusing him of losing touch with his homeland. Angry and distressed after years of critical acclaim, he filed a number of libel suits against his critics, winning most and causing several journals to retract their views.

In 1839, following the publication of his momentous *History of the Navy of the United States*, he was criticized from a new quarter. The descendants of Commodore Oliver Perry took offense at Cooper's failure to support their contention that Perry's second-in-command, Jesse Elliot, had been a coward in the Battle of Lake Erie during the War of 1812.

This decisive naval battle had given the United States control of the Great Lakes, significantly diminishing the British army's effectiveness, and had earned Perry the permanent mantle of a great naval hero. The battle also began a long-running debate over Elliot's role. Although Elliot had performed heroically in other battles, in this case, he kept his ship, the second largest in the action, out of range while Perry's suffered extensive damage, eventually laying dead-in-the-water.

When Perry took command of Elliot's ship, he maneuvered it into a series of effective broadsides to the British line, which ultimately caused the British to surrender. At this point, Perry dispatched his famous line: "We have met the enemy and they are ours, two ships, two brigs, one schooner, and one sloop."

A court of inquiry requested by Elliot officially cleared him of wrongdoing. Initially, Perry had not been critical of Elliot. But when Elliot challenged Perry to a duel, Perry refused and sought to court-marshal Elliot for his performance in the battle.

Cooper examined all the evidence and decided to rely most heavily on Perry's earliest account of the battle, not his later version, which may have been much colored by the growing animosity between the two men. His brief account of the incident did nothing to diminish Perry's heroic exploits. He merely failed to castigate Elliot, an outrage to Perry's relatives and legion backers (Lounsbury, 1883).

Based on Cooper's prior successes in court, he sued Perry's descendants when their criticism appeared in newspapers. In court, the presiding judge, a devotee of arbitration, ordered the parties to arbitrate the dispute. Since arbitration did not require a lawyer to advocate for him, Cooper decided to represent himself. At stake was no more than $250 in damages, plus the loser had to publish the findings of the arbitration panel in newspapers in New York City, Washington, D.C., and Albany (Lounsbury, 1883).

Squaring off against one of the most able lawyers in the country, Cooper prevailed in the arbitration by using his superior knowledge of naval matters based on his years in the navy and by demonstrating how even-handedly he had weighed the evidence on Elliot's behavior. Pleased with prevailing in arbitration and the opportunity to defend himself personally, Cooper became an advocate of arbitration, encouraging others to avoid litigation by using it.

Early Institutional Support for Arbitration

During the last third of the 1800s, business trade groups began to support ADR as a matter of policy—a significant boost for what had been an ad hoc practice.

In 1871, New Orleans, a major port for the shipment of southern cotton, created the New Orleans Cotton Exchange to provide a trading organization for cotton buyers and sellers. The exchange's constitution called for mediation and arbitration to resolve disputes among its members. Similar exchanges or market mechanisms were established in other large U.S. ports for the same purpose in the late 1800s.

Following the example of many other cities, the Sioux City, Iowa, Board of Trade established the Board of Arbitration to resolve disputes between its members in 1873. Like other Boards of Trade, it also encouraged mediation.

The New York Stock Exchange in 1872 went even further by amending its constitution to provide arbitration of disputes between exchange members and their customers, at a time when consumers and customers had few avenues for resolving complaints.

Such business trade groups and associations became even more active in the twentieth century in providing these dispute settlement arrangements for disputes between members.

Federal Government Use of Arbitration

Prior to World War I, Secretary of State William Jennings Bryan aggressively moved the U.S. government to become the leading advocate for and participant in international arbitration. In just over two years as secretary, Bryan negotiated thirty treaties, including arbitration provisions covering both U.S. interests over weapons and territory and also business matters.

The federal government also used arbitration on an ad hoc basis in business disputes to which it was a party. In 1871, the Green Bay & Mississippi Canal Company refused to turn over to the federal government a canal on which it had done repairs until the government paid in full. Secretary of War Elisha Keyes offered to arbitrate the dispute, and the company agreed. The government appointed former Governor William Larabee of Iowa, and the canal company appointed former Senator James Doolittle of Wisconsin. Those two arbitrators selected Paul Dillingham of Vermont as the chairman of the arbitration board. The arbitrators spent most of the summer listening to testimony along the canal route. The government position was that the work done by the company was worthless; the company claimed the government owed $2 million. The arbitrators awarded the company $144,000. Congress subsequently appropriated that amount to settle the claim.

Early Twentieth-Century ADR Precursors in Business

Developments in the early twentieth century greatly strengthened the trend started by trade groups and associations that had begun promoting business ADR toward the end of the nineteenth century.

Although business disputes enjoyed a centuries-long history of turning to ADR precursors, the process had never benefited from a consistent advocate or logistical support. That would change significantly by 1926 after a series of developments in the United States and abroad gave new impetus to the process.

A Permanent Court of International Arbitration

Nicholas II, the last czar of Russia (1868–1918), proclaimed at his coronation in 1894 his intention to maintain peace with his neighbors and Europe. He convened the Hague Conference in 1898 to discuss peace through disarmament and nonviolent dispute resolution. The twenty-four nations participating in the conference made no progress on disarmament, but they succeeded in establishing the Permanent Court of Arbitration at the Hague. Although the Permanent Court of Arbitration was created by national governments, its jurisdiction included business and commercial disputes where two or more nations were involved, as well as international trade agreements that affected business.

The conference of 1898, and a subsequent one called by the czar in 1907, created processes, definitions, and rules for the administration of the ADR processes of inquiry, mediation, and arbitration. Conferees had high hopes that the ADR processes they had established would help prevent wars. Although the world war was not prevented, conferees' efforts did establish international ADR precursors on a stronger footing than ever before.

The League of Nations

A generation later, the establishment of the League of Nations after World War I provided for arbitration and committed member nations to use it in the Permanent Court of International Justice. But neither the Permanent Court of Arbitration nor the Court of International Justice provided education on the processes for using the court. Nor did either court have an active program to encourage nations and businesses to use these international courts. Other reasons also prohibited these international courts from reaching their intended potential until much later.

The U.S. Senate, for internal political reasons, failed to approve the treaty creating the League of Nations, thus removing one of the nations most likely to use the courts. That discouraged other nations from taking issues to the international courts. Following the war, European nations remained angry and suspicious of each other, and national movements toward fascism and communism strengthened the tide against seeking help from international courts.

The Pan American Union

Created in 1890, the Pan American Union (PAU) joined all of the sovereign nations of North, South, and Central America, for the purpose of encouraging trade and cooperation. Beginning in 1923,

PAU member nations began binding themselves together through a network of treaties featuring arbitration covering government and business interests. The result was an increasing reliance on arbitration within the Americas.

Unlike the poor European experience with the international courts, which provided no technical assistance in encouraging court use, the PAU provided member nations with information and training on how arbitration works and the advantages of its use. Thus, PAU nations began to change their culture to favor it.

U.S. Developments

In 1920, through the initiative of the New York Bar Association and the New York Chamber of Commerce, the first modern arbitration law was passed in New York. By 1925, fifteen other states had done the same, and Congress had enacted the U.S. Arbitration Law, which remains the basic commercial and maritime arbitration law.

These state and federal laws provided important underpinnings for arbitration by

- Making agreements to arbitrate future disputes legally valid and enforceable and revocable only as any contract could be revoked
- Closing the courts to parties to an arbitration agreement by requiring them to comply with their agreement
- Authorizing courts to enforce arbitration awards
- Authorizing courts to appoint arbitrators and otherwise expedite arbitration when one party has failed to move forward with the agreement to arbitrate

All of these changes were important, but the one authorizing courts to enforce the award of an arbitrator particularly stands out because it gave the awards a status virtually equal to a court decision.

Help from Visionaries

These new arbitration laws would change the view of arbitration in the court systems, but more was needed to prepare potential users of arbitration and to develop a cadre of available arbitrators. Two visionary New Yorkers, one a businessman and the other a lawyer, saw the need and responded.

In 1922, Moses Grossman, a New York lawyer, persuaded several like-minded colleagues to create the Arbitration Society of America. Grossman and his associates believed that arbitration needed to be promoted before it would be fully used for disputes of any kind. The society attempted to do that and more by conducting conferences and training sessions, issuing pamphlets and a monthly newspaper, identifying and training arbitrators, and establishing administrative processes to connect arbitrators and disputing parties.

In 1925, Charles Bernheimer, a prominent New York businessman, created the Arbitration Foundation with purposes similar to but more conservative than the Arbitration Society. His foundation sought to promote arbitration and mediation by studying, publicizing, and funding these ADR processes. Bernheimer's experience as chairman of the New York State Chamber of Commerce Arbitration Committee had convinced him of the usefulness of arbitration and mediation for resolving disputes outside of court. He was also convinced that too few disputants knew about arbitration and mediation.

American Arbitration Association

By 1926, Grossman and Bernheimer realized that their society and foundation had overlapping purposes and programs, so they decided to join forces by creating the American Arbitration Association (AAA). The new organization subsumed the programs and activities of both its predecessors and added others. With the help and guidance of an active board representing potential arbitration users, AAA created and published rules on how arbitration would be performed under its auspices. It developed panels of arbitrators with knowledge of the arbitration process and technical expertise in specific fields. A fee structure was developed to cover AAA administrative costs, and logistical arrangements were made for hearing rooms and transcribers.

Over the years, AAA has become the premier organization promoting and nurturing business arbitration in the United States, and eventually other parts of the world. When AAA celebrated its seventieth anniversary in 1996, it could look back on its dominant leadership in providing third-party arbitration services to the business world.

AAA maintains an array of third-party panels of individuals who specialize in specific industries or types of business disputes: construction, insurance, real estate, international, antitrust, securities, patents, bankruptcy, discrimination, accounting, health care, intellectual property, computer networks and e-mail, employment, and labor-management. Gradually, it expanded its dispute resolution services to include mediation, fact-finding, and elections.

Concurrent with the growth of AAA, business and trade associations became increasingly active in providing dispute resolution services for their members. AAA worked with many of these associations by helping them establish their internal dispute resolution process or managing their process within AAA.

As many businesses increasingly began operating at the international level, ADR and AAA also stepped onto the world stage. In this sphere, AAA provided the dispute resolution services directly or assisted organizations that provided similar services to AAA in other countries.

Contrasting Business and Labor-Management ADR Use

The effort to establish ADR precursors in business disputes stands in stark contrast with such efforts in labor-management disputes. Typically, when two disputing businesses decide to use a conflict resolution process, they have been largely free to do so without interference or objection. Thus, the progress of ADR development in business disputes has been at the discretion of the business community. The only time a court would become involved was when one or both parties chose to use the court.

Historically, employers in labor-management disputes have viewed these disputes as a zero-sum game, in which whatever the union gains is a loss or a cost to the employer. Therefore, employers have resisted dealing with unions, and in their resistance, they have often had the cooperation of the courts, and occasionally the police or the army. Therefore, the use of ADR was not at the union's discretion. Only when the law provided unions and employees with guaranteed rights was ADR possible in labor-management relations.

Chapter Six

Employee and Union Struggles

Reconstruction to the Coal Wars

When labor and management sit down today in an air-conditioned conference room at an airport hotel to discuss their next contract or an employee's overtime grievance, the negotiations are usually governed by decorum and mutual respect. Representatives from both sides are likely to sport ties and even advanced degrees. Although each side may view the other as an adversary, only rarely does one deny the other's right to be at the table.

It is almost impossible to imagine how different conditions were following the Civil War. Businesses operated in a nearly unfettered legislative environment. The courts were devoted to primacy of property rights. There was little concern for worker safety. Working hours were extremely long, poor pay prevailed, and benefits did not exist. With the system against them, periodic economic downturns and the arrival of 12 million immigrants between 1865 and 1900 producing a labor surplus, workers had little chance of bettering their lot.

A number of unions were formed during this period, but most had short lives. Their only power was the strike, and most of these were unsuccessful. Frequently, they ended with court injunction, police, National Guard, or willing replacement workers.

Struggles for Union Rights

The years from the Civil War to the start of the twentieth century witnessed steady growth in the economy but little, if any, improvement in workplace rights.

At the start of the twentieth century, the United States was an industrial nation dominated by huge trusts, with a small middle class, vast income gaps, a minimal public education system, and a justice system committed to ownership rights. State and federal legislation before 1914 provided for dispute resolution assistance only when the employer was willing to deal with the union, and the vast majority of employers were not willing to do so. None of this early legislation granted employees any rights.

Without recognized rights, worker groups had little success in gaining a voice in the workplace. Government action during World War I provided the only exception to employer dominance in the workplace. Antitrust enforcement and the Progressive era made attempts to shift this balance of power, but the courts resisted.

Commission on Industrial Relations

Presidential commissions attempted to use investigation, study, and reporting as a type of ADR, based on a belief that better-informed citizens and public officials would help resolve conflicts and prevent future disputes.

President Theodore Roosevelt initiated presidential commissions. A citizen group persuaded his successor, William Howard Taft, late in his term to appoint a commission to study and make suggestions on how to bring peace in the capital-versus-labor war. That group, the Commission on Industrial Relations, began its work in the Wilson administration, with three members each from labor, business, and the public. The commission chairman was a charismatic reformer lawyer named Frank Walsh, who had become famous by successfully defending the son of Jesse James.

In 154 days of hearings around the country in 1913 and 1914, the commission heard more than seven hundred diverse witnesses ranging from Mother Jones to John D. Rockefeller Jr., from Clarence Darrow to Henry Ford, from socialists to trust-building capitalists, as well as ordinary people: plumbers and porters, miners and mine owners, doctors and dockworkers, governors and grocers.

Each witness explained how the economic struggle appeared from his or her own life, and many offered insights into how it could be made better. Each hearing gained significant coverage in the popular press, amazing and fascinating readers of every income with the candor of witnesses and the remarkable information they shared.

When the commission chairman asked Mother Jones, a colorful and radical labor leader, "Where do you reside?" she answered: "Well, I reside wherever there is a good fight against wrong—all over the country. . . . Wherever the workers are fighting the robbers, I go there. . . . I belong to a class who have been robbed, exploited, and plundered down through many long centuries, and because I belong to that class I have an instinct to go and help break the chains" (Smith, 1985, p. 367).

John D. Rockefeller Jr., the young New Yorker who controlled the vast empire created by his father, presented a different point of view. In his first appearance before the commission, he denied any knowledge of wrongdoing or mistreatment of his employees, and he made assurances that he would willingly right any wrongs that came to his attention. Aggressive questioning by the chairman drew sympathetic news coverage for the Rockefeller heir and charges of commission bias. His second appearance before the commission was much different. This time, the chairman was armed with personal correspondence between Rockefeller and his underlings at a Colorado miners' strike involving armed resistance to unionization. When state militia and company guards attacked and burned a strikers' tent camp, men, women, and children died in what became known as the Ludlow Massacre of 1914. Under this scathing evidence and questioning, Rockefeller lost his composure, became incoherent, and promised to visit his mine holdings in Colorado immediately. When he visited Colorado, however, his solution was to create company unions to avoid real unions.

The commission hearings were published in eleven volumes, accompanied by a final report that attempted to present what Americans did and thought in the early twentieth century. The key question that the commissioners asked in the consensus section of the report was: "Have the workers received a fair share of the enormous increase in wealth which has taken place in this country during the period (1890 to 1912), as a result largely of their labors?" The commission's answer: "No" (p. 400).

Antitrust Regulation

Except for several recessions, the industrial boom following the Civil War continued for twenty-five years without restrictions by either state or federal regulation. Finally, Congress, recognizing the need for some business regulation, enacted the Sherman Antitrust Act of 1890, providing the government with the legal authority to use fines and court injunctions to stop business restrictions on competition.

President Teddy Roosevelt successfully attacked major business trusts through his bully pulpit speeches and his Justice Department's prosecution of more than thirty corporations under the Sherman Act. These efforts placed the negative impact of anticompetitive business practices before the public. In the cause of expanding rights and protections, Roosevelt, influenced by the Progressive movement, argued strongly for the vote for women and civil rights for African Americans. He pushed legislation in 1903 and 1906 regulating the railroads and started consumer protection in 1906 with the Meat Inspection Act and the Pure Food and Drug Act.

Ironically, in 1908, the Supreme Court applied the Sherman Antitrust Act to union boycotts aimed at companies. The unions themselves acted as a cartel in restraint of trade, the reasoning went. This allowed court injunctions against the unions' most effective weapons in their struggle against employers. In response, Congress enacted the Clayton Act in 1914 exempting unions from the provisions of the Sherman Act. Unions hailed the Clayton Act as their Magna Carta, but the Supreme Court persisted by ruling in 1921 that the Clayton Act did not exempt unions from the Sherman Act.

Eleven years later, Congress tried again with the Norris-LaGuardia Act of 1932, exempting unions from the harsh use of injunctions against their free speech and rights to assemble. In 1938, the Supreme Court agreed, finding Norris-LaGuardia constitutional.

The Progressive Era

The person most often associated with the Progressive era of 1900 to 1915 is Robert La Follette, a Wisconsin political and reformist leader known as Fighting Bob. As Wisconsin governor, La Follette had initiated the Wisconsin Plan, by which university studies were conducted to better inform or provide the basis of legislation expanding and protecting the rights of workers and others and pressing for political reform and social justice. His legacy included primary votes on political candidates, voter initiatives, conservation, and regulation of monopolies. For La Follette, the overriding issue was "the struggle between labor and those who would control, through slavery in one form or another, the laborers" (Smith, 1985, p. 294).

As U.S. senator and presidential candidate, La Follette continued to push a similar agenda but with less success. He always remained an outsider in the Senate. Although he fell far short of his and his followers' hopes for reform, the Wisconsin Plan, his progressive and reform legislative record, and his passionate speeches all had an impact. Some states followed his legislative initiatives, a few politicians carried his issues forward, and a troop of investigative writers and newsmen took up his reform message.

Violence and ADR in Coal Mining

In the early twentieth century, the coal industry was almost as important as railroads because coal was used in home heating and cooking, producing electricity, and powering manufacturing and railroad steam engines. Some examples of the violent relations between labor and coal mine owners highlight the difficulty of instituting the most basic form of ADR: negotiations.

An Odd Couple Using ADR Precursors

Although Teddy Roosevelt was not prolabor, his fair-mindedness in part moved him to intervene in a difficult anthracite coal strike in 1902. The two sides were represented by what can almost be seen as caricatures of good and evil. Speaking for the mine owner was George F. Baer of the Philadelphia & Reading Coal & Iron Co. He had a nearly Old Testament view of the mining company's role in the lives of the workers: "The rights and interests of the laboring man will be protected and cared for—not by the labor agitators, but by the Christian men to whom God in his infinite wisdom has given the control of the property interests of this country" (Pringle, 1956, p. 188). In the opposite corner was the thirty-year-old president of the United Mine Workers, John Mitchell, who began coal mining at age twelve. Roosevelt would come to like and respect Mitchell during the course of the long strike.

After the owners repeatedly refused to meet to hear the miners' grievances, Mitchell called a strike on May 12, 1902, idling 140,000 workers. The owners' refusal to meet and Baer's arrogant words were contrasted with Mitchell's articulation of the miners' conditions—441 men killed in mine accidents in 1901, for example—thus moving public opinion to the miners' side. But the strike continued as the owners ignored appeals from Archbishop Ireland and other notables, including the president.

In October, with winter and a congressional election nearing, Roosevelt, for both political and humanitarian reasons, arranged a New York City meeting with the parties. When the president brought them into the same room, Mitchell behaved politely and reasonably. Baer was crude and insulting, accusing the president of forcing the owners to meet with a criminal, Mitchell, and of failing to have the strikers enjoined under the Sherman Antitrust Act.

Roosevelt, outraged by the owners' behavior and frustrated by his lack of influence, immediately began planning to have the army operate the mines. He sent a representative to urge banker J. P. Morgan to get the owners' agreement to a presidential commission to resolve the dispute. Facing the threat of a government takeover and the banker's pressure, the owners reluctantly agreed to a commission, but insisted that they select the members. After arduous wrangling with owners over commission membership, agreement was achieved and the strikers returned to work. The commission granted a 10 percent wage increase and remedied a few minor grievances but did not grant the union recognition (Pringle, 1956).

This century-old example of ADR was primitive by today's standards. There were no negotiations, since the owners refused to meet with or speak directly to the union leaders. The efforts of the president and banker J. P. Morgan could be characterized as a type of mediation. However, the mediators used threats to achieve the agreement on the commission, and the owners selected the arbitrators.

West Virginia Coal Wars

A description of conditions in West Virginia provides another illustration of the deep-seated conflict between the economic haves and have-nots that existed in the early twentieth century. The conflict between political democratic ideals and what can fairly be labeled economic slavery stood as a barrier to ADR, unless violence interceded or, in the case of anthracite coal, a threatening U.S. president.

Between 1912 and 1920, a series of violent disputes resulted in numerous deaths and extensive property damage in what became known as the West Virginia Coal Wars. Moneyed interests had discovered the coal wealth in the low West Virginia mountains in the late 1800s, and by 1912, they were aggressively extracting coal with little regard for the men digging it. The mine owners attempted to control every aspect of the coal miners' lives by owning the roads, the towns, and all the housing; paying in scrip redeemable only at the company store; prohibiting assemblies of miners to discuss their conditions; and using guards, investigators, and spies for suppression and restraint. The United Mine Workers union attempted to speak for the miners on these conditions, as well as safety, hours, and compensation. Mine owners, backed up by state troopers and militia, local police, sheriffs, and mine guards, resisted unionization efforts with ferocity. The coal wars have been the subject of several movies, including *Matewan*, with James Earl Jones. The anthracite coal region where Teddy Roosevelt helped resolve the 1902 strike is the site of *The Molly Maguires*, starring Sean Connery. This film depicts the violent extremes that miners resorted to when the repression by mine owners allowed no peaceful means of improving their working and living conditions.

Curiously, two individuals named Hatfield—Henry D. Hatfield, the governor of West Virginia, and Sid Hatfield, a local police chief—played critical roles during the wars. The name Hatfield had been linked with McCoy as an example of unending feuds. However, these two Hatfields sought peace.

As governor of West Virginia, Henry D. Hatfield had dealt with the Paint Creek/Cabin Creek strike for months, sending state troopers to enforce the law, repeatedly establishing martial law, asking for federal assistance, encouraging Congress to hold investigative hearings, talking separately with representatives of both sides in a mediatory role, and dealing with the negative coverage by the national press. Throughout the ordeal, he had maintained his neutrality. With the owners continuing to refuse to talk to the union, Hatfield saw no voluntary solution. Therefore, in the spring of 1913, he wrote a recommendation that amounted to compromise for each side, and he urged the parties to accept it in the interest of peace. The governor's recommended settlement included these provisions:

- Granting miners the right to an honest weighman and two thousand pounds to equal a ton
- Establishing a nine-hour workday
- Prohibiting discrimination against union miners
- Requiring fair prices at company stores
- Setting a semimonthly payday

The union accepted, as did most of the owners. Following Hatfield's continuing persuasion, the remaining owners also agreed (Corbin, 1990).

Sid Hatfield's story has a less happy outcome. He was the twenty-eight-year-old chief of police in Matewan, in Mingo County, West Virginia. A former miner with sympathy for the miners' plight, he had been chief for two years on May 19, 1920, when a group of mine detectives came to town to evict striking miners from their homes. Later, Hatfield gave his version of the tragic events that day in testimony in a U.S. Senate hearing.

The city's mayor and Hatfield asked the mine detectives if they had authority to evict the strikers. Their leader said they had a judge's order, but they refused to show it and continued the evictions on the outskirts of town. Later, the detectives returned to town in three cars, armed with rifles. The mayor told Hatfield to arrest them. When Hatfield informed them they were under arrest, the detectives arrested him based on their claim that they had a warrant. The detectives walked Hatfield to the train station intending to take him to jail in Bluefield. At the station, the detectives gave the mayor a paper to prove their authority. When the mayor called the paper bogus, an argument resulted, and a large number of shots rang out, killing ten individuals, including seven of the thirteen detectives and the mayor.

A few months later, on August 1, 1920, mine detectives assassinated Hatfield in broad daylight on the steps of the Welch, West Virginia, courthouse. Unarmed and accompanied by his wife, Hatfield was coming to court as a defendant on another matter (Corbin, 1990).

Slow Growth of Rights

Individual and group rights and protections flow from natural law, philosophers would argue. In the United States, they are made explicit in the Constitution and governmental acts. Generally these legal rights and protections reflect social values, but they often lag behind changes in these values. Disagreements over the existence or application of these rights and protections can lead to violent conflicts or to a court, or to the alternative to both, ADR. Thus, the growth of ADR is tied to the growth of rights and protections, and the exercise of these rights is dependent on an educated citizenry.

The struggle for women's rights was long and difficult. In 1848, Elizabeth Cady Stanton, Lucretia Mott, and other like-minded women convened in Seneca Falls, New York, launching the modern women's rights movement. The movement's purpose was broader than voting rights: it sought equal rights with males in all respects. Their efforts met with passionate resistance. The movement's first success with voting rights came in Wyoming in 1869. By 1916, eleven states had extended the vote to women. Four years later, following a heroic hunger strike led by Alice Paul, the Nineteenth Amendment granted the vote to all women. Other rights would gradually flow from this, but many years were required.

Black Americans had an even more difficult struggle. Although over 400,000 black Americans served in World War I, they returned home to a segregated society that would continue to deny them many rights.

Under the weight of cultural values and the continuing preference of courts for ownership rights over all others, black Americans and women would wait another fifty years before their rights were supported sufficiently to allow them to use ADR. Consumers' experience was much the same, since any challenge of business interests would be moved to a court, where the business interest would prevail.

The economic need for child employment to support most working-class families delayed compulsory school attendance until the early twentieth century. But even then, state attendance laws for children under age fourteen were not vigorously enforced, and attendance requirements could be as short as twenty weeks a year. Thus, universal public education was in its infancy and of little help in expanding ADR.

Prior to the Wilson administration, union and employee rights lacked any standing in the workplace. The only dispute resolution was provided by law, and only if both parties were willing to use it. Since dealing with a union was at the discretion of the employer, unions and employees did not have a right even to dispute resolution. As we shall see in the next chapter, the Wilson administration would change that.

Chapter Seven

Trains and a World War

Pulling ADR into the Twentieth Century

While the West Virginia coal wars of 1912 to 1920 present an image of U.S. industrial relations at their worst, one visionary industrialist saw that the needs of workers and capitalists were not completely at odds.

Henry Ford, whose Model T would begin to transform the nation in so many ways, had a crucial insight when he realized that his workers were not mere cogs in the industrial machine but something far more valuable: potential customers. His "five dollar day" pay plan introduced in 1914 was a critical breakthrough. While fellow industrialists were slow to catch on to the notion that workers could also become customers, Ford's vision would carry the day in the long run.

Meanwhile, studies such as that produced by the Commission on Industrial Relations in the Wilson administration laid the groundwork for government to take a role in establishing peace between labor and management. The crucial railroad industry earned special treatment.

The Special Status of Railroads

Railroads played a key role moving troops and materiel during the Civil War. After the war, they became the backbone of industry, trade, and transportation. The federal government and the states, anxious for the spread of reliable transportation, placed no restrictions on railroads, and in most cases they promoted their growth. Railroad operators became extremely powerful, and they had little motivation to treat the unlimited supply of laborers any way but harshly.

The Impact of Early Violence

Minor and unsuccessful strikes occurred in the first few years after the Civil War. But in 1877, unique circumstance and pent-up worker frustration with repeated wage cuts following the 1873 recession resulted in extreme violence.

In late July 1877, train crews on the Baltimore and Ohio Railroad struck against another wage cut, triggering a chain reaction that President Hayes condemned as an "insurrection." Popular anger over the dispatch of troops to reopen the line spread the strike to Baltimore, where huge crowds clashed with the militia. Simultaneously, work stoppages followed the rail lines across Pennsylvania to small mill and mining towns.

Thousands of Pittsburgh ironworkers and other residents battled with soldiers and burned Pennsylvania Railroad train cars and buildings. Across Ohio and Indiana, workers' committees took over their towns, halting all work until employers met their demands. The strikes and violence moved west from Chicago and St. Louis to San Francisco before the anger played out.

The ferocity of the strikes prompted several states to establish basic laws to attempt to resolve labor disputes. Maryland passed the first such law in 1878, providing for voluntary, binding arbitration with the parties sharing costs. The law simply authorized a state judge, when asked by both parties to a labor dispute, to appoint individuals to an arbitration board on which the judge would serve as chairman. During the following decade, similar laws were passed in New Jersey, Pennsylvania, Ohio, Iowa, and Kansas. In 1886, New York and Massachusetts each created a permanent three-member arbitration board with authority to mediate and arbitrate. None of these state laws was limited to railroad disputes.

The ruthless railroad business practices toward farmers created the Grange movement in farming states as a reaction to unfair shipping rates, which state regulators were unable to influence. Congressional hearings finally resulted in the Interstate Commerce Act of 1887, which established for the first time the principle that the federal government could regulate the railroads. This would ultimately prove to be significant for unions (Rehmus, 1976).

First Dispute Resolution Act

Responding to another major railroad strike in 1888, Congress passed the first federal labor dispute law, the Arbitration Act of 1888. The act provided two methods of dispute resolution: voluntary arbitration and the appointment of a commission to investigate the cause of a specific dispute. Given its voluntary nature, the arbitration provision was never used, but it was retained in subsequent laws. The investigative provision was used only a few times.

In 1898, because of the poor performance of the Arbitration Act, Congress passed the Erdman Act retaining arbitration and eliminating the investigative provision. Most important, the act provided for mediation by the commissioner of labor and the chairman of the Interstate Commerce Commission, at the request of either party. The initial use of this act was minimal, but between 1906 and 1913, the act was used sixty-one times, mostly in mediation cases and in a few arbitrations. In 1913, the law was amended by the Newlands Act, which created a permanent board of mediation and conciliation, authorized to handle negotiation disputes and contract interpretation disputes.

The Federal Government's Role

During World War I, the federal government took control of the railroads, operating them from 1917 to 1920 under the Railroad Administration. The administration negotiated labor agreements with unions and established national boards of adjustment in each agreement to interpret and apply its terms. The latter arrangement, the forerunner of grievance arbitration, would become universal in

U.S. labor agreements by 1950. This special wartime treatment gave railroad unions and ADR practices significant momentum.

The comprehensive Transportation Act of 1920 returned railroad operations to their private owners and created the U.S. Railroad Labor Board to hear and decide all unresolved disputes. The board handled thirteen thousand disputes during its five-year existence. The law continued the use of boards of adjustment to handle grievances. However, both railroad labor and management were disappointed by the 1920 act because it relied too much on the Railroad Labor Board as the final arbiter of disputes and not enough on collective bargaining and mediation. Both the Democratic and Republican parties endorsed revisions, as did both President Harding and Coolidge.

Labor and Management Cooperation

After several bills failed in Congress, President Coolidge in late 1924 urged the railroads and the unions to jointly work out a bill that would ensure peace in the industry and passage by Congress. During 1925, the parties held a series of meetings focused on their best experience in dealing with each other. When they reached an agreement, they jointly presented their bill to Congress, which passed it with large majorities as the Railway Labor Act of 1926.

In testifying on the parties' bill, a railroad witness said: "I want to emphasize again that this bill is the product of a negotiation between employers and employees which is unparalleled, I believe, in the history of American industrial relations." In explaining the reasons for the bill, he said it is "not for the purpose of having governmental power exerted to compel the parties to do right but in order to obtain Government aid in their cooperative efforts" (Rehmus, 1976, p. 8).

The basic features of the 1926 Railway Labor Act remain in place today:

- Protection of employees' right to join a union
- Protection of unions from company dominance

- Collective bargaining assisted by prompt mediation of disputes on rates of pay, work rules, and working conditions
- For disputes not resolved by mediation, use of voluntary arbitration or a cooling-off period and a presidential fact-finding board
- Prohibition of strikes or lockouts during these procedures
- Creation of the National Mediation Board to administer the act

In 1934 and 1936, amendments to the original act expanded coverage to airlines and their employees and authorized the National Mediation Board to establish rules and procedures to determine whether groups of employees wished to be represented in collective bargaining. Under these rules, the board established an election process to impartially determine employee wishes. Such elections could be considered another ADR precursor.

By enduring into the twenty-first century, the Railroad Labor Act of 1926 stands as a remarkable demonstration of the sustainability of an ADR process negotiated by the parties who will use it.

The U.S. Department of Labor

The Bureau of Labor, the predecessor to the Department of Labor, was created in 1885 as a part of the Commerce Department. Believing that objective information about labor problems would help resolve them, President Cleveland (1885–1889) had wanted the Bureau of Labor to objectively investigate the causes of labor disputes and possibly arbitrate them. Congress, unwilling to have the government become so involved in business matters, did not fund the president's plan. Seeking to accomplish part of his goal, Cleveland appointed a highly respected statistician named Carroll Wright to head the bureau, a position Wright would hold for twenty years under both Republican and Democratic presidents. Wright acted as a presidential adviser on labor matters and prepared objective reports on numerous labor issues and disputes but did not become actively involved in resolving disputes (Grossman, 1973).

On his last day in office, President Taft signed legislation to create the Department of Labor in March 1913. President Wilson, following through on his promise to support unions, appointed the first trade unionist to head a major federal department. The appointee, William B. Wilson, was a Scottish immigrant, a former coal miner, a union official, and a member of the Sixty-Second Congress where, as chairman of the Committee on Labor, he played a crucial role in creating the department. The new secretary had left school at age eleven to work in a coal mine. He was a founding member of the United Mine Workers union and once held its second-highest elected office, secretary-treasurer.

U.S. Conciliation Service

The 1913 act creating the Labor Department gave the secretary of labor "the power to act as mediator and to appoint commissioners of conciliation in labor disputes whenever in his judgment the interests of industrial peace may require it to be done." Secretary Wilson quickly ordered his staff to begin mediating labor-management disputes. He then pushed Congress until it approved the U.S. Conciliation Service (USCS) in 1917. Renamed the Federal Mediation and Conciliation Service in 1947, Secretary Wilson's creation would become the oldest continuing mediation institution in the United States.

In implementing his department's mediation function, Secretary Wilson knew he had the active backing and encouragement of trade union leaders; the president's chief aide, Colonel Edward House, himself a skilled mediator and negotiator; and Secretary of State William Jennings Bryan, a former trade union lawyer and skilled negotiator. In his first annual report, Secretary Wilson defined his role. "With reference to labor disputes," he wrote, the secretary of labor's job is to take on "diplomatic duties analogous to those of the Department of State with reference to international affairs. The Department neither dictates nor arbitrates; it negotiates and recommends." As for the duty of the Labor Department, he continued, it is "to represent wage-earners' interests with fairness to all other individuals' interests."

By the end of 1914, the department had mediated thirty-three cases using staff from other functions within the department. With the increase in cases accompanying the buildup to world war, Congress in 1917 provided a budget to create the USCS within the department with its own staff of conciliators. By 1918, the department had mediated 1,217 cases.

To head the USCS, Secretary Wilson turned to his boyhood friend, Hugh Kerwin. The pair had met in Kerwin's father's shoemaker shop in Arnot, Pennsylvania, around the turn of the century. Wilson credited shoemaker Kerwin with promoting his early self-education by encouraging him to read in an extensive library in the shoemaker's back room. This informal public library was the gathering place for young men in the town. With Kerwin's encouragement, Wilson read everything available, including the *Congressional Record* (Babson, 1919).

Years later, the younger Kerwin would serve as Wilson's aide in Congress and during his tenure as labor secretary. Kerwin, as the first director of the USCS, ran the agency for twenty years through, from his point of view, the busy years of World War I, the quieter 1920s when unions struggled to stay alive, and finally, the frenetic 1930s following President Roosevelt's grant of union rights.

USCS at Work

The secretary of labor's first annual report to Congress in 1914 described the first case mediated by the department. It involved the New York, New Haven & Hartford Railroad Company and the Brotherhood of Railroad Clerks, which had jointly requested mediation help on May 24, 1913, when the department was but two months old. The terse report read:

> Mr. G.W. W. Hanger [then chief statistician of the Bureau of Labor Statistics and acting commissioner of labor statistics] having been

thereupon detailed as commissioner of conciliation, the matters at issue were taken up by him in conference with each of the parties at New Haven, Conn. These conferences continued until June 2, 1913, when a satisfactory adjustment was secured, covering all points at issue. The controversy hinged mainly on different interpretations of the prior agreement as to the rules governing wages, seniority rights, and other conditions of employment which had been made by the clerks' organization with a previous general manager of the railroad in January 1913.

"Commissioner of conciliation," used to refer to Hanger, is the title that was used by all USCS mediators, based on the statutory language authorizing the labor secretary to "appoint commissioners of conciliation."

Early on, mediator qualifications were an issue, as a 1918 citizen's letter to the labor secretary suggests: "You have a large and active corps of conciliators who are sent out all over the country to adjust labor disputes. From personal experience, I know some of these men have presented their card with the Union label conspicuously displayed thereon. This immediately suggests that they are not nonpartisan and are not competent to act as impartial mediators" (copy obtained by author from Department of Labor Library).

The letter makes clear the need for mediators to be impartial in fact and in appearance, and that small things are scrutinized to assess those requirements. Of course, anyone with experience in collective bargaining would come from a background representing one side or the other. The charge was often made that most USCS mediators were former union representatives. The USCS's refusal to make public their mediators' backgrounds added to that suspicion. The letter also raises a nomenclature question by using the phrase "adjust labor disputes" to describe the work of the mediator rather than "mediate." The USCS used this language as well. As late as 1931, that expression was still used in a letter from the secretary to a congressman.

Since collective bargaining was not widespread—that term had not been used until the late 1800s—few individuals had much experience in the process. Most who arrived at the bargaining table had had little experience in either negotiations or participation in mediation. Therefore, these early full-time mediators spent much time gently explaining how to bargain and coaching the parties on the process. As late as the mid-1930s, USCS director John Steelman was explaining, "The primary work of our mediator was educating the parties on how to negotiate and use mediation. The parties did not know what they were doing or how to do it" (Steelman, 1975, p. 19).

From the beginning, mediators were made available when labor and management made a joint request for help. If a request was received from only one side of a dispute, a mediator might be assigned to determine whether a joint request could be elicited. In cases in which media coverage suggested the significance of a dispute, a mediator would be assigned to attempt to mediate, even in the absence of a request.

In addition to mediation, USCS in its early years also investigated and prepared reports on disputes, continuing a practice started under the Bureau of Labor. This method of dispute resolution, another ADR precursor, was based on the view that objective information about the facts of the dispute would ease either voluntary resolution or mediation.

In the early years, a typical USCS mediator technique was to persuade the parties to accept arbitration of their dispute. If the parties agreed, the process used an arbitration board consisting of a representative of each party and a chairman appointed by the USCS director or secretary of labor. By the 1920s, USCS mediators continued to encourage parties to use arbitration where appropriate, but they began to use either a staff mediator with arbitration experience or a private citizen as arbitrator.

Even at this early stage, building trades unions argued over which union should perform certain categories of work. Since such jurisdiction disputes often resulted in disruption of work projects,

USCS mediator John Lennon was asked by the American Federation of Labor (AFL), an early association of unions, to assist in creating a process to resolve these disputes. With his help, a board and process were established within the AFL in 1919 that has operated almost continuously since. Currently, the group is called the Joint Board on Jurisdictional Disputes. The mediator's work with the AFL appears to be an early form of what is now called dispute resolution design. Such efforts involved the parties in creating their own process for resolving their own disputes, often with the assistance of a third party.

ADR Machinery During World War I

The U.S. entry into World War I placed greater demand on the nation's production capacity than ever before. Compounding the problem was a labor shortage caused by the absence of men drawn into the military and a significant reduction in immigration. All of this demanded cooperation and coordination. Initial efforts by the government lacked both.

To improve cooperation, President Wilson called labor and industrial leaders together to develop an industrial code. Labor and industry each selected a public member to act as cochairman of their deliberations. In ten weeks, the group developed an agreement on no strikes and no lockouts and freedom for workers to join unions. The group also endorsed the idea of a living wage and eight-hour day. To implement the voluntary code, the first War Labor Board was created with five industry members, five union members, and two public members. The board was remarkably successful in using informal mediation and formal arbitration orders to resolve most conflicts. It succeeded in ending many strikes by offering strikers a hearing and a decision if they returned to work. The board also established dispute resolution processes for union representation elections, appropriate bargaining units, and majority rule. The 1930s New Deal labor relations boards would make use of all these practices.

In the few cases where one or both parties refused to follow a board decision, the matter was referred to President Wilson, who was willing to use strong-arm methods to produce a resolution. When Western Union Telegraph defied a board order, Wilson placed the U.S. Post Office in charge of the company for the duration of the war. The War Department took over a Smith & Wesson munitions plant when management ignored a board order. Strikers in a Bridgeport, Connecticut, plant who ignored an order to return to work were told their draft board would be ordered to reconsider their draft status.

The cooperative arrangements voluntarily adopted to resolve disputes during the war were remarkable given the history of industry hostility toward unionization. The arrangements resulted in phenomenal growth in union membership, soon exceeding 5 million. However, industry extracted significant commitments for its agreement to the code. For example, industry representatives, fearing the code would permanently alter employer-employee relations, insisted on a promise by the public and union members that the arrangement would continue only for the duration of the war. They also resisted a code item requiring collective bargaining with a union. They would agree only to bargain with shop committees of workers rather than experienced union negotiators, demonstrating employer resistance to a "level playing field" and their refusal to make cooperation permanent. Former President Taft, the cochairman selected by industry, said that to achieve industries' approval of the code, "I had to read the riot act to my own people" (Lombardi, 1942, p. 249).

The government made several other arrangements to resolve labor-management issues. The War Department established the Containment Adjustment Commission with the AFL that created the "prevailing rate" process for wage setting. Similar commissions were created to deal with problems in long-shore labor, coal mining, and shipbuilding.

Secretary Wilson appointed Felix Frankfurter as his assistant to establish policy and oversee coordination among the numerous wartime bodies involved in production and dispute resolution. President Roosevelt would later appoint Frankfurter, a law professor and a founder of the American Civil Liberties Union, to the Supreme Court, where he would be a strong supporter of Roosevelt's New Deal. In his policymaking role, Frankfurter required all government wartime contracts to include a dispute settlement process.

USCS During Wartime

An expanded USCS mediator staff was heavily involved in mediating disputes during the war. USCS caseload surged to 1,789 in 1919 from 378 in 1917. Although there were strikes, the mediators were credited with shortening many and preventing even more. USCS mediators also assisted some of the commissions created during the war.

By the war's end, many individuals and groups had gained extensive ADR experience in peacefully resolving issues between workers and employers. In addition to negotiations, mediation, and arbitration, some had gained experience with processes of representation elections, creating formulas for wage settlement, working together in committees with a neutral chairman, and jointly developing policy statements. As remarkable as this extensive use of ADR was, its dismantling following the war, discussed in Chapter Eight, was more remarkable.

With the decline of collective bargaining and trade union strength after the war, the USCS mediation staff and caseload also declined. After the record 1,789 cases in 1919, the average annual USCS caseload was fewer than 560 over the next thirteen years. After the first year of President Roosevelt's New Deal labor legislation, the caseload jumped to 833 and continued to rise until and throughout World War II.

A Private ADR Promoter

Between 1900 and 1920, the National Civic Federation (NCF) had promoted both mediation and arbitration in labor disputes, playing a role much like the Arbitration Society and the Arbitration Foundation did later for commercial arbitration. The foundation, supported financially by a few corporations, had a board including two union officials (Samuel Gompers, president of the AFL, and John Mitchell, president of the mineworkers union) and high-level business representatives (Witte, 1952).

Given the participation of labor representatives and the well-known views of members such as businessman and U.S. Senator Mark Hanna, the NCF studies and papers on social and humanitarian issues found some willing listeners. Senator Hanna, a strong supporter of cooperation with unions, had been an active adviser to President Roosevelt's mediation efforts in the anthracite coal strike in 1902 (Smith, 1985).

Having successfully promoted creating a mediation function in the Department of Labor and cooperation between labor and management during World War I, NCF shifted its interests to other matters after the war. Given the strong business opposition to working with unions after the war, NCF recognized it lacked the strength to oppose the business sector.

The gains in rights for labor and the resulting advances in ADR of the war years would be short-lived. As we shall see, the interwar years, the Great Depression, and Roosevelt's New Deal would take ADR, and the country, on a roller-coaster of boom and bust.

Chapter Eight

Labor-Management ADR, 1920–1945

Bust and Boom

World War I provided trade unions with their first taste of real success. With key industries taken over by the federal government and a sense flowing from Washington that workers were an integral part of the war effort, union membership surged and public acceptability peaked. All of this would decline just as dramatically in the early 1920s with a return to the antiunion practices that dominated before the war. But with the onset of the Great Depression and World War II, the Roosevelt administration would put unionization and ADR on the road to becoming business as usual for vast swaths of the economy.

The End of the Trade Union Golden Era

Following World War I, employers were quick to roll back workers' newfound rights. High inflation and corporate America's aggressive antiunionism resulted in more strikes than ever before. In response, President Wilson called another industrial conference composed of labor, management, and public representatives. Hoping for an outcome similar to the wartime conference, the president asked the conferees to formulate a code for genuine and lasting cooperation between labor and management.

Disappointingly, management adamantly refused to recognize unions beyond the war period, and the conference ended with no agreement. Without government power behind them or the threat of war, the unions were powerless to move management. Within a year of the end of the war, union membership and collective bargaining declined drastically. Two aggressive employer initiatives during the 1920s disabled unions even more: the American Plan and the open shop campaign.

The American Plan and Open Shop Campaign

The war period had created hysteria about foreigners and foreign ideas. Although immigration had stopped during the war, left-leaning socialist and communist unions had earned popular suspicion by opposing the war. Federal Espionage and Sedition Acts and similar state acts during the war added concerns about disloyalty and unorthodox ideas.

The success of the 1917 Bolshevik Revolution in Russia continued to cause anxiety under the influence of a widespread red scare. A heated debate about immigration following the war focused on this wartime experience. The major union federation, the AFL, strongly opposed immigration, yet employers turned this hysteria against trade unions with the American Plan and the open shop campaign in a successful effort to establish their dominance in employment relations. Coincidentally, the effort was bolstered by a two-year economic slowdown that created a labor surplus, further weakening the unions.

During the war, most employers had insisted that they would bargain only with shop committees and not with union officials, having found these inexperienced bargainers much easier to deal with and often intimidate. Therefore, they sought to reestablish this practice under their American Plan.

Under the plan, employers replaced independent trade unions with in-house employee representatives approved by the employer, and thus robbed the trade unions of their unique ADR representation role. The name *American Plan* also helped highlight the employers' argument that outside representation by a trade union was foreign and socialist, if not communist.

Playing on the same distorted view of pseudo-Americanism, the open shop campaign successfully argued that it was un-American to require workers to join a union under arrangements called closed shop agreements. The success of this effort denied unions their only source of income, dues paid by members. The campaign was massive: 150 employer organizations in just New York, Illinois, Michigan, and Connecticut actively supported the campaign under their slogan "equal opportunity for all and special privilege for none." National Association of Manufacturers' president John Edgerton explained the campaign's appeal this way: "I cannot conceive of any principle that is more purely American, that comes nearer representing the very essence of all those traditions and institutions that are dearest to us than the open-shop principle" (Brooks, 1971, p. 145).

Throughout the 1920s, union membership dramatically declined, as did the application of mediation and arbitration to negotiations between labor and management. While railroad unions with their separate legal arrangements fared better than other unions, they declined as well. In 1901, overall union membership was in the range of 1 million; in 1919, membership reached its peak at 5 million. From that peak, it declined dramatically and did not grow again until the 1930s New Deal.

High Rollers Versus the Vast Majority

After a few years of economic adjustment from wartime to peacetime, the economy recovered and in 1922 ushered in seven years of unprecedented prosperity. However, the prosperity was skewed to favor the few. While productivity rose 42 percent during the decade, by 1929 1 percent of the population owned 40 percent of the nation's wealth and the bottom 93 percent of wage earners experienced a 4 percent income drop. During the decade, persons with income of $500,000 or over rose from 156 to 1,489, while a full 80 percent of the population did not earn enough to be taxed.

The high-roller economy rode new consumer credit arrangements, an extraordinary number of bank and business mergers, and an inflated stock market to the 1929 market crash, ushering in high unemployment and the Great Depression.

Presidential Attitudes in the 1920s

The three Republican presidents of the 1920s loved business, and only one of them saw problems in what was happening with the economy.

President Harding's (1921–1923) brief thirty-month tenure in office featured the Teapot Dome Scandal, which sent several members of his cabinet to prison. The scheme involved the secret lease of the Teapot Dome government oil reserves to the Mammoth Oil Company by Secretary of the Interior Albert B. Fall. This major fraud against the government, the president told a friend, was an insider scam, typical of business practices during the 1920s (Russell, 1968). Although Harding himself was not involved in the wrongdoing, the shock of the scandal took a toll on his health, and he died before the full extent of the scheme became known.

Advisers to his successor, President Calvin Coolidge (1923–1928), warned him of inequities in the economy (falling commodity prices with an impact on farmers and modest improvements in wages and benefits of workers compared with productivity gains) and danger signs (excessive power of holding companies, trusts, and merging banks). But Coolidge remained committed to his faith in the primacy of property rights, diminished only by modest taxes and minimal regulation. His most famous and telling remark on his views was, "The chief business of the American people is business" (Ferrell, 1988, p. 61).

Although Coolidge was no supporter of labor unions, he believed strongly in self-regulation and conciliatory handling of conflicting viewpoints. Those views caused him to give strong support to the ADR work of the Department of Labor's USCS in labor disputes (McCoy, 1967) and to urge railroad labor and management to develop what became the Railway Labor Act of 1926.

President Hoover (1928–1932), having been a businessman and secretary of commerce under Coolidge, understood business. But he also understood humanitarian needs from his food relief work in Europe following World War I, and he supported a more activist government than his immediate predecessors had. However, the stock market crash and the Great Depression began during his administration, and he was blamed for it and for the 14 million unemployed as his term ended.

Later historians would treat Hoover more kindly, recognizing that he believed labor, farmers, and government needed to be strong enough to counter the power of business by creating an economic partnership. Such a partnership would have created an excellent environment for ADR. Unfortunately, he had too little time, and no one, certainly not the business establishment, was ready for such ideas.

During President Harding's administration, Hoover took strong stands against business interests to buttress weaker segments of society. In 1922, he opposed the attorney general's sweeping injunction of a railroad strike, viewing it as grossly unfair and excessive in denying union officials' right to even discuss their strike strategy. He believed that a limited injunction followed by mediation would have been more appropriate. At the height of employers' push for the American Plan and the open shop campaign, he urged that mediation be used with shop committees to assist them in negotiations with employers.

In 1922–1923, as secretary of commerce, Hoover successfully mediated an eight-hour day in the steel industry (Fausold, 1985), and as president, he signed two laws that would ultimately aid ADR. In the Agricultural Marketing Act of 1929, the federal government made its first effort to bring negotiations for farmers into crop pricing by providing voluntary marketing arrangements and by creating the Farm Board to coordinate farm production (Fausold, 1985). In the Norris-La Guardia (Anti-Injunction) Act of 1932, Hoover followed through on his strong stand opposing injunctions against trade unions back in 1923.

Hoover would later be recognized by historians as the first president since Teddy Roosevelt to pay serious attention to environmental concerns, an area of disputes in which ADR would have an impact fifty years later (Burner, 1979; Schlesinger, 1979; Schlesinger and Israel, 1971; Smith, 1987).

The Arrival of Franklin Delano Roosevelt

The election of Franklin Roosevelt in November 1932 significantly changed the status of trade unions and ADR in labor-management disputes. As a result of legislation and government support during Roosevelt's years as president, trade unions experienced tremendous growth, as did collective bargaining and mediation.

The Roosevelt administration came to Washington with a plan to reform government, pull the nation out of economic depression, and get the nation back to work. The president's legislative initiatives also supported a large array of innovative social and economic programs.

The New Deal

A two-term governor of New York from a wealthy family, Roosevelt arrived in Washington in the spring of 1933 in the midst of the Great Depression. He came armed with a brain trust of experts, having promised during the campaign to get the country back on its feet and to support "the forgotten man." He would become America's most activist president. During the six months between his election and inauguration, the economy became even worse, and the expectations and pressure on him became even greater.

With a strong Democratic majority in both the Senate and House, Roosevelt's first term was a whirlwind of legislation and administrative action that became known as the New Deal. His first actions focused on economic reform by closing and restructuring banks, abandoning the gold standard, and providing support for farmers and workers.

Norris-La Guardia (Anti-Injunction) Act of 1932

The Norris-La Guardia Act bears the name of two Progressive Republicans who sponsored it: five-term Senator George Norris of Nebraska, a supporter and confidant of FDR, and Representative

Fiorello ("Little Flower") La Guardia of New York, later the colorful mayor of New York City. Their progressive instincts persuaded them of the need for a more balanced relationship between labor and management. Their very brief statute began that balancing effort and almost immediately encouraged increased unionization.

Although the law was not officially a part of the New Deal, since it was enacted just prior to the Roosevelt administration, the Norris-La Guardia Act was very compatible with the New Deal. For years, trade union activity had been halted by court injunctions on the theory that these activities were a restraint of trade and therefore prohibited by antitrust laws; even earlier courts had identified unions themselves as conspiracies and therefore subject to an injunction.

Norris-La Guardia prohibited federal courts from enjoining unions except under very narrow circumstances. Thus, unions were recognized as exercises of free speech and assembly, and their activities of organizing, striking, picketing, and boycotting were recognized as legitimate exercises of their economic interests, on a par with employers' exercise of their economic interests. The law also helped trade unions by outlawing yellow dog contracts, by which individual employment agreements committed the employee to never join or help a union as a condition of continued employment.

Although the Norris-La Guardia Act was extremely important in removing the courts from the relationship between employers and unions, Roosevelt's New Deal would move even more aggressively in support of union and employee rights and the growth of ADR.

National Industrial Recovery Act of 1933

In the first one hundred days of the Roosevelt administration, two major economic recovery statutes were enacted: the National Industrial Recovery Act (to reduce unemployment by shortening working hours, increasing pay, and eliminating unfair trade practices) and the Agricultural Adjustment Act (to support crop prices for farmers). Both would ultimately be declared unconstitutional by the Supreme Court for granting legislative authority to the administration and exceeding the federal government's constitutional authority in regulating private matters.

The National Industrial Recovery Act, typically referred to as the NRA and symbolized by a blue eagle, was abolished when the Court declared portions unconstitutional two years after its enactment. But some of its remaining portions, along with several other new issues, were enacted into several separate new statutes covering minimum wages and hours, child labor regulation, social security, and unemployment insurance.

The National Labor Relations Act of 1935, known as the Wagner Act, carried forward the NRA's new direction in labor-management relations by taking Section Seven of the 1933 act and expanding it by making unions and their activities legal. While the NRA was in effect from 1933 to 1935, the president appointed a nonstatutory Labor Board to assist in resolving labor-management disputes that arose under Section Seven. With Senator Robert Wagner as chairman and prominent representatives of both labor and management as members, the board engaged in informal negotiations and mediation to assist parties in complying with the new law and regulations.

National Labor Relations Act

Senator Robert Wagner of New York was a liberal Democrat who emerged as one of the chief architects of FDR's New Deal. As a state judge, he proved himself a friend of labor by refusing to enjoin unions that breached labor agreements, but he did not show the same compunction when employers broke the rules. Wagner championed the National Labor Relations Act, which came to bear his name.

Given the employer attitudes and the employment practices of the preceding seventy years, the public policy shift announced in Section Seven was truly remarkable: "Employees shall have the right to self-organization, to form, join, or assist labor organizations, to bargain collectively through representatives of their own choosing, and to engage in concerted activities, for the purpose of collective bargaining or other mutual aid or protections." In Section Eight, the law listed unfair labor practices that employers were prohibited from engaging in while dealing with employees or their union. The law made it illegal to interfere with an employee or a union exercising rights under the law, to discriminate against a union member, and to refuse to bargain with a union selected by a majority of employees.

This last measure in the Wagner Act established as national policy the practice of negotiations between employers and unions, thus placing this ADR precursor on a very prominent footing and opening the door for mediation.

To the surprise of many, in 1937, the Supreme Court declared the National Labor Relations Act constitutional by a five-to-four vote.

Since the NLRA was not self-executing, Congress created administrative and enforcement machinery known as the National Labor Relations Board (NLRB), one of the early quasi-judicial boards with a status equal to a federal district court, the lowest-level federal court. The NLRB consisted of a three-member board appointed by the president with consent of the Senate, plus a staff of lawyers, agents, and support personnel.

The three-member board established policy and rendered decisions on unfair labor charges and union representation questions. The board's agents investigated unfair labor practice charges and conducted representation elections. The board's lawyers prepared cases and presented them to the board for decision.

From the beginning, the NLRB was known for its vigorous enforcement of the law. In doing so, it created a new common law of employment relations, replacing employer dominance in the relationship. Its decisions in institutionalizing collective bargaining displayed good insight into the bargaining process.

The board did not require an employer to agree to any particular union proposal, but it did require bargaining in good faith, exchanging proposals and counterproposals, exhausting all reasonable efforts to reach agreement, and putting into written form any agreement reached. In addition to the bargaining process, the board made decisions on the subjects of bargaining. Since the law referred only to wages, hours, and working conditions, the board determined what those words meant in bargaining. When a union sought to bargain on a new issue, vacations, for example, and the employer refused to bargain on that subject, the board would decide if the refusal constituted an unfair labor practice. Thus, the list of issues on which bargaining was required grew. Still, some issues, such as the price of the employer's product, remained outside the scope of bargaining.

The passage of the NLRA had a revolutionary impact on relations between employers and employees. Some employers had great difficulty accepting the new employment conditions. Only the determination of the board and the support of federal courts would diminish their resistance.

Since the act applied to any employment relationship within interstate commerce, its coverage was broad. Only farmers, government workers, rail and airline employees, and employees of very small businesses were excluded from coverage of the NLRA.

The legal recognition of employee and union rights and the restriction of employer rights created a domino effect on union membership, collective bargaining negotiations, and mediation. As the first increased, the second and third increased as well.

Union and Collective Bargaining Growth

After the significant drop in union membership during the 1920s, unions began to regain some of their strength in the 1930s. By 1935, the unionized workforce had grown to 3.5 million, or 13 percent of the nonagricultural workforce. By 1940, the unionized workforce reached almost 9 million, or 27 percent of the nonagricultural workforce, well above the World War I high of 5 million. As World War II ended, union membership reached an all-time high percentage of the workforce: 35.5 percent, or 40 million workers.

U.S. Conciliation Service Growth

The number of USCS mediations increased proportionately with the increase in collective bargaining. The number of mediation cases hit a World War I peak of 1,789 in 1919. Dropping to 802 in 1920, the number of cases would not exceed 600 again until 1932. With the enactment of the National Labor Relations Act in 1933, the number grew to 4,231 by 1938 and to an all-time high of 23,121 in 1945 during the war.

World War II and ADR

World War II required an even greater increase in production than World War I. Therefore, disruptions from strikes could not be tolerated, although some did occur. To meet production needs, the administration put in place numerous boards and commissions to facilitate war production and to resolve labor disputes. The War Labor Board, as well as the existing NLRB and the USCS, all played significant roles in labor-management dispute resolution during the war.

In March 1941, President Roosevelt created the National Defense Mediation Board with four members each from labor, management, and the public. The board was to act as a super-dispute settlement agency handling cases that were not resolved by USCS mediators. By December 1941, when it became clear that a more powerful board was needed, FDR called a conference of twelve industrialists and twelve trade unionists with two neutral cochairmen to make recommendations on new arrangements. The conference recommended a no-strike pledge, that all disputes be settled peacefully, and that the president create a more powerful board. The president gladly accepted these recommendations.

In January 1942, as a replacement for the National Defense Mediation Board, FDR created the tripartite War Labor Board with four members each from labor, management, and the public. A year later, Congress gave the WLB statutory status. The WLB, with both a national and regional structure, drew on academics and lawyers to operate a vast labor-management dispute resolution process involving mediation, arbitration, and policymaking.

Labor-management negotiations that did not achieve an agreement were expected to use the assistance of the USCS before seeking the help of the WLB. This arrangement resulted in competition between the USCS and the WLB, with each eager to get involved in a dispute case. The differences in staff and power increased the competition between the two agencies.

The USCS was staffed by mediators, with a "let's-work-it-out" point of view, content to be armed with only the power of persuasion and with less formal education than WLB staff. The lawyers and economists on the WLB staff were comfortable with more formal hearings, weighing of evidence, and writing decisions. USCS mediators felt that the WLB staff was too eager to get involved, while the WLB staff felt the mediators hung on to cases too long rather than releasing them to the WLB. USCS mediators believed that the existence of the WLB offered labor or management a "second bite of the apple," by which they meant that a party not completely satisfied with the outcome of mediation would move to the WLB for another chance. USCS mediators questioned the purity of mediation conducted by the WLB since the WLB could use the threat of their arbitration authority to reach a mediation settlement. To minimize these problems between the two agencies, USCS director John Steelman placed his assistant at the WLB to coordinate cooperation between them.

One of the most positive actions taken by the WLB to promote ADR involved grievance arbitration. The WLB required that any labor agreement handled by WLB must require arbitration of grievances. The use of such arbitration had been growing during the 1930s with the encouragement of USCS, but this WLB decision would ultimately make grievance arbitration a nearly universal practice.

War's End

By the end of the war, ADR had gained a new level of usage and acceptability. A cadre of experienced mediators and arbitrators had been created by the WLB and the USCS, and many labor and management representatives had gained experience as negotiators and users of mediation and arbitration.

Adjusting to a peacetime economy and a resurgence of employer resistance to unions would mark the years immediately following the war. Reform of the labor law and a restructured mediation service would come soon after.

Chapter Nine

After the War

Taft-Hartley to the Steel Trilogy

America threw everything into the war effort. It sent a huge number of its young men to fight a war on several fronts, and it recruited a fair share of its women onto the factory floor. With wage and price controls and a prevailing sense of sacrifice for the cause, conflict between labor and management was kept to a minimum.

At war's end, an enormous amount of gear grinding was inevitable. As GIs returned home, eager to get back to work and make up for the deprivations of depression and the rationing of the war itself, consumer demand surged. Much as it would have loved to satisfy this hunger, business struggled to keep up. The push and pull of pent-up demand and lagging supply, burgeoning expectations of prosperity, and fears of spiraling inflation led to one of the most intense periods of labor unrest in American history.

Aftermath of War

In the midst of these transitions, it is not surprising that the cooperation of labor and management during the war effort began to unravel with the arrival of peace in Germany and Japan. The aggressiveness of the Soviet Union added a new dimension of fear of communism across the United States and inside trade unions.

Wage and Price Controls

During the war, the Roosevelt administration had assembled a considerable bureaucracy to control inflation. The Office of Price Administration, with a staff of 7,000 employees and 300,000 volunteer price checkers, kept a lid on prices. The Office of Wage Stabilization conducted a similar program limiting wage increases. Both efforts were largely successful.

But with Japan's surrender in August 1945, government oversight of wages and prices became extremely controversial. The Truman administration preferred to continue controls with modifications, fearing runaway inflation. Business and Republican interests wanted an immediate return to a free market economy.

Trade unions had a more nuanced position. Most collective bargaining immediately after the war focused almost exclusively on wage increases. Unions wanted to establish a linkage between prices and wages. As a way to reduce conflict over wage bargaining, some unions attempted to negotiate that linkage. Management vigorously resisted, arguing that only the market should determine prices and that prices should never be subject to collective bargaining. United Auto Workers union president Walter Reuther, the strongest proponent of linking wages and prices, was labeled "the most dangerous man in Detroit because no one is more skillful in bringing about the revolution without seeming to disturb the existing forms of society" (Lichtenstein, 1997, p. 230). For management, linking wages and prices was a revolutionary and disturbing idea.

The concept of free collective bargaining from a trade union point of view meant wide-ranging negotiations between labor and management, supported by public policy, but without negative government interference. Many employers had reconciled themselves to the decade-old public policy requiring collective bargaining. But they felt negotiation topics should be limited and government should not interfere. This controversy over wage-price controls and free collective bargaining would bedevil the transition to a peacetime economy.

Truman's National Labor-Management Conference

In November 1945, President Truman, with congressional encouragement, convened a high-level conference of labor, management, and public representatives, just as President Wilson had done following World War I. Both presidents asked their conferees to recommend ways to improve labor-management relations. Truman viewed it as in the public interest to return to the collective bargaining system that had prevailed before the war: free of the voluntary no-strike and no-lockout pledge by labor and management, respectively, and the government's wage and price controls.

Despite efforts to find common ground for agreement, significant agreement eluded the conferees primarily because of the issues surrounding wage-price controls and the freedom of collective bargaining. A more hidden issue was an employer belief that industry was again strong enough to dominate the relationship, as it had after World War I, if government would step aside (Lichtenstein, 1997).

The conference report showed that the conferees agreed on the value of grievance arbitration and the need to bolster the U.S. Conciliation Service. The report recommended better training for new conciliators, better ways of keeping them up to date, and improved mediation techniques. It also recommended reorganizing and improving the technical services provided by USCS. The technical services consisted of a small staff of specially trained conciliators who were skilled in time and motion studies, piece-rate setting, incentive plans, work load studies, job evaluation plans, and a host of new issues and problems that accompanied the nation's industrialization and massive production effort of World War II. Frequently the conciliator conducted the needed study or supervised the parties in conducting the studies, and frequently wrote factual reports and recommendations for use in negotiation. This form of dispute resolution is another type of ADR precursor.

The director of USCS, Edgar Warren, who had been appointed in September 1945 just two months before President Truman's Labor Management Conference, assumed that Congress would fund the recommendation of the conference. Using funds earmarked for other purposes, Warren immediately began to implement the conference recommendations by expanding the internal mediator training program and upgrading the technical services provided to labor and management. By late in the fiscal year when no additional funds were provided, Warren was forced to lay off mediators despite a proliferation of strikes. Sixty layoffs were required to meet the budget shortfall, leaving a staff of 381 at the start of 1946. Not surprisingly, the layoffs demoralized the staff morale and generated congressional criticism of Warren.

Warren would become very unpopular with several ranking members of the House of Representatives. The House Appropriations chairman would refer to him as "pink if not red." Another House committee member told the labor secretary to stop defending Warren or the committee was "going to cut the heart out of the Department." The department had never been popular in Congress; budget requests had always been significantly cut. The department barely escaped extinction during the early 1920s at the hands of Congress, and following the war, Congress left it looking like a "plucked chicken" in the words of the department's historian (Grossman, 1973, p. 248).

Reacting to the Strikes of 1945–1946

During the winter and spring of 1945–1946, following the end of wartime wage and price controls, more strikes occurred in the United States than in any other period before or since. For several months during that period, nationwide strikes occurred in five major industries: steel, automobiles, meatpacking, coal, and electrical manufacturing, drastically setting back the economy's conversion to peacetime. Five million workers were involved in work stoppages, with 120,000 man-days lost. During this period, more than a dozen state legislatures passed laws attempting to restrict union activities and providing dispute settlement procedures.

Despite these huge strikes, the USCS was both busy and effective in the vast majority of disputes it took on. Between 1945 and

1946, it mediated nearly forty thousand cases, helping to reach a settlement in three out of four cases without a work stoppage.

Labor Law Reform

The November 1946 election produced a Republican majority in both houses of Congress. Given the large number of strikes that had just occurred, the probusiness Congress that began in January 1947 was determine to reform the labor law. On the first day of the session, seventeen bills were introduced to amend the Wagner Act. Hearings on the most significant ones began almost immediately.

Senator Robert Taft's father had been president of the United States and chief justice of the Supreme Court. Elected to the Senate in 1938, Senator Taft earned prominence as a major critic of President Roosevelt. He had lost the Republican nomination for president in 1952 to Eisenhower. In 1947, he served as chairman of the Senate Labor Committee. Representative Fred Hartley of New Jersey, a twenty-year House member with a very antilabor reputation, was chairman of the House Labor Committee. Their names became attached to the bill that finally emerged from Congress and became law.

Two freshmen House members were on the House Labor Committee that drafted the Taft-Hartley bill. Just four months after they had each joined the Eightieth Congress, the Democratic and Republican congressmen were invited to debate the bill before a group in Pittsburgh. The Democrat charmed the audience with a light touch on detail, while the Republican doggedly defended every detail in the bill. The audience of predominantly labor supporters felt the Democrat had won the debate. Late that evening as the two young congressmen boarded a sleeper railcar to return to Washington, they reportedly tossed a coin to determine who would get the upper berth. Richard Nixon won the coin toss and later the vote on Taft-Hartley. Thirteen years later, John Kennedy would win another debate and the presidency (Matthews, 1996).

Taft-Hartley Act of 1947

The Taft-Hartley Act of 1947 was an extensive amendment to the National Labor Relations Act of 1935. Senator Taft would describe the new legislation as a congressional effort to establish a better balance between labor and management.

As a counterbalance to the list of unfair employer practices prohibited by the Wagner Act, the new law added a parallel list of unfair practices by labor. It also prohibited unions from engaging in secondary boycotts—the practice of leaning on an employer with which the union had no dispute in a bid to put pressure on another employer with which the union did have a dispute.

The national fear of communist influences resulted in a provision requiring union officials to sign an annual statement asserting they were not communists. Since no such statement was required of anyone else, trade unionists objected strongly to this questioning of their loyalty. If a union official refused to sign, the union was denied any benefits under that law. Several years later, the non-communist declaration was removed.

Congressional debate favored collective bargaining and mediation as the preferred approach to resolving most labor-management disputes. Most of the congressional debate on dispute resolution focused on procedures for handling major collective disputes that threatened the economy. Compulsory arbitration was considered and rejected. In the National Emergency Dispute section of the law, the president was authorized to seek a court injunction against a strike for eighty days if it was deemed a threat to the national interest. During that cooling-off period, a presidential fact-finding board would determine and publicize the facts. Then, with the clock still ticking, mediation by the fact-finders or the mediation service would attempt to assist a settlement.

The new law also replaced the USCS, which had been under the Labor Department, with a new independent agency. During debate on this topic, members of Congress disagreed over what to call the new agency. The House favored the word *conciliation*, and

the Senate preferred *mediation*. In a perhaps fitting display of compromise, Congress ended up using both words for the new agency's
title: the Federal Mediation and Conciliation Service (FMCS).

The law promoted mediation by requiring that when either
labor or management wished to renegotiate an expiring agreement,
they must give notice to the other side and to the FMCS and any
appropriate state mediation service. Prior to this provision, a mediation agency frequently did not have knowledge of a problem until
a strike was under way.

With full knowledge that his veto would be overridden, Truman
vetoed what he told aide James Reynolds was not a bad bill. He also
told Reynolds that a much more important issue at that time was
getting the Marshall Plan implemented to save Europe and restrict
Soviet expansionism. To accomplish that, he needed labor support
for his 1948 reelection bid (Gross, 1981).

With the veto overridden, FMCS was born on August 22, 1947.
Truman's veto message on June 20, 1947, commented on the creation of FMCS, arguing that it went against the consensus of the
National Labor-Management Conference that the new agency
remain in the Department of Labor:

> The new name for the Service would carry with it no new dignity
> or new functions. The evidence does not support the theory that
> the conciliation function would be better exercised and protected
> by an independent agency outside the Department of Labor. Indeed,
> the Service would lose the important day-to-day support of factual
> research in industrial relations available from other units of the
> Department of Labor [Bakke and Kerr, 1948, p. 881].

The Senate author of the bill, Senator Taft, saw it differently:
"We have set up a Mediation Service. We took it out of the Department of Labor because it was felt, rightly or wrongly, that as long as
it was an agency of the Department of Labor it must necessarily take
a pro-labor slant and therefore could not be as fair in mediating differences between the parties" (Bakke and Kerr, 1948, p. 890).

Even after the passage of Taft-Hartley, the locus of the mediation role within the federal government was not immediately settled. The Democratic party platform on which President Truman won reelection promised to return mediation to the Department of Labor. After the election, Labor Secretary Maurice Tobin attempted to get back the mediation role and several other bureaus that had been transferred to other cabinet departments during the 1947 congressional attack on the department. He used the prestigious Hoover Commission report to argue for the consolidation of similar functions within the same department. His argument succeeded on everything but the mediation role.

Creation of FMCS

Freed of the Labor Department, the new FMCS would soon be led by a director appointed by the president and confirmed by the Senate. The offices, staff, and records of USCS were transferred to the new FMCS. The national office space transferred to FMCS was in the Department of Labor Building, where the independent FMCS would remain for the next thirty years.

The 204 commissioners of conciliation (including two women) were the largest group of the 375 individuals transferred to FMCS. Also transferred were thirty-eight commissioners of conciliation with parenthetical titles, such as regional director and a number of specialist conciliators with parenthetical titles of industrial analysts, job analysts, or industrial specialists from the technical service.

Since FMCS immediately established a policy of no staff arbitrators, the twenty-eight individuals listed as "commissioner of conciliation (arbitration)" never worked for FMCS. Because these arbitrators had been employed by USCS on a when-actually-employed basis, FMCS placed them on a new arbitration roster, effectively giving birth to the private arbitration system we have today.

As the first director of FMCS, President Truman appointed Cyrus Ching, the labor relations director of U.S. Rubber Corporation, who had been active as a management representative on the War Labor Board. Ching enjoyed telling the story of attempts by John Steelman, a Truman aide who had previously served as the director of USCS, to recruit him out of retirement to take the director job. After Ching had turned Steelman down several times, Steelman invited Ching to visit him at the White House. While talking in Steelman's office, the president walked in and continued the sales pitch. Thinking he had the perfect reason for turning the president down, Ching said he was a Republican, to which Truman responded: "That is no reason not to serve your country" (Raskin, 1989, p. 26).

Once on the job, Ching learned he liked mediating and was good at it. Ching was six feet seven inches tall and he was never seen not smoking a curved pipe. Those two characteristics were ideal for cartoonists. During those years of intense media coverage of major disputes, Ching's likeness often appeared on the editorial page, towering above the parties with his pipe billowing smoke.

Ching also used those two characteristics in mediation. He often referred to being five feet nineteen, a size that could not be ignored. In talking about his pipe, Ching explained that during those awkward moments of silence in a mediation session when he wanted a reluctant speaker to talk, he would get very busy with his pipe. The beauty of a pipe, he said, is that it always needs attention—filling it, cleaning it, tamping it down, lighting and relighting it, any one of which can take as long as the smoker chooses. It was during those moments, as he worked his pipe and listened closely with no eye contact, that he would learn something that someone had not intended to say, which could lead to a resolution (Barrett, 1996).

From his Canadian birthplace on rural Prince Edward Island, Ching had an endless store of folksy stories he used to make points while mediating. One favorite he used to explain his reluctance to fight with one of the disputants was to say that his dad told him it was always a mistake to wrestle with a hog because you could not avoid getting muddy, and the hog would always enjoy the experience more than you.

As director, Ching replaced the ad hoc staff arbitrators by creating a roster of private arbitrators from which the parties could select an arbitrator. He also abolished the Technical Services Division and converted the staff to regular mediators. Ching felt the service provided by the Technical Services Division would more appropriately be provided by the private sector.

Ching retained the title "commissioner" for the mediators, but reluctantly. He felt that title was too grand for individuals attempting to mediate between working people and an employer. He retained it out of respect for the title's historic roots. The law creating the Department of Labor authorizes the secretary to appoint commissioners of conciliation (Ching, 1953).

Major Attention for Mediation

John Steelman had risen from a professorship at a small college to become the second director of the Conciliation Service, and during his tenure (1937–1944) he gained a reputation as a very effective, and often dramatic, mediator. Steelman served as assistant to the president under Truman from 1946 until 1953. From his position in the White House, he continued to mediate a number of high-profile disputes, at times upstaging the directors of USCS, and later the FMCS, as well as the National Mediation Board. A gregarious, larger-than-life character, he used the prestige of the White House and a file of everyone he had ever met to settle disputes that made the front pages of newspapers throughout the country.

Perhaps the most dramatic of these was a national railroad strike, which ended with a settlement announcement that resembled a Hollywood script. In early 1946, as 5 million strikers were returning to work ending the most severe strike period in U.S. history, a nationwide railroad strike began. With the nation struggling to adapt to a peacetime economy, a strike in that crucial industry would have brought the shaky economy to a virtual standstill within days. While Steelman mediated, President Truman addressed a joint session of Congress to announce his intention to draft strikers into the army and nationalize the railroads (Bakke and Kerr, 1948). Truman was in the middle of his speech when an aide rushed into the House chamber and handed him a note from Steelman announcing that a settlement had been reached moments before (Clifford, 1991).

The executive director of the War Labor Board, Ted Kheel, who would later become a famous mediator and arbitrator, praised Steelman's extraordinary sense of timing in dispute resolution with this story. While Steelman was director of USCS, he was asked by the board to arbitrate an extremely controversial and high-visibility case on the closed shop, a provision in a labor agreement requiring workers to join the union. This decision was expected to be precedent setting for at least the war years, and it was being awaited with great anticipation by both labor and management. Regardless of how the case was decided, it would be criticized. It so happened that the day that Steelman issued his decision to the parties and the press was the day of Japan's surprise attack on Pearl Harbor. This decision, which would have been front-page news throughout the country, was buried inside and got very little comment for several weeks (interview with Kheel, May 4, 2001).

Steelman's high-profile mediating during a pivotal and formative twenty-year period in America's history both popularized and increased the acceptability of mediation.

Many mediators in USCS, and later FMCS, had feelings about mediation that matched those of high-flying mediators such as Steelman and Ching: the satisfaction of doing important work that not everyone could do, the excitement of entering disputes where angry negotiators agree only on the impossibility of resolution, the exhilarating confidence and exercise of skills to move disagreeable parties step-by-step to a resolution obscure to them, and the satisfying feeling that their mediation effort improved the lives of people and contributed to our democratic way of life.

Growth of Grievance Arbitration

Many arbitrators gained experience during World War II. With the War Labor Board's strong promotion of grievance arbitration, the supply of arbitrators grew to meet that demand. Both the WLB and

USCS had provided grievance arbitrators during the war. In 1947, these arbitrators, who would later be referred to as the War Labor Board Generation, created the National Academy of Arbitrators (NAA) to establish ethical standards and provide an opportunity for professional growth by sharing information about their craft. Both the American Arbitration Association and FMCS had created arbitration rosters for grievance arbitrators. Several state mediation boards created their own arbitration rosters.

The practice of grievance arbitration was sufficiently established after World War II that textbooks on the subject began to appear. In 1946, law professors Whitney McCoy and Clarence Updegraff wrote one of the first, *Arbitration of Labor Disputes*. McCoy would become director of FMCS in 1953.

National Emergency Disputes

The authors of Taft-Hartley felt that most disputes would be resolved by collective bargaining with mediation assistance as necessary. They thought that the national emergency provisions would be used only in exceptional situations. Over the first twenty-five years following the passage of Taft-Hartley, these provisions were used just thirty-four times by a president in cases affecting more than 2 million workers.

Ironically, President Truman, who had vetoed Taft-Hartley, used these provisions seven times during the first year. While all other presidents serving during the first twenty-five years invoked this section of the act, Truman used it the most.

President Truman also set a record for appointing other boards to deal with major disputes. Such boards are generally referred to as nonstatutory boards because they are initiated by executive order, not congressional legislation. They typically consisted of three public members who were asked to determine the facts and attempt to resolve the dispute with recommendations and mediation efforts. In a few cases, the president ordered the seizure and operation of the facility by the government. Beginning in November 1945, Truman would use nonstatutory boards sixteen times. Following Truman's tenure, this process was used only twelve times in the next fifteen years. Truman's heavy reliance on the various tools of Taft-Hartley suggests that the turbulent period following World War II through the Korean War required such drastic actions. After that period ended, mediation by FMCS was sufficient in most cases to manage collective bargaining.

The 1950s and Beyond

With the exception of the Korean War, the 1950s were a much quieter period than the 1940s. Collective bargaining and the use of mediation grew, as did grievance arbitration. The FMCS began a small training program called Preventive Mediation, intended to help labor and management improve their relationship. Typically the training involved sessions with labor and management together and covered topics such as how to handle grievances to avoid or minimize conflict.

Reflecting on Mediation Practice

During the early years, most FMCS staff mediators were reluctant writers. Typically, their jobs required little writing. Case status and final reports provided little detail and no great prose. Then and until much later, FMCS, like its predecessor, had an oral tradition. Often raconteurs by nature, mediators could describe and analyze their cases orally, but they were not inclined to attempt to do so in writing. Given that environment, an event in the FMCS Detroit regional office in 1953 is most remarkable.

Three relatively young mediators wrote a sixty-two-page paper discussing the mediator's job and then named and described 120 mediation techniques. Periodic meetings of the fifteen mediators stationed in Detroit provided an opportunity to discuss cases and share information. The three younger mediators listened to their senior colleagues and made notes. Later they began to draft the paper. When they finished, they gave a copy to their immediate supervisor, the regional director, with this note at the top: "Confidential Use of the Federal Mediation and Conciliation Service Staff Exclusively." Although the mediators doubted that the regional director read the paper, he was sufficiently impressed that he sent copies to his peers, other regional directors, and the deputy director in Washington.

Within a few days, one of the senior mediators went to the regional director with this story: in a mediation session the night before, as the mediator began to use a mediation technique, one of the participants asked, "Mr. Mediator, was that number 29 or 75?" While the embarrassed mediator struggled to respond, everyone else had a hearty laugh at his expense.

The regional director shared the mediator's shock at this development. They both felt that the paper would make a joke of mediation, as if it could be done "by the numbers." The regional director contacted everyone he had given a copy to and told them to return the copy. Then he destroyed them all (Barrett, 1999).

I spent fifteen years at FMCS and had never heard of the paper. Years later while I was interviewing retired mediators, three mediators shared their long-hidden copy of the paper.

The Supreme Court and Grievance Arbitration

In 1960, the Supreme Court handed down several decisions in cases put before it by the United Steelworkers union during the 1950s. These decisions, which became known as the Steel Trilogy, would greatly enhance the status of grievance arbitration.

The Wagner Act of 1935 had made no provision for the enforcement of collective bargaining agreements. When a court enforced a collective bargaining agreement, it was normally done at the state level, following common law practices on contract interpretation. The Taft-Hartley Act attempted to remedy this by giving federal courts authority over violations of collective bargaining agreements.

In the Steel Trilogy cases, the collective bargaining agreement included a provision calling for arbitration of violations, or grievances, of the contract. The employers in each case had refused to submit the dispute to arbitration and sought to have the Court look at the merits of their case. The Court refused to do so, choosing merely to enforce the parties' agreement to arbitrate grievances. It deferred to the expertise of the arbitrators as the appropriate forum for determining the merits of the case.

As a result of the Steel Trilogy, the prestige of arbitration and arbitrators was greatly enhanced. Not only would the federal courts enforce agreements to arbitrate without examining the merits of the case, but the Court would enforce arbitration awards except for very limited reasons: if the arbitrator exceeded his or her authority or was bribed.

Chapter Ten

Branching Out

ADR in the 1960s

The 1950s are often thought of as a time of prosperous conformity, but the administration of President Dwight David Eisenhower also witnessed labor agitation as unions sought to ensure their members a share of the growing national pie. This had two consequences for ADR in the 1960s.

First, and somewhat ironically, the unions' success in helping to spread the wealth may have contributed to the unrest ahead. With rising gross national product and incomes came rising expectations. Long-simmering class, racial, and generational tension would come to a head. Second, the vast experience that ADR practitioners gained from traditional bargaining would serve them well as they moved to address these new arenas of discord.

The 1960s began with the high idealism projected by John Kennedy's election. But the nation would soon be caught up in assassinations, urban riots, and civil rights and Vietnam War protests. These new protests and demands for rights strained, and often exceeded, the capacity of traditional peacekeepers (the police) and dispute resolvers (the courts), and provided an opening for ADR. When public employees joined the ranks of those seeking additional rights, ADR reached a new level of public awareness and acceptability.

Unionization of Public Employees

After President Kennedy's assassination in November 1963, President Lyndon Johnson attempted to implement the young president's idealism through the Great Society—a comprehensive expansion of federal welfare programs first launched with social security under Franklin Roosevelt. For our purposes, the Great Society would lead to one striking result: a boom in state and local public employment. As the ranks of teachers, police, firefighters, social workers, and sanitation workers grew significantly, several unions began organizing these employees. The unions' primary sales pitch urged public employees to unionize if they wanted to be treated as well as private sector employees. Federal, state, and local government employees heard the message loud and clear.

As public employees fought for and increasingly won basic rights to union representation, a national public policy debate emerged around the question of the right to strike by employees deemed essential to everyday life. Citizens expect uninterrupted police and fire services; parents expect teachers to be in the classroom; home owners expect regular trash collection. When a strike threat in one of these vital areas was reported, people noticed. When a mediator or other practitioner stepped in and averted the worst, the public caught a glimpse of the power of ADR.

Federal Employees and President Kennedy

Federal employees entered the 1960s with surprisingly few rights. Most employees were free to join labor organizations, but without guaranteed union representation rights, these groups were largely fraternal. The postal service was an exception. Several large unions, composed completely of postal workers, had long represented these federal employees. Custom and peer pressure ensured virtually universal union membership among postal workers. Lacking traditional bargaining rights, these postal unions had created one of the most powerful lobbies in Washington. The size of their membership and their powerful lobbying could not be ignored at either end of Pennsylvania Avenue.

In 1961, President Kennedy chose Arthur Goldberg as his secretary of labor. As general counsel of the United Steelworkers union, Goldberg had extensive experience as a trade union negotiator and was a strong advocate of mediation and arbitration. While Goldberg served as secretary of labor, the president asked him to mediate a threatened Metropolitan Opera strike. When Goldberg called to report on his efforts, Kennedy joked with him by saying, "Get it settled or forget the Supreme Court appointment" (Goldberg, 1995). Goldberg achieved both an agreement at the Met and an appointment to the high court. One other Goldberg success was persuading Kennedy to use his executive power to provide a framework for federal employees to deal collectively with Uncle Sam.

In 1962, President Kennedy issued Executive Order 10988, a significant, if limited, step toward collective bargaining for federal employees. For the first time, federal agencies were required to bargain with unions of their employees. Still, the bargaining was restricted to a few issues, and any agreement reached was subject to review and approval by the agency head. Some observers said that more subjects were excluded from bargaining than included. Among the issues kept off the table were compensation; fringe benefits; the agency mission, budget, and structure; and all management rights over hiring, firing, promotion, and transferring.

Significantly, the order left in place the 1947 Taft-Hartley Act's prohibition on strikes by federal employees. To emphasize the strike issue, the order prohibited unions that assert employees' right to strike from exercising any rights provided by the order. Historically, the ability to strike has been a part of being unionized. Public employees remain an exception to this day. That sentiment was clearly articulated by Calvin Coolidge, who as Massachusetts governor broke up a police strike with state militia and these words: "No one has the right to strike against the people." Even President Franklin Roosevelt, who held a more favorable view of employee rights than Coolidge, would refer to public employee strikes as "unthinkable." (Later legislation would also preserve that view, and Ronald Reagan, as we shall see, would put it in practice in 1980 when he fired the striking air traffic controllers.)

Kennedy's order also failed to provide dispute resolution arrangements. Mediation was not mentioned, and no other form of

ADR was provided for bargaining impasses. In a number of early federal sector agreements, the parties took the initiative to place a provision for mediation and fact-finding in their accord. Some agreements named the Federal Mediation and Conciliation Service as the source of mediators. Although this was not binding on FMCS, the service did begin to provide public sector mediation on a limited basis in response to joint requests.

The order did permit negotiated grievance procedures, though only advisory arbitration was allowed. The idea of arbitration being only advisory represents an oxymoron for participants in private sector labor relations, where arbitration decisions were typically final and binding. Modified forms of ADR became characteristic of public sector labor relations as governments at all levels argued that giving up any authority to a third party, such as an arbitrator, would violate their constitutional sovereignty.

The Kennedy executive order, while limited in scope and lacking the weight of statutory law, was viewed as the start of the movement to extend unionization to all public employees. And with the growth of public employee unionization came a significant expansion of ADR.

Executive Order 11491

To the surprise of many involved in federal employee relations, President Richard Nixon issued a replacement for the Kennedy executive order in October 1969, after only ten months in office. Never known for his friendship toward unions, Nixon felt that an executive order addressing the complaints about the Kennedy order would keep matters under control and head off any movement in Congress to pass a more sweeping law on federal employees. Nixon greatly expanded the labor relations program for federal employees. Executive Order 11491 attempted to remedy the complaints made about the earlier order by clarifying, expanding, and adding detail to the program.

For ADR purposes, the most important features of the new order were increasing the topics for bargaining, authorizing the

FMCS to provide mediation, creating the Federal Labor Relations Council to establish policy and administer the program, and strengthening grievance arbitration by modifying its advisory nature and making awards binding unless successfully appealed to the Federal Labor Relations Council.

Governments' Mixed Reaction

In 1960, most public employees worked under state or local government civil service systems, which had no provision for union representation. As unions challenged these arrangements, states responded in a variety of ways. Some turned to their attorneys general or the courts to sketch the limits of employee rights. Others passed legislation to grant or restrict state workers' rights. Some used legislation to provide ADR processes to resolve disputes; others provided rights without providing ADR processes (Barrett, 1971).

The result was a patchwork of rights, or lack thereof, as well as a variety of ADR methods to cope with public employee disputes, among them the traditional ADR techniques of negotiation, mediation, and arbitration. But the public sector spawned its own ADR hybrids, including meet-and-confer or consultation (a limited form of negotiations), fact-finding with and without recommendations, cooling-off periods, either-or arbitration (also called final offer arbitration), and other contradictory-sounding processes, such as binding fact finding, binding mediation, and nonbinding arbitration. The public sector also fashioned substitutes for striking, such as the sick-out or blue flu, which involved large numbers of employees' taking a sick day, and working-to-the-rule, whereby employees meticulously and slowly followed every available work rule and requirement (a practice jokingly referred to as "malicious obedience").

Since public employee unions during the period often embraced a social agenda, the growth of public employee unionism sometimes blurred the distinction between labor-management disputes and civil rights and community disputes. Another major assassination of the 1960s dramatized that blurring. Garbage workers in Memphis, Tennessee, called a strike in 1968 after the Memphis government repeatedly refused to recognize or bargain with them. As a show of solidarity with the predominantly black strikers, President Walter Reuther of the United Autoworkers union made an appearance and gave the strikers a check for fifty thousand dollars. Tragically, the Rev. Martin Luther King Jr. was also there to support the strikers. While standing on the balcony of his Memphis Hotel, King was shot by James Earl Ray on April 4, 1968.

Studies and Assistance to Public Employment

Because of the grave concern in most states about the unionization of public employees and its implied threat of disruptive strikes, numerous studies by academics and politically appointed commissions delved into the topic. Most of the ADR processes that emerged from this dialogue were fashioned as substitutes or alternatives to strikes. Some were particularly concerned with preserving government sovereignty—the belief that government could not surrender any of its authority through an ADR process, particularly arbitration.

Although most of the studies covered just one state, the problem was seen as national. Thus, the U.S. Department of Labor created a small office to provide assistance to state and local governments and organizations of their employees. The Division of Public Employee Labor Relations issued a number of publications listing available literature and summarizing the legal framework for employee relations within each state, including available ADR processes. The division conducted conferences in which state and local officials shared information, sponsored training sessions on ADR, and provided consultation and some dispute resolution assistance (Barrett, 1971).

State Mediation Boards and Agencies

Even before 1960, a number of industrialized states—New York, Massachusetts, Pennsylvania, Michigan, Wisconsin, and Minnesota—established agencies to provide mediation in private sector labor disputes and, in a few cases, grievance arbitration and processes for resolving issues of union representation. As public employee unions demanded attention, these existing state agencies began to offer assistance, and in some instances, state legislation authorized an expansion of their authority to provide public sector ADR assistance and a statutory basis of employee rights.

In states where bargaining was allowed but no staff or funding was provided for mediation, the FMCS provided mediation on a limited basis. In other states, legislation created new labor relations agencies exclusively for public employee disputes. States as diverse as New York and Nevada also enacted new public employee laws in the late 1960s.

New York State's Taylor Law

Both New York City and New York State had long-standing mediation agencies with staff mediators to handle private sector labor disputes. As public employee unionization expanded, the legislature could have widened the authority of these existing mediators to include public employee disputes. The newness of public employee unionism, with limits on striking and a questionable scope of bargaining, cast doubts on whether the private sector model was applicable. Many experienced private sector mediators expressed the same doubts, wondering how a dispute could be settled without a strike threat or a broad range of bargaining topics. Their concern displayed the limits of their practice of mediation since they relied so heavily on the presence of those two factors.

In 1966, an illegal strike by the thirty-five thousand employees of the city-owned transit system crippled New York City. Governor Nelson Rockefeller appointed George Taylor to head a commission to study and recommend legislation that would balance worker rights with the public interest. Taylor, professor of industrial relations at the Wharton Business School, was an ideal choice. Often referred to as the father of grievance arbitration, he began his conflict resolution career with the War Labor Board and had gone on to be appointed by five presidents to help resolve major national disputes.

The public employee law that Taylor fashioned became known as the Taylor Act of 1967. All public employees were prohibited from striking by the new law, and strikers were subject to having two days of pay withheld for each day of striking. As a substitute for the right to strike, Taylor provided mediation, followed by fact-finding with recommendations to the government's legislative body. Funds were provided for both staff mediators and fact-finders. This comprehensive law would become the model for other states in the 1970s and 1980s.

As the 1960s ended, ten states had no statutory coverage of public employee relations and another twenty had very modest coverage prohibiting strikes or covering a limited category of employees—police and firefighters, for example. Although most states aggressively prohibited public employee strikes, a 1969 Montana law allowed public hospital strikes if no other strikes were under way at other health care facilities within 150 miles. In contrast, the highly unionized state of Ohio relied on a 1947 law prohibiting public employee strikes with very harsh penalties, but frequently it did not enforce that law against strikers (Barrett and Lobel, 1974).

In the face of many state governments' refusing to recognize their rights, public employees and their unions used strikes and work disruptions to achieve the opportunity to use ADR. Other nonlabor groups followed this same pattern to secure the right to use ADR.

Other Reactions to Turmoil in the 1960s

Faced with growing urban unrest, continuing civil rights marches, and the closing down of some college campuses to protest the Vietnam War, the nation groped for solutions. New legislation, foundation-funded projects, presidential studies, and expansion of labor-management dispute settlement processes beyond their usual boundaries were some of the results. All of these developments increased opportunities for the growth of ADR.

Civil Rights Act of 1965

President Johnson, never shy to propose a grand legislative solution to problems confronting the nation, put all of his considerable skills of persuasion behind the Civil Rights Act of 1964. Often considered the most important U.S. law on civil rights since Reconstruction, the legislation aimed to end discrimination based on race, color, gender, religion, or national origin. It faced a fifty-seven-day filibuster by southern conservatives in the Senate. Clark Clifford, a Washington insider and adviser to presidents, called Johnson the most skilled legislator of the twentieth century. His one-on-one persuading, called "the treatment," had moved many strong politicians from intractable positions. Johnson knew the leaders of the southern opposition from his years in the Senate. Using his knowledge of weak and failed civil rights bills during the 1950s, Johnson, working one-on-one, persuaded southerners that they had better accept this bill because the next one would be even harder for them to swallow. Johnson eventually prevailed. With the new rights won by minorities and women, ADR practices found a new area of growth.

The act created the Equal Employment Opportunity Commission (EEOC), which investigates charges of discrimination based on religion, race, sex, color, national origin, age, or disability. Significantly for ADR, violations identified by EEOC staff members were assigned to mediation for resolution. The law would use court action only if mediation failed. A number of state laws were enacted during this period that paralleled the federal law, including the use of mediation.

Community Relations Service

The Civil Rights Act also created the Community Relations Service (CRS), a new federal program to mediate community and civil rights disputes. CRS mediators acted as peacemakers in community conflicts involving race, national origin, and class conflict.

In addition to mediating, they helped head off problems by developing strategies and processes with local leaders to prevent violence and resolve conflicts. In many cases, the disputing parties were unprepared for negotiation or mediation—one side being content to march, demonstrate, and point out the wrongs, while the other side expressing outrage at the inconvenience and unfairness of being targeted by the protesters. The role of the CRS mediators was to move the parties from this unproductive stance to an effective ADR process.

Cornell University in New York captured national public attention in 1969 when media coverage showed black students armed with rifles and cartridge belts across their chests. The media had covered other campuses where students demonstrated, sometimes engaging in sit-downs in administrative buildings. But at Cornell, the students had gone a frightening step further by taking over the administration building and holding the university president captive in his office. The CRS dispatched a team of two mediators, one black and one white. After learning as much as they could about the armed students and their issues, the mediation team persuaded the students to designate a small group to leave the administration building to talk with the mediation team, while the majority of the black students remained in control of the building.

At the time, the expression *black power* was popular within the black community. After a long session of listening to strong rhetoric and seeing weapons brandished, the mediators attempted to convince the group of students that black power was useful only if it resulted in change. Having used their takeover to get the administration's attention, the mediators argued, the students now needed to propose solutions that the mediators could take to the administration to attempt to achieve the students' goals. While allaying the students' fears that negotiating with the administration would appear to be "selling out," the mediators needed to convince the students that the time was ripe for an agreement. The administration was close to exercising its power by calling in the National Guard, expelling the students, and denying them their degree.

Once the students reluctantly agreed to draft some demands with the mediators' help, the mediators met with an administrative team. Before the administrators could hear the student demands, they needed to express their outrage over the students' behavior: Hadn't they been taught to seek civil discussion rather than armed conflict? The mediation team began by convincing the administration that calling in the National Guard would be a disaster and that threatening to expel them or deny their degrees would only inflame the situation. Next, the team persuaded the administration to consider some reasonable options. The one they agreed to involved granting two student demands and promising to consider the remaining once order was restored and weapons were removed. After several more round-trips between the two sides, a resolution was achieved (Laue, 1970).

CRS waded into other important topics for dispute: protests of housing and employment discrimination, lack of public services to minority neighborhoods, police aggressiveness and brutality toward minorities, and underfunding of minority schools and services (CRS Oral History, 2000). In its early days, CRS received FMCS training in mediation and preventive mediation. Consultation between the two mediation services resulted in information sharing and other areas of cooperation.

National Advisory Commission on Civil Disorder

During the summer of 1967, an unprecedented number of riots rocked cities across the country, bringing home to many citizens the seriousness of the problems. President Johnson responded by appointing Illinois governor Otto Kerner to head the National Advisory Commission on Civil Disorder to study the causes of the riots and make recommendations.

Kerner issued a report in 1968 concluding that the urban riots resulted from prejudice, bigotry, and racial injustice, which were pushing the country toward two separate and unequal societies.

The report urged immediate remedial action in education, employment, open housing, and welfare reform.

Private Sector Funding

Immediately following the Kerner Report, the Ford Foundation began to fund ADR activities to address racial unrest. In 1968, it funded the two earliest and most prominent projects using ADR in community and racial disputes: the National Center for Dispute Settlement (NCDS) and the Center for Mediation and Conflict Resolution in New York City. Although the NCDS in Washington, D.C., was created by a grant to the American Arbitration Association (AAA), it operated quite independent of AAA for the first several years to provide the maximum opportunity for experimentation without harming the reputation of AAA.

NCDS began under the leadership of Willoughby Abner, an African American and former FMCS mediator, and two other labor management neutrals, one from AAA and one from FMCS. The primary purpose of NCDS was to attempt to use labor-management ADR in new conflict arenas. The small staff began their task with strong convictions about the labor-management model. But with few examples of where the model had been applied successfully outside of labor disputes, they sought to demonstrate the practicality of their beliefs.

Many of those early initiatives have been fully developed—for example:

- The mayor of Cleveland invited Abner to help resolve a disruptive, and sometimes violent, month-long dispute with black municipal employees. During a marathon mediation session, Abner repeatedly stood in the doorway alternately blocking each party's spokesman from leaving. The articulate black mayor felt frustrated by his inability to overcome distrust and reach understanding with the black union members; the very experienced white union leader felt equally frustrated by having lost the confidence of his angry members. Abner ordered sandwiches and promised regular toilet breaks, but insisted that no one could leave until a settlement was reached. Twenty-three hours later, Abner and the two bedraggled spokesmen announced a settlement before TV cameras.

- In Philadelphia, two NCDS staff members created what may have been the earliest courthouse open door or multidoor program in which court cases were routinely diverted to mediation. In what was called the Philadelphia 4A program, NCDS provided classroom training to novice local mediators, followed by on-the-job training with an NCDS staff member mediating a neighborhood dispute diverted from the municipal court. (Arlen Specter, now a U.S. senator from Pennsylvania, was the district attorney with whom this arrangement was made.)

- In Rochester, New York, which had been rocked by a series of violent riots, NCDS helped start one of the nation's first community mediation centers. With local funding and several local activists leading the center, NCDS provided guidance and training to provide ADR services to the community.

- NCDS was invited to Wilberforce University, a black school in Ohio, to help with a conflict involving the administration and the students. Since the invitation was unclear about the cause of the unrest, NCDS asked that a series of interviews be arranged with a cross section of students, faculty, and administration. When two NCDS mediators, one black and one white, arrived, they spent a full day questioning and listening to groups share their opinions on the demonstrations and hostility on campus.

  Before a mass gathering later that evening, the two mediators shared their impressions of the causes of the unrest. They first identified several minor issues before discussing a problem with the two senior administrators heading the counseling office. Many students considered their behavior demeaning and patronizing, and when the two administrators began justifying how they ran their office, the students' angry shouts drowned them out. After restoring order, the mediators suggested that the two administrators' behavior was conveying a very negative impression. Then several students were asked to explain their impression of how they were treated in the counseling office. After several students spoke without interruption, the university president asked to speak. He began by saying: "I got it. I hear what the students are saying." He closed by promising to fix the situation by meeting with the two administrators in the morning and giving a report at an assembly the next afternoon.

- An early NCDS strategy was to promote ADR with community and college groups and other interested parties, including what was then referred to as the establishment—leaders of business, churches, unions, foundations, schools, and government. These discussions focused not only on how ADR works but also on how disputing parties can gain access to ADR and how to participate effectively in ADR processes. The staff conducted a semester-long class on negotiations and mediation at Federal City College, now the University of the District of Columbia, a predominantly black institution.

- Another way that NCDS promoted ADR was by regularly briefing AAA headquarters and field management on the ADR projects and successes that NCDS was having in the new areas.

Given its small staff, NCDS sought strategies to identify and develop more mediators. In doing so, it struggled with the issue of mediator acceptability to disputing parties. The question was, Should NCDS train experienced labor-management neutrals to work in community and racial disputes or train community leaders in dispute resolution skills? Most experienced mediators were white. Newly trained community mediators might be rejected by black community leaders as sellouts. Unsure of what was best, NCDS did both.

Abner was familiar with these issues on a firsthand basis. Before his appointment to NCDS, he had served as a national troubleshooter mediator for FMCS. He worked throughout the country at a time when black faces were rare in leadership positions at the bargaining table. When he started in the mid 1960s, there were only four other black FMCS mediators.

When I asked him how he managed to mediate successfully with racially bigoted southern parties, he offered an interesting interpretation based on what he believed to be the parties' capacity for self-delusion. The parties needed a settlement but had failed to achieve one in direct bargaining and with the mediation assistance of the local FMCS mediator, so the matter escalated to the national director of FMCS, who assigned national troubleshooter Abner to mediate. The parties had no choice but to accept Abner. To overcome their prejudice toward blacks, the southern parties chose to identify this particular black as different from any other black person they had ever known. In their adjusted view, Abner was not just a good mediator, he was exceptional; in fact, better than any other mediator. Abner believed that as a result of this self-delusion, the parties credited him with exceptional skill and treated his ordinary actions and suggestions with great respect and deference, thereby allowing him to have a greater impact on their settlement than he felt was warranted. Abner's reflections on this phenomenon combined amusement and amazement and reflected his sincere humility.

The Ford Foundation also funded the Center for Mediation and Conflict Resolution (CMCR) in New York City with a role similar to NCDS. The grant was made to Automation House, a labor-management project headed by Theodore Kheel, a nationally renowned labor-management mediator and arbitrator. In its first few years, Kheel headed CMCR, focusing it on training community leaders in negotiation and mediation. Two floors of Automation House were devoted to training rooms. An expert evaluation and training development staff was hired to develop training materials, which CMCR shared with others. On another front, Kheel earned great credibility for the center by successfully mediating high-visibility racial, gang, housing, and school disputes.

California Grape Boycott

California's huge agriculture industry relied on Mexican migrants for laborers. These workers, sometimes including entire families, were poorly paid and worked under extremely poor conditions. Cesar Chávez, a charismatic Mexican American farm laborer, began organizing his fellow farmworkers in the late 1950s. In 1962, he founded and began to lead the United Farmer Workers union, whose efforts met with stiff resistance from farm owners. The police broke up numerous confrontations between the groups.

Since the Taft-Hartley Act specifically excluded agricultural workers from legal protections to unionize and collective bargaining, the status of these employees was similar to public employees in states that lacked a public employee statute. But the on-again, off-again nature of agricultural employment made unionization even more difficult. An itinerant workforce moving regularly to new locations following the harvest was difficult to keep in touch with, let alone unionize. The limited duration of the harvest made replacing dissident workers easy. Employers could also drag out talks with empty promises until the work was complete. With large corporations dominating the industry and controlling employment practices, the union seemed to have little chance at success.

Taking a page from Gandhi and Martin Luther King, Chávez hit on a nonviolent form of protest: he called for a nationwide boycott of California grapes, using informational picketing and hand billing at large supermarket chains. Gradually, the farmworkers' cause captured the support of consumers, students, civil rights groups, and other unions. Senator Robert Kennedy called Chávez "one of the heroic figures of our time." Martin Luther King corresponded with Chávez about their common cause in seeking a more just society.

In 1969, with thirty grower strikes under way and the grape boycott having an effect on the chief target, DiGiorgio Corporation, California governor Pat Brown invited Ronald Haughton to intervene as a mediator. Haughton, an experienced labor-management mediator and academic from Michigan who would later head the CMCR in New York City, entered an extremely complex set of disputes. Since neither state nor federal law provided any process or procedures, Haughton had to negotiate an agreement for voting to determine whether employees wanted a union at each grower site. Once that was accomplished, he achieved an agreement for a thirty-day negotiation period at each bargaining unit with unresolved issues subject to binding arbitration. And finally, Haughton mediated an end to the grape boycott.

Although these agreements were not easily achieved, Haughton found enough evidence that public support for the farmworkers was shifting the tide. Other growers, seeing the success of the grape boycott, worried about that powerful tactic being focused on their product. The fight had become too costly and tiring and had the potential to get worse. Mediator Haughton used these facts and parties' doubts to move the parties to a resolution. The union got its long-sought recognition and opportunity to bargain; the growers avoided an industry-wide agreement in favor of their own site agreements. They both got an end to a long, exhausting, and expensive struggle (Haughton, 1983).

A Widening FMCS Scope

The legal jurisdiction of FMCS was restricted to private sector labor-management cases that have an impact on interstate commerce. Therefore small businesses, public employment, agricultural employees, and health care facilities were excluded from the protection of the law. Since FMCS performs a nonregulatory function, recipients of its help seldom challenged its jurisdictional limits. FMCS needed to be concerned only about congressional budget oversight. Given the general concern about the unrest, Congress did not raise questions about a modest amount of mediation done by FMCS beyond its legal jurisdiction during the 1960s.

With the growth of public sector collective bargaining in the 1960s, FMCS used an ad hoc policy for mediating public sector disputes, providing mediation when requested by the parties or, in some cases, a public official such as a mayor or governor.

Many federal mediators were reluctant to get involved where strikes were prohibited. Even after the Nixon executive order directed FMCS to provide mediation in the federal sector, mediators found the work boring and unchallenging because of the limited scope of bargaining topics and the absence of the right to strike.

One FMCS mediator in the late 1960s wrote two journal articles suggesting to the protesters how they could use the labor-management ADR model to address racial, community, and Vietnam War issues (Barrett, 1967, 1969–1970). But few FMCS mediators were ready to expand their work even into the public sector, much less into these newer dispute arenas. That would change in the 1970s.

Chapter Eleven

New Rights and New Forms

ADR in the 1970s

In many ways, the 1970s was an age of limits. The United States saw the limits of its power in Vietnam, the limits of its natural resources with the Organization of Petroleum Exporting Countries (OPEC) oil embargo, and the limits of prosperity with the stagflation of the Carter years. In other ways, the decade was an expansive time, as Native Americans, women, the elderly, and other groups won new recognition based on the model of the civil rights movement.

Both of these trends—limits and expansion—provided new areas of growth for ADR. The realization that resources are finite brought a greater willingness to find common ground in less adversarial settings. Similarly, as minorities continued to press for expanded rights, the government and the complainant groups alike realized that ADR processes offered a more productive way of working out differences than violent demonstrations or lengthy legal battles. New forms of ADR developed to address these new challenges.

The Effect of Enhanced Rights on ADR

Just as the Wagner Act in 1935 granted employees and unions rights that allowed them to take advantage of ADR, the 1970s saw a similar transformation in the rights of environmentalists, prisoners, and the aged. In most cases, the new rights came through laws that provided for an administrative agency for enforcement, and most leaders of these agencies were open to some form of ADR prior to any court action.

Environmental ADR

On April 22, 1970, Americans celebrated the first Earth Day, a brainchild of Wisconsin senator Gaylord Nelson to get the country behind environmental issues. President Nixon that same year created the Environmental Protection Agency. Both these events contributed to a new way of looking at the earth: it has rights too.

This new perspective would soon create new forms of conflict. Environmental issues create some of the most complex and unwieldy of disputes. They usually involve multiple parties and focus on complicated environmental rules. An entire specialty of ADR would develop around this field.

Probably the first environmental mediation case in the United States concerned a proposed flood control dam on the Snoqualmie River in Washington State. In 1973, Governor Daniel Evans appointed Gerald Cormack and Jane McCarthy, two experienced mediators, to attempt to work out a compromise all sides could support. The issue had been simmering for years after a major flood in 1959 had caused $8 million in property damage (Dembart and Kwartler, 1980).

The Snoqualmie snakes out of the Cascade Mountains and empties into Puget Sound north of Seattle. The Army Corps of Engineers had proposed building a dam on the river's middle fork, a plan that all agreed was the best from a flood control standpoint. But that was far from the end of the story.

Fishermen and kayakers prized the stretch of river above the proposed dam for its challenging rapids and prime fishing spots. Others deplored the loss of natural beauty in an area just a few miles from downtown Seattle. Many feared rapid development in the area once the threat of flooding was removed. Farmers wanted the benefits of flood control, but they were also concerned that their land would become so valuable that farming would become uneconomical, forcing them to sell out to developers. Some landowners, of course, were thrilled at the prospect of the dam and were more than eager to cash in.

Cormack and McCarthy, who were looking for a small environmental dispute to mediate, spent months deciding whether to wade into the sprawling dispute and several more figuring out whom to include in any mediation process. After extensive interviews with a wide swath of concerned parties, they identified a group of people representing the various interests: farmers, sportsmen, environmentalists, landowners, and home owners. One group they did not include proved to be critical: local politicians. The mediators were afraid that politicians would bring hardened positions—and too much public pressure—into the delicate process. Many participants felt that no deal could have been struck if politicians had been part of the group. Nevertheless, the group's ultimate decision was much harder to implement because elected officials were excluded.

A major focus of the process was finding the core issues that all involved could agree on. One key early development involved a landowner who held a parcel at the confluence of the river's three branches that would have soared in value with the protection afforded by a dam. He agreed to accept a similar-size parcel elsewhere to allow his property to be converted into a park.

Much of the progress that was made in the surprisingly quick four-month process came not at the bargaining table but when participants in the mediation process went back and discussed various issues with their constituents. Farmers, for example, wanted flood control, but they wanted land use protections even more. They thus became very invested in reaching a settlement and were willing to compromise on some key issues to bring one about. They eventually agreed, for example, to a proposal by environmentalists to move the dam to a different fork of the river, which provided less-than-perfect flood control but also left intact the precious whitewater. The farmers realized that moving the site of the dam was the only acceptable option to the constituents of the environmental representatives. The farmers then pushed for greater land use controls to preserve their farms and also a system of dikes as a backup to the less effective dam.

The group reached consensus on a plan that carefully balanced the various parties' interests. But the agreement faced serious obstacles in implementation because of the lack of political participation. Governor Evans remained a strong backer of the process and the final outcome. But many of the group's proposals required action by multiple local jurisdictions and the federal government. Without a good way to enforce the group's decision, it would be many years before the dam would be built. Even today, many of the issues the group wrestled with remain concerns (Dembart and Kwartler, 1980). Still, the ambitious mediation process itself was judged a qualified success. Never before had anyone attempted to resolve such an ungainly dispute through mediation.

Within ten years, groups of environmental mediators were operating in a dozen states. The largest of these groups was Resolve, a nonprofit organization founded in 1978. Over the next twenty-five years, Resolve would create a remarkable record of success in these extremely complex disputes. Using consensus building among interested groups while informing them with scientific and engineering knowledge, Resolve's staff of group process dispute resolvers patiently worked through conflicts over water and fishing rights, timber cutting and mining practices, wetlands and forest protection, energy use and clean air. The conflicts ran the gamut from locating a trash dump to global warming concerns. Difficult disputes such as these proved to be a fertile field for mediation.

Prisoner Grievance Arbitration

A simple misunderstanding at the Attica State Correctional Facility, thirty miles east of Buffalo, New York, would lead to one of the bloodiest incidents in American history and add a new word to the nation's vocabulary of protest: "Attica, Attica, Attica," as Al Pacino famously chanted in *Dog Day Afternoon* and John Travolta later mimicked in *Saturday Night Fever*. Two inmates believed to have fought were taken out of their cells for punishment. A rumor spread that they had been beaten. Neither the fight nor the beatings ever took place. Nevertheless, the next day, September 9, 1971, prisoners took several guards hostage as they gained control of an exercise yard. When state troopers moved in four days later to end the insurrection, forty-three people, including more than ten guards, were killed in what one official called a "turkey shoot."

Clearly there was more behind the prisoners' rage than the immediate spark. One result was an effort to address prisoner complaints better. The courts had opened the door to constitutional challenges of prisoner treatment; however, the courts lacked the capacity to consider the number of complaints raised.

In 1973, New York and California began pilot programs to test whether a formal grievance procedure would provide a measure of justice and an outlet for anger. The pilot grievance procedure ended in advisory arbitration in which the arbitration decision was not binding on either party. Like a grievance procedure in a labor agreement, the process used several levels of examining the grievances and attempting to settle it prior to arbitration. In some cases, a joint committee of guards and inmates made the final effort to resolve the grievance before arbitration. To the surprise of many, the joint committee often was able to reach consensus or a majority vote on the appropriate resolution. Volunteers drawn from the labor arbitration panel of AAA in California and from the Public Employee Relations Board in New York acted as arbitrators. Subsequently, other states developed similar dispute resolution systems.

Typical cases involved rule infractions, extent of punishment, disparate treatment, prior disciplinary record, transfers, and loss of some privilege. Such issues strongly resemble labor-management grievances, which involve gathering the facts, assessing credibility, comparing differences in punishment based on an inmate's discipline record, and applying the relevant rules. Thus, labor-management mediators or arbitrators could handle these prison cases easily and bring a sense of fairness to the process.

Other states developed processes with features such as an ombudsman program in which an individual who is not a part of the chain of command investigates prisoner complaints and attempts to negotiate or mediate a resolution.

Age Discrimination Mediation

The Age Discrimination Act of 1975 prohibited discrimination based on age in providing benefits or services in federally funded programs. The Department of Health, Education, and Welfare (HEW), designated as administrator of the act, asked FMCS to mediate discrimination complaints under the new law. FMCS selected and trained outside mediators to mediate these cases. Typical cases involved a complaint by a forty-five-year-old man denied admission to a medical school receiving federal grants and a complaint by a sixty-five-year-old woman denied employment at a federally funded day care facility. Based on the agreement with HHS in 1979, FMCS began mediating such age discrimination cases on a routine basis. With budget cuts in the early 1980s, regular FMCS mediators replaced the ad hoc mediators in mediating these cases (Barrett and Tanner, 1981).

Presidential Peacemaking

Probably the best-known use of ADR in the 1970s involved the president of the United States. For thirteen days in September 1978 at the Camp David presidential retreat, President Jimmy Carter worked with Prime Minister Menachem Begin of Israel and President Anwar Sadat of Egypt to fashion an agreement that earned Carter a Nobel Peace Prize.

Accompanied by a team of international experts and conflict resolvers, Carter mediated a historic settlement between Egypt and Israel and popularized a new ADR process called the one-text procedure. Harvard law professor Roger Fisher, coauthor of *Getting to Yes* (1981), is generally credited with initiating this procedure.

Preparation for Carter's work included extensive briefing books on the parties' history, prior efforts at resolutions, options on all issues, and even lengthy psychological profiles of Begin and Sadat.

But the most remarkable tool at Carter's disposal was the idea of focusing the entire process on the creation of a single negotiated text.

Egypt and Israel had remained in an official state of war since Israel's founding in 1948. But Sadat had recently extended an olive branch by traveling to Israel and speaking before the Knesset. In the negotiations, Carter repeatedly asked questions to move the parties away from discussing their fixed positions on specific issues and tried to get them to focus on their common interests in regional affairs. After listening carefully to these discussions, Carter and his team drafted a single text agreement. Over the course of the thirteen days, the Americans wrote draft after draft of the agreement. Each draft was shared with the parties, followed by more discussion focused on their interests. Each successive draft satisfied more of both parties' interests and thus approached an agreement acceptable to both. The twenty-third draft achieved the signed agreements, which contained a framework for peace between the two nations, Israel's withdrawal from Sinai, and a guarantee of passage for Israeli ships through the Suez Canal. The agreements came to be known as the Camp David Accords.

Public Employee Disputes

The 1970s saw new federal and state legislation that influenced further ADR growth. Some new federal laws endorsed and required ADR.

U.S. Post Office

By the mid-1960s, the U.S. Post Office was in such trouble with increasing volume, rising deficits, old equipment, and outmoded work practices that the postmaster general said the organization was "in a race with catastrophe," according to a press report at the time. A 1968 presidential commission report recommended privatization and significant reorganization. The administration submitted its reorganization bill to Congress and predicated any postal wage increase on congressional passage of the reorganization bill.

Postal unions, accustomed to dealing directly with Congress on wages and benefits through their very powerful lobby, felt suspicious of a corporate boss and resisted the reorganization bill. While the bill moved slowly in Congress, postal workers grew restless over delayed wage increases and the uncertainty of their future. The media reported the unrest and rumors of a strike. But federal employees had virtually never struck, so no one viewed the possibility of a strike as a serious possibility. Nevertheless, in March 1970, an unauthorized strike started at postal facilities in New York City and spread to other locations. Over nine days, the striking continued on and off around the country, crippling mail delivery. At its peak, 200,000 employees had joined in.

Because the strike was illegal and there was no bargaining relationship between the postal unions and the Post Office, FMCS director Curtis Counts refused to get involved. After some agonizing over the union's request for help, the Department of Labor agreed to let Assistant Secretary Bill Usery attempt to mediate.

To end the immediate crisis by getting employees back on the job, Usery persuaded management that blaming the union leadership for the strike or seeking to punish the strikers would not solve the problem. Instead, he persuaded managers to negotiate with the union on the issue of a wage increase and reorganization. As a condition of starting negotiation, the unions agreed to urge their members to return to work; although the strike did not totally end, the number of strikers greatly lessened. Following several weeks of mediation, on April 2, 1970, Usery and the parties announced an agreement on a wage increase, with no striker discipline until a joint policy was established by the parties, and a jointly bargained and sponsored reorganization of the Post Office Department.

The president signed the Postal Reorganization Act on August 12, 1970, converting the U.S. Post Office into a semiprivate corporation, the U.S. Postal Service. The act prohibited striking and gave FMCS a larger role in impasses, including mediation, fact-finding, and arbitration.

At the conclusion of his successful mediation of the strike, Bill Usery told Postmaster General Blount of his interest in a postage stamp honoring the institution of collective bargaining. As a result, a ten-cent first-class stamp honoring collective bargaining was issued on March 13, 1975.

Rights for Government Workers

More states enacted legislation giving public sector employees representation and bargaining rights. By 1973, twelve more states had passed laws granting such rights and creating ADR procedures. This trend continued into the 1980s until virtually every state had provisions for at least some of their employees.

The experience gained by federal employees and the U.S. government under the series of executive orders beginning with Kennedy's 1962 order was converted into a statute in 1978 in the Civil Service Reform Act. With only minor changes, the new law essentially converted President Nixon's executive order into a statute. The ADR provisions remain unchanged today.

New Health Care ADR

In the early 1970s, a combination of factors placed the plight of employees of nonprofit health care facilities in dramatic contrast with the employees of the for-profit portion of the industry. Rapidly rising costs in the industry were forcing state and federal officials to make high-profile efforts to control costs. At the same time, the civil rights movement used marches and protests to call attention to low-wage black workers in the industry, while unionizing efforts in the heavily unionized states of New York and California began focusing attention on the disparity between these employees' rights and those of most other employees.

In that environment, Congress amended the Taft-Hartley Act in 1974, extending its coverage to nonprofit hospitals and other private health care facilities. Because of health and safety issues in that industry, the new law mandated unique ADR provisions. Negotiators subject to the amendment were required to use mediation if their negotiations reached an impasse. This distinguished the 3-million-member health care industry from all other industries covered by the Taft-Hartley Act, for which mediation was voluntary.

Health care disputes not resolved in mediation could be subjected to a board of inquiry (BOI) appointed at the discretion of the FMCS director before a union was free to strike. Strikes were allowed in health care after mediation and after a BOI, if one was appointed, and after a ten-day notice to the employer.

The BOI, usually consisting of one individual, often an arbitrator, was required to hold a hearing and report findings with nonbinding recommendations within fifteen days. The BOI report, if not accepted by both parties, was to be used in further negotiations or mediation. To make the BOI process as effective as possible, an FMCS mediator remained in close contact with the BOI before and after the report. As FMCS gained experience with the BOI process, it found the process less and less effective compared with mediation alone (Tanner and Barrett, 1986).

Farther Afield for FMCS

With some legislative directives, changing social circumstances, concern about unrest, and FMCS's own initiatives, the mediation service expanded its role into the nonlabor-management sector during the 1970s and added additional ADR techniques to its labor-management toolbox.

FMCS Mission Statement

In 1974, FMCS's director, Bill Usery, convened a planning retreat of his management team where a mission statement was adopted signaling FMCS's ambitions of expanding its dispute resolution role beyond labor-management. Most of the mission statement focused on FMCS's traditional role in labor-management disputes. But part of it asserted this FMCS mission: "Developing the art, science and practice of dispute resolution." This statement looked to FMCS seniority in the dispute resolution field, extending back sixty years to the creation of its predecessor, the USCS. During that long period, FMCS had evolved and improved the practice of negotiations, mediation, and arbitration, and it continued to do so. FMCS was prepared to share its expertise with others and extend its own practice beyond labor-management disputes.

FMCS Nonlabor Work

The newly created FMCS Office of Technical Service (OTS) accepted this mandate to begin programs responding to opportunities in nonlabor work in federal agencies, the Washington, D.C., area, and the private sector.

OTS provided negotiation and mediation training to numerous federal agencies in the 1970s: the Community Relations Service, the FBI, the Law Enforcement Assistance Administration, the Equal Employment Opportunity Commission, the Veterans Reemployment Office of the Department of Labor, the Civil Rights Office in the Department of Health and Human Services, and the Department of Housing and Urban Development. It helped develop a dispute settlement process at the Division of Standards and Regulations at the Environmental Protection Agency, the Environmental Office at the Department of Energy, the Council on Environmental Quality in the Executive Office of the President, and the Science and Technology Office of the Department of Commerce.

In the early 1970s, the Federal Highway Administration asked FMCS to help it find a better way to do one of its toughest jobs: acquire land for highway construction. OTS staff met with state highway officials in Virginia and Maryland to understand their problems better. They found individuals who seemed to believe that engineering principles and studies should govern whether a highway should take someone's front yard or pass between a farmer's house and barn, and they typically presented their arguments to a neighborhood group or at a condemnation hearing in that fashion. Several negotiation training sessions were planned and presented to state highway engineers to help them see the human side of these issues.

OTS used the Washington area as a clinic to test labor-management techniques in emerging disputes. As a result, the office mediated a racial dispute between black and white firefighters in Washington, D.C., and a racial dispute between teachers and custodians in Arlington County, Virginia. They trained the Montgomery County Consumer Complaint Office in negotiation and mediation and set up a dispute settlement office for landlord and tenant conflicts in Washington, D.C.

The media attention given to civil rights and other protests encouraged more people to assert their right to protest. The National Association of Home Builders found their members increasingly drawn into court or confronted by noisy protestors. In response, the association created Home Owners Warranty (HOW), which offered training for individuals drawn from the industry to act as mediators and arbitrators. FMCS provided HOW with training over several years and in the processes expanded its knowledge of another emerging dispute area.

The Oil Crisis

In the wake of the OPEC oil embargo, a gasoline shortage hit the United States in 1974. The crisis, characterized by long lines of cars and angry drivers waiting to fill up at gas stations in most cities, garnered great national media attention. One of many conflicts during this crisis pitted the independent truck drivers, frustrated by excessive fuel prices eliminating their motive to work, against government regulators, whom the drivers saw as unhelpful.

The dispute was not a typical FMCS case: it involved no labor-management relationship. Because the independent truckers hauled 85 percent of all commercial products, their strike quickly affected manufacturers, farmers, and consumers. In addition, violence directed toward nonstriking drivers and their equipment became a safety concern, as bricks were dropped from highway overpasses onto trucks.

FMCS director Usery had recently been appointed special assistant to the president from a White House seeking to associate with a colorful mediator. Always eager to explore new territory, Usery seized this opportunity to apply his mediation skills beyond labor-management disputes. He had come to Washington, D.C., as assistant secretary of labor in 1969 from a union representative position at Cape Kennedy and quickly became active as a mediator. Even before becoming FMCS director, he had staked out an unchallenged presence in the normal jurisdiction of both FMCS and the National Mediation Board (NMB). Former astronaut and president of Eastern Airlines Frank Borman explained mediator Usery this way: "I don't really know what he does, but he is the absolute best at it" (Borman, 1986).

The independent truckers were represented by a number of associations whose primary function was lobbying in Washington and state capitals for trucker-friendly regulations. For the truckers, the oil crisis became a survival issue as fuel prices rose and squeezed against fixed freight rates. Many truckers simply parked their rigs and took time off. As manufacturing layoffs rose and supermarket shelves emptied, more truckers parked their rigs, and the untraditional strike grew. The poorly defined sides and spokespeople made the mediator's job puzzling.

After Usery located the relevant government officials and leaders of the truckers, he assembled them in several meetings. The result was an end to the strike based on a fourteen-point federal program addressing the truckers' issues.

A New Process for Labor-Management

From its birth, FMCS had developed programs to help labor and management improve their relationship. This work, called preventive mediation, is distinct from the mediation of a collective bargaining dispute. The two components of preventive mediation were training labor and management, usually jointly, to handle grievances and problem solving better, and to facilitate labor-management committees, during the term of a labor agreement, with a focus on improving communications, anticipating problems, and solving them.

FMCS introduced a new preventive mediation initiative, Relationships by Objectives (RBO), in 1975. Mediator John Popular developed RBO based in part on some earlier work by mediator Jerry Ross. The process combines organizational development with mediation and training skills to help a labor-management group examine their relationship and develop plans and commitment for improvements. It is most often used with relationships that are not working well. Because of its high success rate, RBO almost immediately became a mainstay of the FMCS preventive mediation program and an excellent form of ADR. RBO remains part of the preventive mediation work of FMCS (Popular, 1976).

Labor-Management Cooperation Act

In 1978, Congress passed the Labor-Management Cooperation Act urging FMCS to encourage and support the establishment and operation of labor-management committees. FMCS had been doing this work for at least fifteen years as part of preventive mediation. Such committees at a work site provided a regular opportunity for representatives of labor and management to share information and address common problems in an informal setting, as opposed to the adversarial setting characteristic of collective bargaining meetings or grievance processes. Many labor-management committees (LMCs) experienced great success in improving productivity, morale, and communications in the workplace.

Such committees had also proved helpful at industry and community levels, each with a similar focus. A famous community-level LMC was in Jamestown, New York, where Mayor Stan Lundine provided strong leadership, and ultimately rode on the LMC success to his election as lieutenant governor of New York State in 1986. An old industrial town with a reputation for quarrelsome negotiations and numerous strikes, Jamestown had seen manufacturers leave because of the city's poor reputation regarding labor. With help from FMCS over several years, the Jamestown LMC dramatically reversed that trend by monthly meetings playing up the positives about the community and sponsoring training and information programs about cooperative relationships. Soon the outflow of jobs stopped, several enterprises expanded their workforces, and several new businesses arrived. Chambers of commerce have always been cheerleaders promoting the business environment of their community. A community LMC has the local trade unions seeing that as a mutual interest and joining the business leaders in promoting their community.

Labor-management committees anticipate problems and issues, and address them before they become overheated or, as in the case of Jamestown, they confront a negative trend and help reverse it. To encourage these efforts at nurturing labor-management cooperation, the act also provided funding for an FMCS grant program to help LMCs at all levels.

Native American Mediation and Elections

Geographically the largest Indian reservation in the United States, covering 2.5 million acres in northeast Arizona, the Hopi-Navajo reservation was created by executive order in 1882. In the ensuing years, the two tribes had fought bitterly over land use. Traditional dispute resolution procedures in the courts and the Bureau of Indian Affairs (BIA) produced only partial and temporary success. As the BIA tired of continuing skirmishes between the tribes, Congress came to their aid by passing a 1974 statute directing FMCS to mediate the dispute.

FMCS hired former director Bill Simkin as the lead mediator on the project. Appointed director by President Kennedy and reappointed by President Johnson, Simkin had been a full-time arbitrator his entire adult life before joining FMCS. He stayed at FMCS to become the longest-serving director, nearly eight years, because, as he said many times, he came to love mediation more than arbitration.

Of all the issues mediation faced, the most difficult concerned sacred burial grounds. As property boundaries were proposed during the negotiations, often they either intersected a burial ground or isolated one in the other tribe's land. Reluctantly, and frequently with great emotional pain, some burial grounds had to be moved. Congress had appropriated just $500,000 for the Hopi-Navajo mediation itself. It provided another $50 million for other agencies to help implement the settlement by relocating fences, villages, families, monuments, and the burial grounds.

After nine months of work, settlement was reached in principle on all major issues, and the federal court ordered enforcement of the agreement. Since questions remained on implementation, the tribes and the court asked that the mediation effort continue. For the next year, Simkin continued to help the parties with implementation as needed. He later referred to the dispute as his longest mediation case and his most satisfying because it ended such a long-standing conflict and demonstrated that talking is always the best solution.

This mediation effort won praise from the court, the tribes, the BIA, and the media for having succeeded where earlier efforts had fallen short. Treaties, litigation, court orders, executive orders, and acts of Congress had addressed narrow questions, whereas mediation allowed the parties to deal with their needs and desires—as well as long-simmering angers and misunderstandings—in a way that allowed them to develop workable solutions.

The Oglala Sioux occupied the second largest U.S. reservation, the Pine Ridge Reservation in South Dakota. When controversy persisted over a tribal election among the twelve thousand members, tribal leaders contacted FMCS for help in 1975. FMCS had little experience in elections, but the tribe trusted FMCS because of its work with the Hopi and Navajo in Arizona. FMCS assembled a staff of mediators with NLRB election experience and a few

NLRB retirees to organize and monitor the election at twenty-one polling places on the 2 million acre reservation. A primary and general election were held in January 1976 without a hitch.

Wounded Knee

In the early 1970s, the American Indian Movement (AIM) began demonstrating and protesting to call attention to the treatment of Native Americans by the federal government. The organization was the first national and highly publicized civil rights organization representing the interest of Native Americans. In 1973, to dramatize what they felt was the federal government's blatant disregard of their culture and violations of treaties, the AIM took over the Bureau of Indian Affairs (BIA) building in Washington. To gain maximum publicity for their cause, they occupied the BIA building for days while the federal government puzzled over how to deal with this aggressive protest. After causing a lot of damage to the BIA building, AIM members left in a caravan heading for the Pine Ridge Reservation in South Dakota to protest the actions of Dick Wilson, the elected tribal chief, whom they accused of nepotism and improper use of federal funds and civil rights violations.

Assuming that AIM intended to take over the BIA building in Pine Ridge, heavily armed U.S. marshals and BIA troops prepared to meet the caravan of two hundred vehicles at the Pine Ridge building. Avoiding that confrontation, AIM took over the historic village of Wounded Knee. The choice of Wounded Knee, the site of a massacre of hundreds of Sioux by federal troops in 1890, was both a strategic and symbolic coup for the protesters. By avoiding the main force arrayed against them, they were able to dig in and hold the town for seventy-three days, creating a tense situation and a public relations nightmare for the government. CRS sent a mediation team to act as intermediary, while armed FBI agents, BIA, and customs officers stood by threatening to forcibly dislodge the AIM occupation.

Although the CRS and the FBI were both in the Department of Justice, they played vastly different roles. The FBI came to resent the CRS mediation role, believing that by talking peace and seeking solutions, CRS prolonged the takeover.

Although AIM faced internal disagreements, some issues were clear: recognizing Wounded Knee as a historic site, renegotiating treaties, congressional attention to their issue, White House talks on their issues, and a government investigation of the civil rights violations under Wilson's regime at Pine Ridge. In negotiating sessions in the meetinghouse in Wounded Knee, CRS acted more as a facilitator and sought to keep the events from exploding (although there were a few killings).

Dissension within AIM, the AIM interest in calling attention to its cause with media coverage of the siege, and the difficulty in finding some way to end the siege peaceably, an effort that required cooperation and consent all the way up the White House, all contributed to the difficult mediation role that CRS played. The ultimate resolution was that a delegation from AIM would meet with someone at the White House, there would be consideration given to their demands, a memorial would be established at Wounded Knee, and the Civil Rights Division would investigate complaints on the reservation. Also the leaders of the takeover would be tried for felonies.

The best way to characterize CRS's role was not in terms of reaching a settlement but in calming the warring factions and allaying their fears of the violence about to be inflicted by their foes—in short, to keep them talking rather than resorting to actions such as those twenty years later in the Waco, Texas, siege, where many lives were lost. While the talk continued, accommodation could be made to some of the AIM demands and interests.

Although much of the action of ADR in the 1970s involved new rights granted or new initiatives taken by the federal government, there was also much going on among private groups.

Chapter Twelve

Outside the Federal Realm

New Groups Pick Up the ADR Torch

The growth of ADR was driven for years by federal actions—new laws, studies, or initiatives. But private efforts played a role as far back as the 1920s with the creation of the American Arbitration Association. As we have seen, private groups also backed key initiatives during the 1960s. In the 1970s, these private efforts began to come into their own, underscoring that ADR was maturing as a practice and a profession.

The SPIDR Story

The story of the Society of Professionals in Dispute Resolution (SPIDR), founded in 1972, exemplifies the story of ADR expansion in the 1970s. The founding, development, and membership growth of SPIDR demonstrate the spread of ADR from the labor sector into the emerging dispute arenas. Within a decade, SPIDR would have a thousand members representing an array of new dispute areas (Barrett, 1997).

Background

Most professional groups have an association that satisfies members' needs for training, updating, and promoting their field, as well as developing and upholding professional standards or ethics. Labor-management mediators and arbitrators had had several such organizations for a number of years. The National Academy of Arbitrators (NAA) and the American Arbitration Association

(AAA) were available for arbitrators' professional needs. Federal mediators had their own agency, the Federal Mediation and Conciliation Service (FMCS), which was large enough to provide for their professional needs, and state and local mediators had the Association of Labor Mediation Agencies (ALMA). The charters of these organizations, however, did not allow for expansion beyond their traditional membership of labor-management dispute resolvers.

Even with the continuing racial, community, and campus conflicts, ADR impact remained minimal at the start of the 1970s. But as media attention increasingly focused on these disputes, citizen concern and anxiety rose. Those charged with protecting public safety and property showed little evidence of having effective strategies in place, even as the situation appeared to be worsening.

Beyond the protective service ranks, another group with a capacity to aid the situation was labor-management dispute resolvers. However, early on, only a few showed any interest. A few had written articles suggesting the labor-management model as a way to address these new disputes, and only slightly more had begun working in the new areas, primarily at the NCDS and CMCR (Barrett, 1967, 1969–1970).

Laying the Foundation

David Tanzman, a long-time FMCS mediator from Detroit and an early SPIDR president, had asked each FMCS director on appointment to support the idea of a professional organization of labor-management mediators. He believed that mediation would never achieve the status of a profession without a professional association. He had in mind an organization similar to the National Academy of Arbitrators, which was limited to experienced labor-management arbitrators admitted to membership through a rigorous peer review.

Each succeeding FMCS director had no disagreement with the idea, but none gave practical support to it until Curtis Counts did so in 1971. Confidants of Counts later reported that he embraced the idea because of rumors within FMCS that the mediators were starting to unionize. Thinking that this outside professional organization would mute the unionizing effort, Counts gave Tanzman travel funds and time off from mediating to assess the extent of interest in such an organization. Tanzman interviewed state and federal labor-management mediators and a few private labor-management arbitrators.

After Tanzman interviewed Robert Helsby, head of the New York State Public Employment Board and president of the Association of Labor Mediation Agencies, Helsby later reported, "I grabbed the ball and ran with it." With staff and other resources at his disposal, Helsby used his organizing skills to make things happen. He formed a working group, asked several members to draft a proposal for an organization of neutrals, and explored the idea with many others. By the summer of 1972, Helsby and the working group had developed a proposal endorsed by an extensive group of contacts. They began planning for a September inaugural of what would become SPIDR.

A Wider Vision for SPIDR

Helsby's vision for the organization was very broad. Since he worked in the newest area of labor-management, the public sector, he felt empathy for the newcomers in the nonlabor-management arenas. He wanted membership open to all dispute resolvers. As the proposal for the organization evolved, the definition of membership was strongly debated. Helsby's view prevailed with two categories of membership: regular members needed three years of full-time dispute resolution experience, and associate membership was available for those with less experience but an interest in dispute resolution. Membership was offered to anyone involved in dispute resolution, not just those in the labor-management field.

In September 1972, SPIDR was formed, and charter memberships were issued to 146 individuals. In Chicago a month later, the

34 members at the first SPIDR meeting signed the certificate of incorporation. The group was predominantly male and focused on labor-management issues. Seven of the signatories would later become SPIDR presidents. But the initial group also included four women, two nonlabor-management practitioners, and four labor-management practitioners who were working in the new dispute areas. The gathering selected Robert Helsby as SPIDR's first president. Subsequently, eighteen other labor-management dispute resolvers would be elected president before Wallace Warfield's election in 1992 would break that pattern. Warfield, an experienced mediator and faculty member at George Mason University's Institute for Conflict Analysis and Resolution, had once headed the CRS.

In 1973, two hundred dispute resolvers participated in SPIDR's first annual conference in Reston, Virginia. The agenda of the conference focused exclusively on labor-management concerns, with great emphasis on public employment. This labor-management emphasis was not accidental. The leadership and conference planners were not ignoring dispute resolvers from the emerging dispute areas. The leadership felt the best way to help was to admit these newcomers to membership and encourage them to attend SPIDR's annual conference, where they would be exposed to labor-management ADR. They believed that the labor-management model was the proven one, and once it was understood, it could be adapted to new dispute areas.

Membership Shifts

At the 1973 conference, Helsby's welcoming speech noted that SPIDR membership had grown to six hundred in a year and that dispute resolvers from the nonlabor sector were well represented at the conference, although he did not provide any numbers.

In the fall of 1974, the annual conference agenda changed only slightly, adding two sessions that were not on labor-management ADR. This slow trend continued throughout the 1970s, gradually moving away from exclusively labor-management concerns. Instead of shifting its focus to the nontraditional dispute areas, the conferences spotlighted new ADR processes within the labor-management settings—public employee disputes, for example. Even foreign labor-management dispute resolution got more attention at SPIDR conferences than new dispute areas. It would be the 1980s before nonlabor ADR would achieve much attention on SPIDR conference agendas.

As the conference agenda shifted slowly, the membership composition shifted from an overwhelming labor majority to a nonlabor majority ten years later. SPIDR president Sam Sackman, a longtime FMCS mediator, puzzled over the fact in his 1981 inaugural address that only 10 percent of the FMCS mediators remained members of SPIDR. Many labor dispute resolvers by the end of the 1970s had dropped out of SPIDR, preferring the familiarity of FMCS, AAA, NAA, and ALRA.

The diversity of ADR practitioners continued to expand in terms of both processes—mediation, arbitration, fact finding, ombudsmen, training, med-arb—and dispute arenas—environmental, marriage and family, commercial, court annexed, and community and racial. Later, each common practice area developed a sector within SPIDR with its own workshops at the annual conference.

Another aspect of diversity influenced by ADR expansion was the increase in women, minorities, and younger people in SPIDR's membership. With these changes, SPIDR began to deal with issues of certification, membership qualifications, ethics, and a wider range of training topics.

The SPIDR initial logo presented an interesting debate. The logo featured a spider web extending in two directions from the word *SPIDR*. Vigorous debate over that logo caused it to be abandoned after several years. One side felt the web suggested intrigue, maybe even conspiracy; the other viewpoint suggested that just as the spider's web captured unwanted bugs and insects, SPIDR members caught unwanted confrontations and violence (Barrett, 1997).

Other Initiatives Aiding ADR

Having proved itself in the labor dispute arena and shown its applicability in the civil rights area, ADR began to attract a number of new players in the 1970s. Bar associations, law schools, universities, states, and nonprofit organizations acted to promote ADR.

The Pound Conference

Roscoe Pound, a celebrated Harvard law professor and legal scholar, had earned a reputation for promoting court reform and improvements in the administration of justice in the first half of the twentieth century. In 1976, a conference used his name to emphasize a similar interest in seeking improvement in courts and justice administration. Chief Justice Warren Burger called the Pound Conference of lawyers to examine and discuss the inefficiencies of the justice system. Addressing the conference, the chief justice spoke forcefully in support of more ADR in the justice system. As a result, the conference resolved to seek opportunities to promote the use of ADR throughout the system. Some writers credit this conference with the beginning of the court-related ADR of today (Baer, 2002).

Most reports indicate that 80 to 90 percent of lawsuits are settled before a court judgment. Typically, lawyers call this process a settlement conference—basically a negotiation between opposing counsel. For all their litigious tendencies, lawyers are actually frequent users of a basic form of ADR.

At the Pound Conference, participants discussed Rule 16 of the Federal Rules of Civil Procedure that encouraged judges to use pretrial conferences to identify ways of moving the case efficiently through the process. In the pretrial conference, judges could urge the parties to consider using ADR.

Participants also considered other forms of ADR that would be compatible with legal practice. For example, law professor Frank E. A. Sander suggested his idea of a "multidoor" courthouse at which an aggrieved individual could choose among a number of alternative methods to resolve a conflict. The basic forms of ADR—negotiation, mediation, and arbitration—were discussed, as were the more lawyer-familiar forms of ADR: moderated settlement conference, mini-trial, summary jury trial, and early neutral evaluation. These four are used most often with parties who have a need for their day in court, to the point that they feel mediation does not afford adequate legal advocacy. Each uses a neutral third party who facilitates the process, while the final resolution remains with the parties. Each also allows for discovery of relevant facts from the opposite side and significant preparation.

In a moderated settlement conference, each side presents a summary of its case to a panel of attorneys. In a mini-trial, each side presents a summary of its case to an audience of the clients and lawyers. In a summary jury trial, each side presents its case to a jury and judge, usually a magistrate or visiting judge. Early neutral evaluation often takes place before discovery or major preparation. Brief case summaries are presented to the evaluator, who may ask questions and challenge evidence, before presenting the parties with a written and confidential evaluation, usually with a percentage of expected liability and damages.

Private Sector Labor Relations

Although arbitration of grievances—alleged violations of the labor agreement—has been widely used in private sector labor-management negotiations since World War II, the parties traditionally use mediation to resolve their collective bargaining impasses. They seldom use arbitration for bargaining impasses, since private sector negotiators are reluctant to allow an outsider to decide such important issues. In 1973, the steel industry made a dramatic break from that practice.

The use of strikes by steelworker unions had developed into a nearly ritual process that was beginning to take a toll on both sides. To maintain a steady supply of steel for regular customers, the industry had begun stockpiling steel during the year before contract negotiations as a hedge against a strike. If no strike occurred, lay-offs started shortly after the settlement to reduce the built-up inventories. Union members thus felt punished by reaching a settlement without a strike.

In response to this dilemma, the steel industry and the United Steelworkers union reached an unprecedented agreement to submit any issues not resolved during 1974 negotiations to final and binding arbitration. By submitting the issues to an impartial arbitration process, both sides felt they could get a fair outcome without the union's resorting to a strike or management's holding out the implicit threat of post-settlement layoffs. Their agreement, called experimental negotiating agreement (ENA), was reached a year before the contract was to expire. Satisfied with their first experience with the new bargaining process in 1975, the parties continued to use it in the 1977 and 1980 negotiations with only minor modifications.

ENA set out a rigid schedule for concluding its collective bargaining. Negotiations started on February 1 and ended on April 15. All issues not resolved would be submitted to arbitration on May 10, with the arbitration due on July 10. Any contract language and other arrangements the parties failed to work out in implementing the arbitration award would be resolved in arbitration by July 31, and their agreement would become effective on August 1. This transparent schedule helped to assure both sides that there would be no surprises—and no need to take punitive actions against the other side.

Agricultural ADR

Tractor fuel prices during the oil embargo in the 1970s added greatly to the usual problems caused by fickle rainfall and other unpredictable elements in the life of farmers. Michigan legislators attempted to bring a measure of fairness to farming with a 1973 law creating a forum for farmers and growers to collectively bargain with the food industry processors and distributors. The new law closely paralleled the state's labor-management law. The Agricultural Marketing and Bargaining Act required bargaining over sales of agricultural products, provided for mediation and final-offer arbitration, and made refusing to bargain an unfair practice.

Ronald Haughton, who acted as both mediator and arbitrator under the statute, said the ADR process worked very well. Haughton, an experienced labor-management mediator and arbitrator, said that although he knew nothing about the pricing or grading of fruits or vegetables, he was able to quickly learn enough from the parties to make substantive contributions to the process. In a paper on the transferability of labor-management ADR skills, he used that and other experiences to argue that experienced ADR practitioners from one dispute area, if motivated and open-minded, could work effectively in more than one area (Haughton, 1983).

American Arbitration Association

Having been established in 1926 and having created a successful niche providing arbitrators for commercial and labor-management disputes, the American Arbitration Association (AAA) was, like FMCS, timid about moving beyond its traditional work into new dispute areas. In 1968, it had accepted a Ford Foundation grant to create NCDS, but it had maintained an arms-length relationship with NCDS for the first seven years. Then in 1975, NCDS was renamed Community Disputes Services and became a formal part of AAA.

With that move, AAA made a strong commitment to promote the new dispute areas as much as its other programs in labor-management, commercial, international, insurance, construction, and union representation elections. By expanding its extensive roster of ADR experts to cover the new dispute arenas, AAA could make available professionals with the skill to help resolve virtually any dispute. AAA also expanded its capacity to promote peaceful dispute resolution and assist an even wider variety of industries and organizations in developing dispute resolution systems.

In 1993, the name of its long-time journal, *Arbitration Journal*, was changed to *Dispute Resolution Journal*, emphasizing the increasingly significant role played by the association in all types of dispute resolution in the United States and internationally.

National Commission for Industrial Peace

Presidential Executive Order 11710 in April 1973 created the National Commission for Industrial Peace to study the industrial relations climate in the United States and make recommendations for improvement. While collective bargaining in the early 1970s was extensive and vibrant, problems were resulting from the oil embargo and the imposition of wage and price controls to calm inflation.

Arbitrator David Cole, a former director of FMCS, served as commission chairman with leaders of major unions and employers participating. The commission's final report strongly endorsed the FMCS work in mediation and preventive mediation, and it urged adequate funding to support its work. It further recommended that the Department of Labor provide labor and management with data needed for sound bargaining.

Neighborhood Justice Centers

In the late 1970s, the Justice Department funded pilot programs in Kansas City and Los Angeles that provided local part-time mediators to relieve courts from handling small cases—landlord spats over security deposits, domestic squabbles, neighbor complaints about barking dogs or noisy motor bikes, and the like. The cost in both money and time of getting such disputes resolved by a court prohibited them from ever being addressed.

An example illustrates the difficulty of relying on the courts to resolve small problems. When an angry estranged husband put sugar in his wife's gas tank and broke her apartment door, the woman learned that to get him to pay repair costs would require a police investigation, an arrest, and conviction. Then she would need to file a claim in another court and go through another process there.

President Carter's attorney general, Griffin Bell, who as a former federal judge understood the barriers to getting satisfaction in the courts, initiated the neighborhood justice centers, another by-product of the 1976 Pound Conference. The success of the pilot programs in Justice Centers resulted in legislation introduced by Senator Ted Kennedy providing funds for grants to underwrite similar programs.

As with any other new field, participants disagreed on some important details. Beginning with the violent protests of the late 1960s and early 1970s, one viewpoint insisted that change could come only from aggressively challenging the system. Although that viewpoint had been somewhat muted based on progress made by the later 1970s, that aggressive viewpoint persisted. In its most extreme form, it viewed negotiations and mediations as a sellout, a lack of commitment. Many of the people involved in the Justice Centers viewed ADR with misgivings because of its close ties with the law and lawyers. They felt that real social change was needed, and it could not be accomplished with legal entanglements.

National Peace Academy

Senator Spark Matsunaga of Hawaii was a much-decorated veteran of World War II who strongly opposed the Vietnam War. He first introduced legislation to create a peace academy while he was in the House of Representatives in 1963. Matsunaga sought to create an institution on a par with the military academies to teach and promote peace and peaceful methods for resolving disputes.

When he moved from the House to the Senate in 1976, his idea for a peace academy gained the support of several prominent senators, including Senator Jennings Randolph of West Virginia. A coalition of citizens and organizations began a campaign pushing the idea. Finally, Congress created and funded the Commission on Proposals for the National Academy of Peace and Conflict Resolution. Senator Matsunaga served as chairman of the commission, which was composed of other public individuals. Following extensive hearings and research, the commission recommended creating a peace academy in 1981. A long legislative process finally produced the U.S. Institute of Peace in 1984, an organization of scholars who study conflict resolution and issue research reports. The organization also makes grants for such research and provides a place for foreigners to study peace. Although the U.S. Institute of Peace is focused primarily on international matters, it is generally recognized that useful dispute resolution practices honed in one sector find their way into others.

Senator Matsunaga's consistent support of peace and the peace academy idea earned him the B'nai B'rith International Peace Award in 1986, and the Institute of Peace at the University of Hawaii, where his public papers are housed, was renamed to honor him posthumously.

Reflections on ADR in the 1970s

The 1970s extended the progress of ADR into more new dispute areas and reinforced its use in traditional disputes. The decade ended with labor-management mediation books dominating bookshelves and the term *ADR* not yet in common usage.

Writings on Mediation

The 1970s began with two excellent books on labor-management mediation by former FMCS staff members: former FMCS director William Simkin's 1971 book, *Mediation and the Dynamics of Collective Bargaining*, and former director of the Office of Mediation Walter Maggiolo's 1971 book, *Techniques of Mediation in Labor Disputes*. Although these books dealt exclusively with labor-management mediation, individuals from the new dispute areas used them because others did not exist. By the 1980s, this lack of research on nonlabor disputes was remedied by a storm of papers, articles, and books by practitioners and scholars, which accelerated into the next century.

The ADR Label

No one was yet using the term *ADR* in the 1970s. For example, in the 1977 SPIDR Annual Conference Report, repeated references are made to "nonlabor disputes" and "new dispute areas" to refer to emerging disputes. FMCS used the same expressions to refer to its own work outside labor-management disputes.

When most labor-management dispute resolvers used the words *negotiation, mediation,* or *arbitration,* they were referring to the labor-management setting. From their perspective, the realms of conflict were international, handled by war or diplomacy; criminal and civil, handled by the courts; labor-management, handled by mediators and arbitrators; and these new areas, which they labeled nonlabor, handled by want-to-be mediators and arbitrators. All of this would begin to change in the 1980s as labor-management dispute resolvers increasingly took a back seat to the new areas.

Chapter Thirteen

Crisis and Rebirth

Labor-Management ADR in the 1980s

Throughout the postwar period, labor-management mediators came to think of themselves as ADR professionals who could handle any crisis. They had waded in to crippling steel or coal strikes and violent building trades disputes; some had been challenged to resolve civil rights protests and armed insurrections on college campuses. They had proved themselves adept at handling other people's problems. In the 1980s, these mediators and the institution of collective bargaining faced their own crisis, causing a major adjustment in ADR efforts.

Changing the Guard

The long postwar expansion gave way in the late 1970s to a period of stagflation, defined as a period of falling economic growth and inflation—something the country had never seen before. President Carter, lowering the thermostat at the White House and putting on a sweater to demonstrate the era of diminished expectations, chalked up the problem to a growing sense of malaise in America. His successor, Ronald Reagan was not a malaise kind of guy. At his inauguration in 1981, he looked the very part of a nineteenth-century capitalist donning a morning coat at his inauguration and sporting a white tie at the record nine inaugural balls. But there was more than symbolism behind the change of guard. Reagan ushered in a period of government cutbacks and probusiness policies that would seriously shake up an American economy that was indeed stagnating.

From World War II onward, the United States had led the world in the production of goods and services. But by the 1980s, its lead was fast eroding, and foreign competition increasingly was pushing it into the role of the world's consumer. In 1978, domestic steel production and profits had reached an all-time high; three years later, half of the Steelworkers union membership had been laid off, and the industrial region of the Midwest, once the pride of the American economy, was rapidly turning into a Rust Belt. Mini steel mills and Japanese auto plants popped up in antiunion (euphemistically, "right-to-work") southern states. Deregulation of telephone, trucking, railroads, airlines, and later utilities created nonunionized competitors such as Sprint and MCI. The accelerating changes in technology saw old-line manufacturers such as Westinghouse shift from an 82 percent unionized workforce in 1982 to 10 percent in 1990 by introducing new technology only at new factories and closing older, unionized plants.

All of these developments would significantly hobble the labor movement, which for years had been a primary source of prestige and legitimacy of ADR. A strike by federal air traffic controllers in 1981 would come to symbolize the dead end of traditional collective bargaining and the beginning of a significant rethinking of the relationship between labor and management.

Air Traffic Controllers Strike

The Professional Air Traffic Controllers Organization (PATCO) represented twelve thousand controllers employed by the Federal Aviation Administration (FAA). These highly trained professionals handled traffic in the busiest air travel system in the world.

In mid-June 1981, FMCS assisted PATCO leaders and FAA management in reaching an agreement on a new labor agreement. In a subsequent vote, PATCO members rejected the accord. The parties returned to mediation in mid-July with five issues separating them: union participation in selecting technology, a retirement plan, pay levels, sick leave accumulation, and a shorter work week. The union insisted that if agreement were not reached in two days, it would call a strike. When agreement evaded the parties, the union struck, stranding travelers and cargo across the country.

President Reagan warned the union that employees who did not return to work within forty-eight hours would be terminated. When the deadline passed, the FAA fired all strikers, a significant portion of the workforce. Within a few days, military controllers and FAA managers returned air traffic to near normal. This decisive action by the new president in ending an illegal strike was widely praised by businesspeople and the traveling public. It would come to stand for a new day in dealing with unions.

PATCO members had made several wrong assumptions. They had assumed that other unions would support the strike, but none did. They assumed that they could not be replaced, but they were. They assumed the precedent established by the 1970 postal strike would prevail; it did not. And, finally, they assumed that Reagan, as former head of the Screen Actors Guild and the first trade union leader ever elected president, would be sympathetic—even more so since PATCO had broken ranks with the AFL-CIO to endorse him. Again, they were wrong.

The greatest significance of the PATCO demise was the emboldening of management to take on unions. It represented a symbolic shift to a new day in labor-management relations, one that, aided by other realities, made trade unions a significantly smaller player in employment relations. When the president fired strikers, some socially unacceptable practices swiftly became acceptable. Replacing strikers or locking out workers during a dispute, rare occurrences in the past, now became real options. Suddenly unions could be portrayed as part of the problem, not the solution, to the nation's economic ills.

Collective Bargaining and Labor-Management Relations in the 1980s

For years, collective bargaining had operated under a fixed pattern: the union would raise issues, and contract negotiations would focus on them. In the ever expanding American economy, employers could afford to raise prices to satisfy union demands for improvements in compensation, benefits, and working conditions. Employers seldom raised issues of their own. Industry and pattern collective bargaining—the practice of following the industry leader on pay and benefit improvements—also aided in taking labor costs out of competition because competitors' labor costs increased together.

Pattern bargaining worked as long as everyone followed the pattern. But when foreign competitors and domestic nonunion competitors ignored the wage-benefit standards, the fabric began to unravel. Suddenly it was the employers that were making demands and the unions responding.

Collective bargaining in the 1980s became concession, or giveback, bargaining. The union strategy shifted from the "more and more" of Samuel Gompers long ago and a rush to the bargaining table to win new ground to a desire to stay away from the table as long as possible in a bid to hold on to what had already been won. Another new union strategy was to bargain for employment security by agreeing to employer-demanded concessions—accepting a wage cut in exchange for an employer commitment to protect a percentage of the workers from layoff. The United Steelworkers, once one of the strongest unions in the country, gave up wage increases as a concession for the right to appoint a corporate board member of U.S. Steel. Some unions tried delaying tactics: where employers had insisted on including a provision extending the agreement for one year if the union did not give the employer notice of its intention to renegotiate, unions simply refused to give notice. The move put off any givebacks for at least another year. This sea change in labor-management bargaining featured lower wages and less generous benefits for newly hired employees, striker replacements, and lockouts.

If the new employer attitude was not enough for the unions and their members to recognize the new day, there were also production cutbacks, layoffs, and rising unemployment announced regularly in the media. A new concept was added in the 1980s to bedevil trade unions even further. The concept of a union-free environment gained popularity in management circles, accompanied by an army of consultants and lawyers dedicated to that outcome.

Union organizers in the past had asserted that poor management was the greatest help in unionizing a workforce. In the 1980s, enlightened management practices caught on. They drew concepts from union labor agreements: a grievance procedure (a few included arbitration), ombuds programs to deal with employee problems more effectively than union shop stewards, and employee handbooks that resembled labor agreements. To that they added processes encouraging employee involvement and better working conditions.

When some employees, believing the handbook was a contract, sued the company to enforce its provisions, employers stopped issuing handbooks. State courts began to enforce employment-at-will, meaning that employees who are not protected by a law or a labor agreement are considered at-will employees, who work at the discretion of the employer.

Impact on FMCS

Since mediation has always been closely tied to collective bargaining, the changes in collective bargaining in the 1980s had a significant impact on FMCS. The trend toward longer labor agreements and the smaller number of strikes reduced the need for mediation. Employers pushing the union hard for major changes were less inclined to use mediation.

The Reagan administration budget cuts, necessitated by the dual policies of lower taxes and increased defense spending, reduced the FMCS budget in eighteen months from $26.7 million to $22 million, causing the elimination of seventy-five positions at FMCS from a staff of fewer than five hundred. That included five mediator-managers and the entire clerical field staff of seventy. To save funds and provide work for permanent staff, regular field mediators replaced the part-time community conciliators handling age discrimination cases. FMCS also began charging for some services. Beginning with charging fees for arbitrators to be listed on the

FMCS arbitration roster, the practice spread to charging labor and management fees to get lists of arbitrators, and finally requiring fees for some training under the preventive mediation program.

The diminished volume of collective bargaining allowed FMCS to eliminate the Office of Mediation Services in the national office. Since the early 1960s, this office had provided assistance to mediators in the field by sending a national representative, or "paratrooper" mediator, to bring greater attention and mediation effort to major disputes. These national mediators also coordinated the mediation of industry and pattern bargaining cases. As the number of these significant negotiations diminished, the national office role shrunk to one special assistant to the director from between six and eight mediators.

The rapid decline of collective bargaining in the 1980s stood in sharp contrast with the previous thirty years. All earlier administrations had a ranking White House staffer knowledgeable on labor matters who served as a contact with the FMCS director. President Johnson and other presidents had moved major negotiations to the White House to demonstrate their significance. In the 1970s, it was not unusual to see a press conference at the FMCS national office announcing a settlement or for the media to wait on the sidewalk in front of the building for the latest on high-profile negotiations. By the 1980s, collective bargaining was no longer the headline news it used to be.

These developments had an impact on the esprit de corps of FMCS and particularly its mediators. They had taken seriously the Wagner Act assertion that collective bargaining was the preferred method for resolving industrial conflicts. To both FMCS and USCS before it as the go-betweens with labor and management, the agency's mission was to nurture and defend the institution of collective bargaining. FMCS mediators took that as a personal mission; it brought them together as colleagues doing important and exciting work.

Some mediators were as puzzled by the changes in collective bargaining as trade union negotiators were. They had rarely mediated wage and benefits reductions and were not sure they wanted to, since it clashed with their paradigm of mediation and collective bargaining. It was a struggle for them. For some, the introduction of interest-based negotiations and other forms of cooperation provided a new direction and reenergized their work.

Shifts at the National Labor Relations Board

The National Labor Relations Board makes and enforces formal rules for collective bargaining under its responsibility for keeping the relationship even-handed between labor and management. This regulatory role is done by decisions made on cases brought to the board.

With President Reagan's appointment of a new member in 1983, a Republican majority assumed control of the board and immediately began to shift board policy and precedent to match the tenor of the 1980s. Subsequent board decisions allowed employers to refuse to provide the union relevant information for bargaining and at the same time gave more weight to competitive business considerations than to a stable collective bargaining relationship. Other decisions made it easier for management to implement unilateral decisions without bargaining with the union and to insist on bargaining on topics that previously required mutual agreement before bargaining.

The board chair showed his hostility to the institution he was charged with regulating when he wrote this about collective bargaining: it "frequently means labor monopoly, the destruction of individual freedom, and the destruction of the market place as the mechanism for determining the value of labor" (Dotson, 1980, pp. 39–40).

Impact on Unions and Membership

The unionized portion of the workforce declined significantly during the 1980s. At the start of the decade, there were 20.1 million union members, accounting for 23 percent of the workforce,

according to the Bureau of Labor Statistics. By 1990, union membership had shrunk to 16.7 million, or 16 percent of the total workforce.

With this stunning drop in membership, many unions had difficulty covering their expenses. To cut costs, they reduced staff,
conferences, travel, and newspapers. Union mergers also resulted
from the decline of membership. Many old-line unions had to
overcome long-standing rivalries to enter mergers just to maintain
adequate service for their members.

Between 1980 and 1989, forty-two union mergers occurred,
twenty-six of them involving AFL-CIO unions. One of the largest
mergers joined the 50,000-member Brotherhood of Railway Car-
men and the 175,000-member Brotherhood of Railway, Airline
and Steamship Clerks. Both the United Telegraph Workers and
the International Typographical Union joined the Communications Workers of America. The United Food and Commercial
Workers combined with the Packinghouse Workers. The American Federation of State County and Municipal Employees and the
Service Employees International Union both added a number
of small, independent unions to their ranks. The Carpenters and
Joiners assimilated the International Tile, Marble and Terrazzo
Finishers and the Shopworkers & Granite Cutters International
Union. The National Marine Union combined operations with
the National Marine Engineers Beneficial Association.

A generation of older union representatives retired, and some
left because of staff reductions. Trade unions would miss their experience and skills as the unions faced significant decline in their
power and influence during the 1990s.

Responding to Change

The changes affected unions and management in so many ways
that they could not be ignored. Questions as to whether the
changes were temporary or permanent confused decision makers
and delayed responses. Labor-management pairs, who saw the new
situation differently or had a history lacking trust, were held back
by suspicions about the other side's motives. Ultimately, this process

would lead to a rethinking of ADR, with a new emphasis on getting more deeply into the relationships between union and management and not simply settling disputes as they arose.

Union Response

The labor movement initially reacted to its declining fortunes with anger, disbelief, and frustration. Although collective bargaining had never been easy, it had been largely institutionalized since World War II. It had consistently provided an improving standard of living for both unionized and nonunionized workers, a rising tide that had lifted all boats. Now with the most basic form of ADR, negotiation, being seriously challenged, the labor movement lacked a real alternative to vigorously engaging in collective bargaining and grievance handling.

At the 1985 AFL-CIO Thirtieth Anniversary Convention, the leadership talked about becoming more active politically, lobbying for improved labor legislation and jobs programs, reviewing several studies on what to do about the array of problems facing them, and placing more staff into organizing and better coordinating organizing efforts among unions. With membership numbers continuing to fall, the AFL-CIO did not appear to have a new strategy.

By the late 1980s, the AFL-CIO was achieving limited success with what it called its corporate campaign. This effort involved using aggressive public relations to embarrass, and even harass, corporations and individual representatives. Banking officials on the corporate board of a company involved in a labor dispute might find their bank building or their personal residence being picketed with informational signs announcing the banker's connection to the dispute. Michael Moore would keep the tactic alive in the 1990s with his film *Roger and Me*, in which the native of Flint, Michigan, keeps the cameras rolling as he repeatedly tries to ask the CEO of General Motors why he closed the huge plant there.

From a later perspective, it became obvious that the labor movement needed to rethink the entire labor-management relationship of the early 1980s. That process is much easier to consider theoretically than in practical terms, so change occurred very slowly.

Typically in the early 1980s, humor and ridicule were used in place of rethinking. President William Wimpinsinger of the International Association of Machinists liked to tell a story at conferences and union meetings. A Swedish trade union leader told him, he said, that cooperative labor-management programs in his country were called HONK. Then he would deliver this punch line: "HONK is not an acronym. It stands for what management does just before they run over the union."

Since World War II, labor-management relations had displayed a modest amount of cooperation with joint labor-management safety committees and some joint involvement in community issues, but cooperation was the exception, not the rule. That would change in the 1980s. With Japan's dramatic record of productivity improvements and the real fear that the Japanese would soon steal the mantle of world economic leadership from the United States, corporate America began examining Japanese and northern European work practices and labor-management relationships.

Ironically, Japan's Quality Circles, which were producing better quality at lower cost than U.S. industry, had been introduced to Japan during postwar reconstruction by an American named W. Edwards Deming. The son of a small-town lawyer, Deming went on to a distinguished academic career in mathematics, physics, and statistics. In the 1930s, he became interested in the idea of quality control, and in the 1950s, he was asked to give a lecture to Japanese industrialists on his ideas of continuous improvement. The Japanese eagerly took to his ideas, which involved systematically tallying product defects, analyzing their causes, correcting them, and then recording the effects of the corrections on subsequent product quality.

By the mid-1980s, many labor-management pairs had begun to recognize they must stop treating each other as adversaries and identify their common enemy: foreign competition. Quality of Work Life programs became popular at many major corporations interested in engaging their entire organization in cooperation.

Such efforts used labor-management committees at various levels within the organization to identify, promote, and oversee opportunities for cooperative efforts of all kinds.

The result was an array of new ideas and practices, some aimed at improving how labor and management worked together, including jointness, partnerships, and labor-management committees at the plant, industry, and community levels. Others included changing the way work was done, including work teams, self-managed teams, and joint problem solving using workers and managers to brainstorm options for solving production problems. All of these have some characteristics of ADR because their purpose and intent is to help resolve issues among individuals and groups.

Previously, management vigorously and successfully protected its prerogative to manage the business, allowing only modest input from workers through suggestion boxes and an occasional award for a good idea. To make cooperation work, both parties needed to move away from seeing every encounter as a win-lose opportunity. Many were successful in this effort, but the work was never easy.

Traditional front-line managers presented the biggest obstacle to the needed changes in management. They had struggled to achieve their supervisory position in which they commanded their subordinates. They had never been collaborative types, and now they were being asked to do just that. And the most threatening idea to their security was self-directed work teams, that is, teams that did not need a supervisor.

Employer Options to Competition

A study of employer reaction to the serious market competition of the 1980s identified three types of strategies and assigned them catchy names: flee, fight, or foster (Walton, McKersie, and Cutcher-Gershenfeld, 1994):

- Flee. These employers moved away from the union to an offshore site or to a new domestic site, often called a greenfield. There they were free to start anew in a union-free environment. Westinghouse was one of the best-known examples of this, but there were many others.

- Fight. These employers attempted to force change on the union and workforce. Depending on the union strength and determination, the results could be easier or harder to achieve. Eastern Airlines and Caterpillar manufacturing both attempted to force their very strong unions into big changes that management wanted in order to improve the bottom line. After years in an untrusting relationship, even a perfect management approach would have made this a hard sell. In these cases, management opted for a fast pitch followed by threats of layoffs or other drastic measures—the goal being acquiescence rather than cooperation.
- Foster. Other employers energetically promoted cooperation with their unions. This involved selling ideas to the union leadership and union members and building trust into the relationship. This is a slow process, but a powerful one because it develops the buy-in of all the stakeholders and fully engages the employees in the enterprise.

Two factors were crucial in successful cooperative efforts. First was an honest and respectful effort to win the hearts and minds of workers, to get them to see the commonality of their and their employer's interests. This required a convinced workforce, which would then provide the discretionary effort in the best interest of the organization and themselves.

The second factor was an understanding of the difference between labor cost and unit labor cost. Employers who do not appreciate the difference put all their effort into reducing labor cost, when unit labor cost is more important. For example, an employee paid $10 an hour who produces 2 units per hour is less valuable to the organization than an employee paid $15 an hour who produces 4 units an hour. The unit labor cost of the worker with the lower wage is $5 per unit. The higher-wage employee actually has a lower unit labor cost: $3.75 per unit.

Changes in the 1980s Workforce

The educational level of the workforce was higher in the 1980s. U.S. society in general was experiencing a greater desire for work self-actualization. Therefore, employees had higher expectations about having input on the job. These expectations had grown gradually from the 1950s, when employees took direction on the job much more readily. As the much-indulged baby boomers played a growing role in the workforce in the 1980s, they expected, and often demanded, similar treatment on the job.

Bureau of Labor-Management Relations and Cooperative Programs

The Department of Labor created the Bureau of Labor-Management Relations and Cooperative Programs to address and assist with these issues in the early 1980s. John Stepp, a former FMCS mediator who headed the bureau, said the bureau spent its first five years playing Paul Revere, attempting to get the word out that there were new ways of envisioning the traditionally hostile union-management relationship. With meetings, briefings, conferences, publications, training materials, and a series of videos called *Work Worth Doing*, the bureau alerted labor and management to the economic changes, their implications, and the best practices for dealing with them.

After 1985, the bureau shifted from spreading the word on what was coming to helping labor and management find and apply solutions. For example, it joined with FMCS to develop a training program called Committee Effectiveness Training, an extensive skills training program seeking to help labor and management to work together. The training exercises focused on dealing with difficult people, understanding personality differences, communicating in nonthreatening ways, identifying body language, and engaging in cooperative decision making such as consensus building and brainstorming.

FMCS and the bureau also developed the Partners in Change (PIC) program, which used organizational development theory to help labor and management jointly identify their relationship problems and the ideal relationship they both desired. Next, the parties would develop a plan for getting from their present state to their desired future state. PIC was field-tested with labor-management pairs in a variety of work settings: city employees, health care workers, high-tech manufacturing, construction workers, white-collar federal employees, and railroad workers.

The typical labor and management pair left the two-day workshop with an agreed-on list of items they would work on jointly, with time commitments and assigned responsibility. Equally important is their greater trust and regard for their opposite number, and strong expressions of their belief that they can and will act as a team to move their relationship to the improved goal they have set. FMCS made PIC part of its preventive mediation program (Barrett, 1989).

Positive ADR Developments in Labor-Management

In addition to these cooperative efforts, the smaller labor movement of the 1980s began to experience two other improvements in labor-management ADR: interest-based negotiation and grievance mediation.

Interest-Based Negotiation

Since improvements in labor-management cooperation did not deal with the parties' bargaining relationship, the traditional bargaining process remained out of sync with the day-to-day phase of those relationships, which increasingly featured real cooperation. It became unrealistic for labor and management to set aside a day-to-day cooperative relationship when traditional adversarial bargaining started, and then expect to resume cooperation after tough bargaining ended. The bureau initially focused on this bifurcated relationship by producing a video introducing the idea of interest-based negotiation.

In traditional bargaining, the sides begin from fixed positions—specific proposals on wages, benefits, and working conditions, for instance. Bargaining is merely a case of horse-trading, in which the two sides make offers and counteroffers supported by arguments until reaching a settlement. To a large extent, the settlement will reflect the relative power of the parties.

Interest-based negotiations attempt to look more deeply at their relationship and to focus on their separate and common interests: beating the competition, maintaining a quality workforce, and improving productivity. With this new focus, both sides can begin to share information more freely, building trust and eventually reaching a point where their positions on specific issues are no longer a question of "take it or leave it" or "take it or we'll strike." Their focus on interests will help both parties develop and select options that satisfy their mutual interests.

Later, a bureau staff member with experience in collective bargaining and mediation produced the P.A.S.T. model of interest-based negotiation and a two-day training program to jointly instruct labor and management on interest-based negotiation (Barrett, 1990).

"P.A.S.T." stands for principles, assumptions, steps, and techniques. The principles and assumptions replace the negatives of traditional bargaining with the positives of an interest-based approach. The steps and techniques provide a sequential process using mutual interests to select options that meet mutual standards to achieve a win-win outcome. The process uses brainstorming and consensus decision making that focus at all times on the parties' interests to arrive at the best available options.

As of the mid-1980s, Humvee, a maker of rugged vehicles for the military, and its industrial union had never reached an agreement without a strike in more than twenty-five years. Both parties thought of themselves as being as tough as the oversize jeeps the company cranked out. The local union took pride in saying they had put Studebaker, the prior owner of the plant, out of business in the late 1960s. Just prior to the training, managers told the trainer, "They won't put us out of business."

The first two training exercises, to the great surprise of both parties, showed them that their adversarial approach, their drive to win at all costs, had in fact produced a solution that was not good for either side. Both saw that if they had cooperated just a little, they could jointly create a bigger pie to divide rather than fighting over what they perceived as a small pie. Then the trainer provoked them with this: "The behavior you demonstrated in these exercises is the same as your behavior in your collective bargaining. Do you want to continue that with the same results, or would you like to learn a better way?" They agreed to continue the training, which involved practicing new skills and learning a different approach to bargaining. Without great enthusiasm, they left the training agreeing to try interest-based bargaining.

One of the most surprising moments in their negotiation came on the issue of subcontracting of component parts. The facilitator insisted, much to their mutual annoyance, that they continue to discuss their interests until they found at least one mutual interest on this issue. Once they agreed that good-quality parts was a mutual interest, they quickly discovered several more mutual interests. That led to an agreement to create a joint committee to examine the subcontracts to determine whether employees could perform the work better and at lower cost.

While their bargaining required more days than previous negotiations, the union spent no days on the picket line. The facilitator had to keep them from slipping back into old habits many times during their negotiations and regularly encourage their continuing efforts. When they reached settlement, both sides expressed pride in what they had done and claimed it was their best settlement.

FMCS has been using the P.AS.T. model with increasing frequency in its labor-management work, as well as its international work.

In the late 1980s, the use of interest-based negotiating increased slowly at first, initially attracting K–12 education bargainers, but winning many adherents in the next ten years. This interest-based concept would animate the cooperative movement of labor-management relations, replacing in many relationships the traditional positional approach to dealings between labor and management.

Grievance Mediation

Grievance procedures became a standard provision in labor agreements during World War II to provide an opportunity to resolve disputes over the interpretation and application of the agreement, without disrupting work. Using face-to-face discussions between escalating levels of authority at each step, the process provided an opportunity to share facts and seek a resolution. When the parties' discussion failed to resolve the grievance, final and binding arbitration was used as the last step to bring finality.

The functioning of the grievance procedure in collective bargaining agreements was also scrutinized in the 1980s. The cost and delays involved with grievance arbitration encouraged consideration of mediation as a way to reach resolution more quickly. Mediation also provided the opportunity for dialogue, seeking solutions that addressed the interests of the disputants. This approach contrasted favorably with the traditionally adversarial arbitration process that featured narrow issue statements and tight evidence elicited through lawyers' questions, objections, and cross examination.

FMCS had traditionally done a very small amount of grievance mediation, primarily because the Taft-Hartley Act had said such efforts should be used only as a "last resort and in exceptional circumstances." The service had taken "last resort" to mean that a strike might occur and no other process was available to prevent it. "Exceptional" was taken to refer to the essential nature of the product involved. Since more than 95 percent of labor agreements provide for grievance arbitration, FMCS mediated a small number of grievances. That restriction was lessened in the 1980s as collective bargaining mediation declined. By the 1990s, FMCS would be announcing its grievance mediation role on its Web site.

Stephen Goldberg, a law professor and arbitrator, had conducted a grievance mediation experimental program in the coal industry in the late 1970s that proved very successful in reducing costs, the grievance backlog, and the time between grievance filing and resolution. Goldberg's research also showed a high level of participant satisfaction with grievance mediation.

Those findings encouraged Goldberg to create the Mediation Research and Educational Project to promote the use of grievance mediation and conduct research on the results. More important, Goldberg's project created a roster of mediators who could perform grievance mediation. Typically mediators doing grievance mediation handled two cases per day, further reducing costs and increasing the speed of resolution.

The 1980s ended much differently than the decade had started. While the crisis in collective bargaining had produced a smaller labor movement, it also had provided new ADR processes focused on cooperation and recognition of the importance of mutual interests.

Chapter Fourteen

The Era of Win-Win

Nonlabor ADR Becomes a Force of Its Own

While mediators and other participants in collective bargaining were watching the world they had known for more than thirty years crash down in the early 1980s, a very different thing happened in the nontraditional world of ADR. New organizations and individuals jumped into the field, academic departments sprouted, and suddenly everyone from corporate CEOs to the guy at the corner deli was spouting a new catch phrase: win-win bargaining.

The 1980s spawned an explosion of new organizations to fund, promote, and support ADR. Some wed the peace movement with conflict resolution, at home and overseas. Others began supplying ADR information and technical assistance to business groups and other areas of conflict. Two important organizations began funding ADR projects. Many new providers of ADR services hung out their shingles. Ten years after its founding, SPIDR was joined by new associations for third parties. All of these new groups served constituencies to aid the growth of ADR.

The 1980s boom of new organizations demonstrated that ADR was not simply an array of activities but a movement in need of better organization and structuring. The dispersed individuals doing conflict resolution across the country were on the verge of becoming an industry.

An Interest-Based Approach

Amid this blizzard of activity, nontraditional ADR was undergoing a significant shift that paralleled that of traditional ADR: a switch to an interest-based approach.

For generations, disputes had been conceived as win-lose propositions. When two parties face each other in court, out of court, or on the battlefield, there have always been winners and losers. Even in the ADR proceedings of arbitration and mediation, the two sides often come at the situation from the perspective of maximizing their gains and minimizing those of the other side.

As we have seen, many traditional cultures practice ways of looking at conflict that do not use the adversarial practices traditionally found in the West. In the early twentieth century, Mary Parker Follett (1868–1933), a Quaker social worker and pioneer in the areas of informal education and community building, had talked about interest-based conflict resolution. Her books *The New State* (1918) and *Creative Experience* (1924) also developed the subject. A book of her speeches, *Dynamic Administration*, published posthumously in 1935, also advanced her arguments for an interest-based focus. Follett was one of the first people to apply psychological insight and social science findings to the study of industrial organization and conflict.

In 1965, a textbook, *A Behavioral Theory of Labor Negotiations: An Analysis of a Social Interaction System*, contrasted interest-based and traditional collective bargaining. The authors, Walton and McKersie, were the first to systematically identify collective bargaining topics that most easily lend themselves to an interest-based way of bargaining.

But these ideas did not really take off until the 1981 publication of *Getting to Yes: Negotiating Agreements Without Giving In* by Roger Fisher and William Ury. The best-seller did much to popularize the concept of interest-based negotiation and win-win bargaining. Using everyday examples, such as an interaction between a person trying to buy an antique and a shop owner, and easy-to-understand language, Fisher and Ury injected the language, if not the actual practice, of ADR into the mainstream.

As the title of the book suggests, negotiating for most people was based on fear—fear of getting a big no, of losing, of getting ripped off, or of not getting the best possible deal. *Getting to Yes* went a long way toward convincing a skeptical public that it was possible to be more open and honest in negotiating and not be taken advantage of. Both Fisher, a Harvard Law School professor who had helped Jimmy Carter prepare for the Camp David Peace Summit, and Ury, an anthropologist, went on to do groundbreaking work on the academic and practitioner side of conflict resolution.

Academic Attention

The 1980s witnessed the start of major academic interest in conflict resolution. The two most prominent examples began at Harvard University and George Mason University in Virginia. By the year 2000, there would be more than a hundred higher education programs offering degrees, concentrations or certificates in dispute resolution.

Institute of Conflict Analysis and Resolution

In 1981, the conflict resolution program founded at George Mason University became the first in the world to offer a master of science in conflict management. By 1989, the program now known as the Institute for Conflict Analysis and Resolution (ICAR) became the first to offer a Ph.D. in the field. With no model to follow, ICAR sought to blend theory with practice and maintain relevance to practitioners and scholars alike.

Founder Bryant Wedge drew early faculty with an interest in conflict resolution from departments of law, sociology, psychology, and international relations, as well as conflict resolution practitioners. This integrated faculty and the newness of the endeavor caused Wedge to tell early students, "Those of us trained in the traditional disciplines are too tied to our intellectual frameworks to create the new field. As the first students ever trained in an interdisciplinary program, you will invent the field of conflict resolution" (Blechman, 2004).

ICAR drew students seeking second careers, recent college graduates, and foreign nationals. Some ICAR doctoral graduates would eventually join or start new university programs in conflict resolution at other institutions.

In addition to the academic programs of teaching, research, and publication, ICAR expanded the opportunity for students to get experience in conflict resolution. The Consortium of Peace Research, Education and Development and the National Conference on Peacemaking and Conflict Resolution both accepted ICAR's invitation to locate on the campus. In addition, some students and graduates created the Northern Virginia Mediation Service to provide conflict resolution services in the local area. It was based on centers already established in Richmond, Harrisonburg, and Roanoke, all in Virginia. An innovative, nationally known practitioner group, the Conflict Clinic Inc., also moved to the George Mason campus, adding James Laure, an early ADR practitioner of community disputes, as a faculty member.

When Hampton, Virginia, reached a stalemate over plans to build a road to relieve congestion on the city's main thoroughfare in the late 1980s, the city turned to the Conflict Clinic. It helped the city assemble and train a group of concerned citizens, environmentalists, home owners, real estate agents, and city planners to reexamine the city's master plan and eventually circle back to the controversial road project. While the city planners and traffic engineers could point to traffic counts and other pieces of hard data to show the necessity of building the road, home owners only needed to look out their back windows to see the picturesque wetlands that the new road would pave over.

Over more than a year of weekly meetings, the various sides slowly built trust to the point where home owners began to talk like city planners and city planners gained a deep understanding of the home owners' position. Although the sides continued to disagree over the necessity of building the road and the amount of environmental damage it would cause, they eventually did agree to allow the city to buy key parcels of land before they were developed. The land would be held in trust as a city park, while leaving open the option of someday building the road if it ultimately seemed necessary. The Conflict Clinic conducted a similar process in Fort Worth, Texas.

In 1987, ICAR turned its attention and mission "to advance the understanding and resolution of protracted and deeply-rooted conflicts among individuals, groups, organizations, and communities throughout America and other nations." This new emphasis demanded thorough analysis of conflicts to determine root causes of protracted disputes that defied resolution by traditional negotiations, mediation, or improved communication. The faculty undertook this approach not with an expectation of early and clear results, but recognizing that such disputes will be resolved only by scholars and Ph.D. candidates willing to study such disputes patiently and thoroughly. The ICAR Web site list of faculty accomplishments is dominated by these protracted conflicts, from Northern Ireland to Rwanda.

Program on Negotiations

In 1980, Roger Fisher brought together faculty with an interest in dispute resolution from universities in the Boston area. His idea was to initiate collaboration in research and teaching of all phases of conflict resolution. Following several years of collaboration among the universities, the Program on Negotiation (PON) was officially recognized by Harvard University in 1983. The prestige of Harvard greatly enhanced the program and encouraged grant support.

The remarkable number of participating schools and departments resulted in an extraordinary collection of scholars on conflict resolution—legal scholars Roger Fisher and Frank Sander, anthropologist William Ury, urban planner Lawrence Susskind, industrial relations expert Robert McKersie, and many others. The schools included Massachusetts Institute of Technology, Boston College, University of Massachusetts/Boston, Tufts University, New England School of Law, Wellesley College, Suffolk University, Brandeis University, Radcliffe College, and Simmons College.

PON rapidly became known for practical seminars on applications of conflict resolution, excellent training case studies, its quarterly *Negotiation Journal* and other publications, and a commitment to an interest-based approach to conflict resolution.

Initially, PON had five programs:

- The Dispute Resolution Program to promote research and experimentation with mediation, arbitration, and the use of ombudsmen as alternatives to court systems
- The Negotiations Project to improve the theory and practice of negotiations, especially in legal and international contexts
- The Negotiations Roundtable dialogues on business conflicts to develop case studies and working papers
- The Nuclear Negotiation Project to explore how negotiations can reduce the risk of nuclear war
- The Public Dispute Program to conduct action research to demonstrate that mediation and negotiations can enhance fairness in public sector decisions

Law Schools and ADR

U.S. law schools began offering courses on ADR in the 1980s. A 1983 American Bar Association survey found that only forty-three law schools, or about 25 percent, offered ADR courses. By 1986, a majority of law schools offered courses or clinics on ADR. By 1998, law school accrediting standards began recommending that ADR be covered in curricula, and today ADR is a standard law school topic. Some schools even include ADR in all basic first-year courses.

Three law schools support ADR journals: *Journal of Dispute Resolution* from Missouri/Columbia, the *Ohio State Journal of Dispute Resolution*, and the *Negotiation Journal* from the Harvard Program on Negotiation.

Books on ADR in the 1980s

A host of books appeared in the 1980s that provided nonlabor practitioners with books of their own, beginning with *Getting to Yes*—for example:

- Moore's *The Mediation Process: Practical Strategies for Resolving Conflict*, which would become a standard text in mediation training sessions
- *The Fundamentals of Family Mediation* by Haynes, and his *Divorce Mediation: A Practical Guide for Therapists and Counselors*, which were added to the bookshelf of every family mediator
- *Getting Disputes Resolved: Designing Systems to Cut the Cost of Conflict* by Ury, Brett, and Goldberg, which turned ADR practitioners' attention to an additional level for their practice
- *Dispute Resolution* by Goldberg, Green, and Sander, a useful collection of writing on ADR before the mid-1980s
- *Breaking the Impasse: Consensual Approaches to Resolving Public Disputes* by Susskind and Cruikshank, which presents a compelling case for resolving difficult public disputes without courts and lawyers and with speed and fairness on all sides
- Kolb's *The Mediators*, which describes and contrasts the mediation styles of labor mediators from FMCS and the state of Massachusetts
- *Mediation Research*, by Kressel and Pruitt, which depicts mediation research attempting to keep up with rapidly developing practice

Competition for SPIDR

SPIDR had no competition for ten years as it expanded to serve an increasingly diverse membership. In the 1980s, four new membership organizations appealed to narrow segments of the growing

ADR field, in family issues, education, law, and ombudsmen. While the most obvious activities of these membership organizations were at the national level—conferences, newsletters, and journals— their local activities of meetings, informal gatherings, and networking provided a vital support system to the growing field.

Academy of Family Mediators

Divorce cases are some of the most difficult and emotionally charged areas of the law. They involve messy issues—property distribution, alimony, child support, and custody—as couples seek to disentangle their lives. With the explosion in divorce in the 1970s and 1980s, many people began to recognize that these wrenching issues often got only worse in the traditional adversarial setting of the courtroom.

Some judges began ordering couples into mediation to attempt to work out their differences in a way that both sides would find satisfying. In one case chronicled in the *New York Times Magazine*, a couple walked through weeks of sessions in which they not only settled the issues of money and property, but each came to have a better understanding of the fundamental flaws that ultimately caused their marriage to fail (Thernstrom, 2003). In one of their mediation sessions, the two recounted a tale that was emblematic of the problem. Out bird watching, they had a vicious argument over the identification of a bird each had spotted. After several heated exchanges, they realized that they were looking at different birds in the same tree. They came to see that in their marriage, they were often passionately split over arguments in which they were both wrong and right at the same time.

Created in 1982 as a nonprofit organization, the Academy of Family Mediators (AFM) set out to promote family mediation. In its eighteen-year history, AFM grew to several thousand members, 60 percent of them in private practice. AFM members demonstrated their professionalism by creating a journal, the *Mediation Quarterly*, and developing standards for training courses and ethics.

The organization worked with the Association of Family and Conciliation Courts on setting standards of practice. The AFM newsletter and annual conference contributed to keeping members well informed. When it merged with SPIDR and CREnet in the late 1990s, AFM became the Family Section within ACR, the organization's largest section.

Because of the frequent imbalance of power in divorce conflicts, professional ethics raised tough questions about mediator conduct and practices. These questions were made more difficult as society struggled with the issue of women's growing independence during this period.

Conflict Resolution Education Network

One of the most exciting ADR developments in the 1980s involves children. Growing up in America is growing up in a very competitive environment where pushing and shoving, physically or verbally, is too often a first response. Since children's lives are increasingly filled with TV and movie violence and the fear of strangers, as well as real disputes and bullying within their schools, an effort by ADR specialists to address conflicts in young lives is a welcome step.

ADR programs for children present information and training in dealing with conflict using peaceful strategies. Equally impressive are programs using children as mediators. Called peer mediators, these children receive training in mediation skills before being given a colorful T-shirt imprinted with "MEDIATOR" across the chest. These peer mediators take turns mediating playground conflicts. To prevent these young mediators from getting in over their heads, teachers stay alert to provide appropriate intervention. Peer mediators also work on conflicts brought to them by teachers and other students as a substitute for the usual school discipline route. Making children aware of peaceful options where no one gets hurt represents hope for a future in which ADR is the preferred response to conflict.

One of the earliest school mediation programs was started in San Francisco in 1982 by the Community Board (Davis and Porter, 1985). The program has three major components: a conflict resolution course taught in high schools, classroom meetings conducted in kindergarten through fifth grade where alternate conflict resolution methods are taught, and peer mediators trained to mediate disputes on the playground. Students from grades 4 and 5 are selected by their peers based on leadership ability and represent the gender division and racial-ethnic identity of the school. They receive fifteen hours of training in active listening, problem solving, critical thinking, teamwork, assertiveness, open communication, and conflict management. They wear "conflict manager" T-shirts and, using a simplified version of the mediation process, make themselves available on the playground to help students resolve disputes.

Evaluations from the Community Board projects in San Francisco show that conflicts in the school decreased. The principals of the four schools using the Conflict Manager program stated, "Conflict managers make significant contributions to a calm, friendly atmosphere on the playground." They noted "what students learn about resolving conflicts on the playground is carried into the classrooms" and results in less teacher time on "refereeing disputes." These principals also observed that "conflict managers teach what they have learned to parents, siblings, and friends" (p. 124). The success of these early school mediation programs encouraged replications in most states.

Conflict Resolution Education Network (CREnet) began in 1984 with the creation of the National Association for Mediation Education (NAME) at the University of Massachusetts to foster the use of conflict resolution in educational settings. Having started a number of programs with the assistance of the National Institute of Dispute Resolution (NIDR), NAME accepted an invitation to join NIDR in Washington. In doing so, the organization changed its name to Conflict Resolution Education Network to reflect its recognition that linkages with many others in conflict resolution education would be more effective for everyone.

American Bar Association

In 1977, the American Bar Association (ABA) created the Special Committee on the Resolution of Minor Disputes to study the potential for using mediation in criminal, misdemeanors, and civil small claims courts, referred to as the multidoor approach. The committee subsequently recommended establishing experimental pilot multidoor courthouse programs. Demonstrating its slowly growing interest in ADR, the ABA moved gradually to give ADR greater prominence.

In 1987, six years after launching the multidoor courthouse idea, the ABA established the Standing Committee on Dispute Resolution, an indication of the ABA's greater comfort with ADR. The committee's purpose was to "study, experiment with, disseminate information concerning and identify appropriate integration of methods for the resolution of disputes other than the traditional process."

Finally, in 1993, the ABA converted the Standing Committee into the Section of Dispute Resolution, with a mission "to provide its members and the public with creative leadership in the dispute resolution field by fostering diversity, developing and offering educational programs, technical assistance and publications that promote problem solving and encourage excellence in the provision of dispute resolution services." The Section of Dispute Resolution quickly grew to six thousand members and has continued to increase its membership. Today, it has a large annual conference, several smaller regional and specialized meetings throughout the year, and a quarterly magazine.

U.S. Association of Ombudsmen

Ombudsmen, or ombuds for short, came on strong in the 1980s. By 1983, over one thousand individuals were operating as ombuds in government, private industry, and universities. Ombuds had an organization of their own, the U.S. Association of Ombudsmen (USAO). Like other organizations starting during the 1980s, USAO received help from National Institute of Dispute Resolution.

Ombuds combine several ADR processes: negotiation, mediation, investigation, fact-finding, arbitration, and simply listening and referral to where help is available. Its flexible nature makes it comparable to the multidoor courthouse. It is sometimes described as the union-free answer to the union grievance procedure, since the ombuds process provides an outlet and solutions to complaints within organizations. By providing several routes for dispute resolution or problem solving, the ombuds process allows the user a critical sense of choice in how his or her problem will be resolved, thus creating a sense of empowerment.

The best known of these programs in the 1980s operated on the MIT campus under the direction of Mary Rowe. She often referred to the process as upward feedback, since it provides needed information to managers in an orderly, timely, and supportive manner. The MIT ombuds program includes faculty, students, and employees not covered by a labor agreement.

Typically an individual comes to the ombuds office complaining about a concern: a student denied the opportunity to retake an exam, an employee whose recent paycheck is lower than expected, or a junior faculty member who feels he or she is not getting a fair shake from the department chairman. In each of these situations, the ombuds role is flexible. Counseling might be used with the student, referral of the employee to the payroll office for an explanation of the pay question, and mediation of the faculty issue.

SPIDR

Although SPIDR now had competition, it remained dominant for much of the decade. Its growth continued during the 1980s, with members involved in new areas of disputes greatly outnumbering the previously dominant labor-management practitioners. The annual conference agenda clearly began to reflect the change in the membership composition. As the decade ended labor-management was still represented but had become a minority in SPIDR.

The SPIDR annual conference agenda dramatizes the expansion of the new dispute areas in the 1980s. Conference speakers addressed environmental mediation, mediation by telephone, court promotion ADR, neighborhood justice centers, family and consumer mediation, CRS interventions in violence, home construction arbitration, the ombuds role, and others.

To deal with the increasing diversity of the practice areas, SPIDR created practice sectors to provide common meeting grounds for individuals doing similar work, such as labor-management, marriage and family, and environmental ADR. SPIDR practice sectors eventually grew to thirteen, plus a number of committees that could eventually become sectors.

As SPIDR moved beyond its youthful growing pains, it began to discuss and address ethical questions, the merits of qualifications and certifications standards, and concerns about state government regulation and ill-advised regulations. Conference workshops, committees, and actions by SPIDR officers addressed these issues. SPIDR uses qualified members who are willing to testify at state hearings on issues related to ADR.

Funding and Reshaping ADR

Even when unpaid volunteers were used, nontraditional ADR projects were hard pressed to find funds because of the uncertainty of success and clients who were frequently unwilling or unable to pay.

Research and evaluation to help the field grow were even more difficult to fund. For these reasons, promoters of ADR turned to foundations. Small local foundations did help, but their funds were limited. In the late 1960s and early 1970s, the Ford Foundation generously funded a few early projects. Fortunately for ADR growth, two other organizations began to provide critical funding in the 1980s: the National Institute for Dispute Resolution (NIDR) and the Hewlett Foundation.

National Institute for Dispute Resolution

In the rapidly expanding ADR field, foundations and other potential sources of funds were being confronted by a bewildering variety of proposals. NIDR attempted to bring some order to this chaos. NIDR was established as a foundation in 1983 specifically to solicit grant funds for the promotion of ADR. The initial funds came from such large foundations as Ford, Hewlett, MacArthur, AT&T, and Prudential. The initial board of directors included a former president of the Corporation for Public Broadcast and the University of Michigan, the secretary-treasurer of the AFL-CIO, a former dean of the National Judicial College, the chairman of Aetna Life and Casualty, and a U.S. ambassador.

Taking a wide view of the entire ADR field, NIDR attempted to act as a broker, or regrant organization, to nurture and rationalize ADR development. Through its staff, who provided technical assistance, and its grant program, NIDR supported research and publications, experiments, evaluations, and educational programs on ADR. Many of the organizations that promoted ADR during the 1980s owe much to NIDR help. With its prestigious board and activist staff of twenty, NIDR aggressively promoted ADR from its Washington headquarters. By funding resource centers at universities, a research and experimental program, and numerous meetings and conferences, NIDR established itself as a major player in growing and sustaining ADR.

In 1999, after sixteen years of operations, the NIDR board decided to terminate the organization because it was experiencing increased difficulty in securing grant funds. Although NIDR had not achieved all its goals, it had had a very positive impact on the ADR field.

Hewlett Foundation

In 1984, the William and Flora Hewlett Foundation, named for one of the founders of Hewlett-Packard and his wife, created a conflict resolution program as its focus for grant making in ADR. It emphasized general support to a small number of recipients aimed at three goals: building ADR theory, encouraging practitioner organizations, and promoting the growth of the conflict resolution field. Within ten years, Hewlett was supporting twenty university-based theory centers covering a wide range of ideas and approaches.

From a grant program of $1.8 million in 1984, the program expanded to $3 million by 1991. The three major membership organizations—SPIDR, AFM, and CREnet—each received crucial financial assistance from Hewlett to supplement membership dues and conference fees, which were inadequate to support the organizations' programs. Later, a Hewlett grant supported the merger of these three organizations in 2001 into the Association of Conflict Resolutions (ACR), helping to eliminate duplication of efforts and expand services.

Hewlett's dealing with the three membership organizations and later ACR illustrates how deftly the foundation supported, encouraged, and moved with the growth of the field. By funding activities that remained open to many possible ideas and approaches, Hewlett allowed many flowers to blossom when the field was still developing.

Peace and Conflict Resolution

In the 1980s, three peace-promoting organizations joined ADR students and faculty—two at the George Mason University Institute of Conflict Analysis and Resolution (ICAR) and one at Emory University in Atlanta. By locating these three peace organizations on university campuses, both ADR and peace interests were enriched.

National Conference on Peacemaking and Conflict Resolution

In 1982, the National Conference on Peacemaking and Conflict Resolution (NCPCR) was founded to provide forums where individuals working on and researching peacemaking, conflict resolution, and social justice could gather to exchange ideas and learn.

In its twenty-one-year history, NCPCR has provided ten international gatherings of nonviolent peacemakers committed to diversity and inclusiveness in working toward peace.

NCPCR and its adherents represent the successors to the flower children of the 1960s, who were often dismissed as immature and unrealistic dreamers. The 1980s version presents a more persuasive case for the cause of peace with a full menu of workshops and exhibits at their gatherings, such as: Native American practices and beliefs, religious and pacifist examples (St. Francis, Martin Luther King, and Gandhi), music, poetry, meditation, yoga, and tai chi. By examining traditional and culturally based peacemaking practices and emphasizing respect for diversity, NCPCR seeks to offer a great variety of approaches to peacemaking.

Consortium of Peace Research, Education and Development

The Consortium of Peace Research, Education and Development (CPRED) shared a constituency with NCPCR: people interested in peace and conflict resolution. However, CPRED interests were more focused on peace research and education at universities. In 2001, CPRED issued a directory of universities with peace studies programs. The volume listed nearly five hundred universities worldwide with peace studies programs in forty countries. Many of the universities granted degrees in peace studies or conflict resolution.

In 2002, CPRED merged with the Peace Studies Association (PSA) to form the Peace and Justice Studies Association (PJSA).

The Carter Center

Founded in 1982 by former President Carter and his wife, Rosalynn, the Carter Center is a nonprofit organization in partnership with Atlanta's Emory University. The Carters view poverty, hunger, disease, and discrimination as the root of conflicts in poor nations, and so the center has addressed all of these problems in the cause of peace. Within a decade of its founding, the center had programs in sixty-five countries nurturing democracy and human rights, helping economic opportunity and farm productivity, and preventing diseases.

The center also used ADR. The former president has used his good offices to monitor elections and mediate disputes. The center, often with Carter personally participating, has sent monitoring teams to elections in the Americas, Africa, and Asia. These include Guyana (1992), Haiti (1994), Venezuela (1998), Mozambique (1999), Nigeria (1999), Indonesia (1999), East Timor (1999), Peru (2000), Mexico (2000), China (2001), and Jamaica (2002). Interestingly, three governments that invited Carter's election assistance—Panama (1989), Nicaragua (1990), and Dominican Republic (1991)—lost their election. After monitoring just a few elections, Carter concluded that monitoring elections was a new and useful way of dealing with conflicts.

After more than twenty years of fighting in Ethiopia, President Mengistu was persuaded to meet with several revolutionary factions including Eritreans. In 1989, meetings were held with Carter in Atlanta, but renewed fighting in Ethiopia caused those talks to be discontinued. In 1990, the U.S. government picked up where Carter had left off and began formal peace talks that produced an agreement in July 1991. The agreement provided for a transitional government and Eritrea's right to a UN-supervised referendum on independence in 1993. Throughout the long process, Carter promoted the idea of resolving the dispute through an election process with the parties accepting the result. In 1993, Ethiopia acquiesced, accepted the election results, and recognized Eritrea.

Carter brokered an agreement between Sudan and Uganda in December 1999. Following the agreement, the center staff worked tirelessly to get the accord implemented. The success of that effort included the exchange of seventy-four prisoners of war and the return to Uganda of more than two hundred Ugandan children abducted by the Lord's Resistance Army, a northern Uganda rebel group based in Sudan.

Carter also mediated in Venezuela and between North and South Korea.

New Practices and Processes

The 1980s brought new processes and practices to the expanding ADR field that took ADR well beyond negotiations, mediation, and arbitration. The new processes were often more sophisticated and handled problems in a more complex manner with better outcomes than the earlier methods.

Regulatory Negotiations (RegNeg)

Statutory law generally lacks the detail necessary to provide for reasonable application and enforcement. That leaves government agencies charged with enforcing the law to issue regulations or rules to fill in the holes. As they make their rules, agencies invite public comment. In the past, after issuing a notice of intent to issue new regulations, the agency would invite written comments and take testimony in formal hearings. These proceedings tended to be very adversarial as each interest group attempted to secure a regulation most favorable to it. Following the written comments and testimony, it fell to the agency to draft regulations giving appropriate weight to the information offered by interest groups.

RegNeg, also called negotiated rule making, offers much less formality and a consensus outcome that allows for creative solutions grounded in the experience of those who will be involved in following the rules. Prior to the RegNeg process, an investigation identifies all interest groups affected by the proposed rule, the issues that need to be resolved by the rule, and the information needed for the resolution.

In 1983, the Federal Aviation Administration (FAA) was the first government regulator to attempt to use RegNeg to establish a new rule. FMCS mediator Nicholas Fidandis was asked to lead the rule-making meetings. The issue involved a safety rule on maximum hours for pilots on flight duty. The rule had not been altered in thirty years, despite significant changes in equipment and practices. Prior discussions and litigation had been unsuccessful in resolving the issue.

Seventeen groups were involved in meetings extending from fall 1982 to fall 1983. During the course of the meetings, several expectations had to be changed. The initial meetings were open to the public and media, with a public transcript created of each meeting. When that proved unworkable because it prevented flexibility and candor, Fidandis called executive sessions limited to the seventeen groups. Also, the FAA administrator expected that the meetings would produce recommendations, which he could use at his discretion in creating the new rule. When it became clear that the participants wanted assurance of more direct input, the administrator was persuaded to accept the meeting output as the new rule. At the outset of the meeting, it was assumed that a consensus would be achieved among the participants. That proved unworkable because several groups could not publicly agree to a new rule for political and internal reasons.

The mediator did have one thing on his side: the participants all recognized that a less acceptable rule would be imposed if they did not work together to fashion a new rule. With input from the parties, the mediator wrote a rule that the majority of the participants endorsed and the FAA administrator issued in spring 1984.

The process developed by this initial and successful RegNeg became the model for subsequent rule-making efforts. Later FMCS mediators led RegNeg with the Environmental Projection Agency, Department of Transportation, and Occupational Safety and Health Administration.

Based on several years of RegNeg practice, the ABA and other organizations recommended that Congress enact the Negotiated Rulemaking Act in 1990. Most government regulatory agencies have used the process to their satisfaction and that of interested parties.

Many states have used RegNeg and similar formal consensus-building processes. They include Arizona, California, Colorado, Idaho, Indiana, Maine, Massachusetts, Montana, New Mexico, New York, Ohio, Oklahoma, Texas, Virginia, and Washington. These projects have dealt with a wide variety of issues, including transportation planning, air and groundwater standards, pesticide emissions, oil and gas controls, access issues for the disabled, pollutant discharges in the Great Lakes, utilities regulation issues, fertilizer containment, and natural resource management.

As of mid-1996, at least three states (Florida, Montana and Nebraska) had passed negotiated rule-making statutes, one (New York) has promoted it by executive order, and several others have referenced the procedure in statutes to encourage its use (Idaho, Indiana, Maine, Oklahoma, and Washington).

Financial Institutions and ADR

By the mid-1980s, the volume of legal actions against banks, brokerage houses, and other financial institutions had become extensive and costly. In reaction to these unwanted issues resulting from new and novel theories of liability, financial institutions began turning increasingly to ADR. Gradually, they began placing arbitration in their agreements with customers to reduce liability and court expenses, particularly high jury awards. The American Arbitration Association (AAA) became the administrator for many of these programs or at least the source of arbitrators from its commercial arbitration panel.

Faced with similar cost and liability issues to financial institutions, other industries came to favor ADR; among them were real estate, construction, insurance, and automobile sales. Also like financial institutions, these areas began to use mediation as an alternative to the courts. AAA helped these groups create their systems, and in some cases it still administers the dispute resolution process.

Building Dispute Resolution Systems

The coal industry work of Stephen Goldberg, mentioned in Chapter Thirteen, started as a research project attempting to determine the causes of the multiple unauthorized strikes, called wildcat strikes, in the 1970s. The coal industry's long-standing grievance resolution system in the 1970s increasingly showed signs of dysfunction. The increasing incidence of wildcat strikes, rather than using the traditional multistep grievance procedure ending in arbitration, brought the problem dramatically to the attention of industry and the United Mineworkers union.

Goldberg's research revealed that the grievance procedure took too long, and the arbitration process too often provided answers to very narrow questions rather than seeking to understand underlying problems needing resolution. His work is notable for two reasons: it was an early example of the ADR practice of building improved dispute resolution systems in contrast with just resolving a single dispute, and it resulted in the growth of labor-management grievance mediation.

The building of a dispute resolution system combines research with an effort to find the best ADR practice for a given category of conflict, as well as sound collaboration with groups affected by the dispute resolution system. The ADR practice that in the 1990s would be labeled dispute resolution design (DRD) was first spelled out by *Getting Disputes Resolved* (Ury, Brett, and Goldberg, 1988).

Yet in its infancy in the late 1980s, the DRD of the 1990s demonstrated the growing sophistication of those ADR practitioners venturing into this field. The comprehensive model set out in *Getting Disputes Resolved* continued to be enhanced and improved during the 1990s as experience accumulated.

Prophetic of the future, the 1990 SPIDR annual conference was called "Designing Dispute Resolution Systems." A book by two practitioners elaborated DRD further. *Designing Conflict Management Systems: A Guide to Creating Productive and Healthy Organizations* quickly became the text for understanding DRD (Costantino and Merchant, 1996).

Organizational Development and ADR

Organizational development (OD) is the term attached to behavioral science work aimed at improving organizations. The development and expansion of OD into a more clearly defined field parallels the development of ADR since the 1970s. The ADR work of dispute resolution design demonstrates the overlap of portions of OD and ADR. Both, for example, focus on systems; collect, analyze, and feed back data to participants; use small group activities and interactive training; and place emphasis on trust building, openness, collaboration, and problem solving. Both also use negotiation, facilitation, and mediation, and both have benefited from this overlapping and borrowing.

Theory and practice from other fields, such as social work, counseling, psychiatry, and probation work, have benefited the expansion and improvement of ADR as well.

Two FMCS programs mentioned earlier have borrowed from OD. Relationships by Objectives and Partners in Change both use OD concepts.

Campus Mediation

An early example of experimentation with mediation on campus began in 1979–1980. Sponsored by the American Arbitration Association and called the Center for Mediation in Higher Education, it operated for five years, encouraging mediation use to resolve disputes involving university administrations and staff or faculty.

One of the earliest campus mediation programs began in 1980–1981 at the University of Massachusetts. Others included the University of Hawaii and Oberlin and Grinnell colleges. Most of the early programs primarily addressed faculty and administration disputes, but over time, programs expanded to serve everyone on campus, and the ombuds role was added on many campuses. The University and College Ombuds Association (UCOA), established in the mid-1980s, remains the central organizing body for campus ombuds.

The mid- to late 1980s saw a growth of writing about campus conflict resolution approaches. In 1985, a manual, *Peaceful Persuasion: A Guide to Creating Mediation Dispute Resolution Programs for College Campuses*, was published by the University of Massachusetts Mediation Project and the National Institute for Dispute Resolution

(Girard, Rifkin, and Townley, 1985). Folger's and Shubert's research on student grievance mechanisms indicated growth and sophistication in these processes (Folger and Shubert, 1986).

By the spring of 1990, sufficient interest in campus mediation had developed to support a national conference. The first National Conference on Campus Mediation Programs was hosted by the Campus Mediation Center at Syracuse University. By 1998, there were 165 conflict resolution programs on college campuses.

New Providers of ADR

The number of providers of ADR services grew substantially in the 1980s. Those described here offer an illustration of the range and variety. They included large and small enterprises, for-profit and nonprofit organizations, and outfits narrowly focused on a single industry or practice area and broad ranging, all-embracing partnerships. Some were limited to lawyers, and others not.

Law Firms

The ADR movement has changed the image that law firms have tried to project. With U.S. Supreme Court Chief Justice Warren Burger promoting it, the ABA warming to ADR, law schools teaching it, and some clients demanding it, law firms began to try to create an appearance of being ADR-friendly. However, conflicts of interests and the fact that fees paid for working as a third party are less than law firms' typical billing rates made that work unattractive to law firms. Representing a client in ADR processes is attractive because that work is done at the usual billing rates. Consequently, numerous law firms purport to offer neutral ADR services. In reality, they are more likely to represent clients in ADR. Perhaps the difference between reality and appearance explains why little has been written about law firms' providing neutral services.

Representing clients in arbitration and mediation, as well as settlement negotiations, was not new for law firms. The newer

ADR processes were lawyer friendly and easily accommodated at the going billing rate

A recent strategy has been to add to the firm a retired judge to perform ADR, because the judge's reputation could attract other business and create a protective shield, allowing the judge to handle other selected litigation without being viewed as engaging in conflicts of interests.

Search for Common Ground

Founded in Washington, D.C., in 1982 with two employees and a handful of supporters, Search for Common Ground (SCG) within twenty years had a staff of 360 with activities on four continents and offices in fourteen countries. SCG was started by John Marks, a newsman who had written a critical analysis of the Central Intelligence Agency. He became disillusioned with the destructiveness of unresolved issues and began thinking about win-win solutions. With the support of some friends and a prestigious board, he attempted to get international discussions started on arms control and terrorism.

In the United States, he started similar discussions between supporters and opponents of abortion and between progun and antigun advocates. The organization used a format requiring each side to listen fully to the other and then attempt to find anything, however minor, on which they could agree. SCG helped the parties in abortion discussions identify adoption as a mutual interest. Similarly, the gun dialogues agreed on the desirability of safety. The discussions were broadcast on television, showing that even these seemingly hard-line opponents could establish some common ground.

Later the group began more long-term efforts in countries where confounding disputes persisted, Burundi, for example. After developing a plan in cooperation with local groups and individuals, SCG would seek project funds. It has received funds from USAID, the European Union, Japan, and the Netherlands for such projects.

These admittedly long-range efforts, SCG believes, enhance other conflict resolution efforts, such as negotiation and mediation.

In addition to these dialogues, SCG uses other communications methods, including sponsoring training programs in conflict resolution in Gaza, Jordan, and Ukraine; operating six bilingual, interethnic kindergartens and coproducing a dramatic television series for children to help strengthen cross-ethnic understanding in Macedonia; and producing television programs that treat contentious issues within a common ground framework in South Africa and Angola. SCG has conducted workshops for journalists to diminish inflammatory reporting and promote mutual understanding in the Aegean region and the Middle East, produced a peace song sung by pop singers on both sides of the war in Burundi, and sponsored soccer matches between Hutu and Tutsi youths who were previously involved in violence. The group has also provided conflict resolution training on its Web site for use by any nonprofit organization.

SCG has a U.S. domestic program, Search-USA, which has used common ground discussions on prisoner reentry issues in a community, faith-based questions, and a variety of community issues from land use to parking.

Judicial Arbitration and Mediation Service

Retired Judge Warren Knight of Orange County, California, started Judicial Arbitration and Mediation Service (JAMS) in 1979, based on his belief that lawyers and their clients are inclined to trust retired judges because of their experience on the bench. Judges' experience and judgment prepare them for the full range of ADR work. Their experience helps them see the strengths and weaknesses of a case, identify possible solutions, and help the parties negotiate a resolution, or mediate or arbitrate a resolution.

By the mid-1980s, JAMS claimed to have the largest roster of former judges and experienced ADR lawyers in the country, with a settlement rate of 90 percent. Later, JAMS would merge with EnDispute, another very successful ADR provider headquartered on the East Coast, thereby creating JAMS/EnDispute.

CPR Institute for Dispute Resolution

General counsels of five hundred major corporations, leading law firms, and prominent legal academics founded the Center for Public Resources (CPR) in 1979. The group's aim is to lead the way in new and high-quality forms of dispute resolution, in both the public and private sector. It funds research, education, advocacy, and dispute resolution. It considers itself a leading proponent of "self-administered ADR," meaning conflict resolution managed by the parties assisted by a highly qualified neutral.

Support from New and Old Quarters

Following the theme he set at the Pound Conference in 1976, Chief Justice Burger continued to promote ADR with bar associations and within the federal court system. In connection with the bar associations and judge training, he tried to affect everyone in the system—federal and state. The chief justice was a true friend of ADR, promoting it at every opportunity. In August 1985 before a AAA conference, he said, "I cannot emphasize too strongly to those in business and industry—and especially to lawyers—that every private contract of real consequence to the parties ought to be treated as a 'candidate' for binding private arbitration."

Court Dispute Resolution Programs

In 1985, the Washington, D.C., Superior Court established the Multidoor Dispute Resolution Division as one of three experiments sponsored by the ABA. The other two were in Tulsa, Oklahoma, and Houston. Harvard law professor Frank Sander's proposal in 1976 and the Philadelphia AAA model established by NCDS in the late 1960s inspired these new efforts.

When the program proved successful at resolving cases at a small cost and relieving court congestion, it became a permanent adjunct to the court in 1989 with these sections, or doors: Small

Claims Mediation Program; Family Mediation Program; Civil Dispute Resolution Program; Community Family Information and Referral Center; probate, tax and complex civil cases; and Child Protection Mediation Pilot Program (which was added in 1998 to deal with child abuse and neglect cases). Volunteer mediators, selected and trained by the program, and a full-time staff mediator handle the cases.

Federal Courts and ADR

The continuing success of court ADR programs encouraged the creation of similar arrangement throughout the country, and not just in state and local courts. Before the end of the 1980s, federal district courts, and even U.S. courts of appeal, were establishing similar mediation programs to handle major public policy and other complex cases. In such courts, administrative offices were selecting and training volunteer mediators, as well as evaluating their ADR programs.

Administrative Conference of the United States

The Administrative Conference of the United States (ACUS) was established in 1968 by Congress to study the efficiency, adequacy, and fairness of administrative agencies and make recommendations for improvements. In the 1980s, ACUS would become the strongest supporter of ADR use in the federal government. By 1990, it had issued seventeen reports supportive of ADR in administrative agencies.

An example of ACUS leadership in ADR was its sponsorship in June 1987 of the Colloquium on Improving Dispute Resolution: Options for the Federal Government, which brought together members of Congress, judges, high-level executive branch officials, private practitioners, and academic experts on administrative law and dispute resolution. That same year, ACUS issued the comprehensive *Sourcebook: Federal Agency Use of Alternative Means of Dispute Resolution,* just one example of its role in providing information to agencies interested in implementing ADR programs.

After ACUS had worked for years pushing and promoting ADR in the federal sector, including draft legislation that would later be adopted, the ABA's Section on Administrative and Regulatory Law was persuaded to join the effort in 1989. Through their joint efforts, two major ADR laws were enacted in 1990: the Negotiated Rule Making Act and the Administrative Dispute Resolution Act.

Ironically, as we shall see, despite its energetic work on ADR, ACUS did not survive the next decade.

State Offices of Mediation

In 1985 the National Institute of Dispute Resolution (NIDR) gave matching grants to five states because states had done so little to promote ADR:

- In New Jersey, a Center for Public Dispute Resolution was located in the State Department of Citizens' Complaints and Dispute Settlement, which had existed since 1974 to deal with community disputes. By 1985, four programs were operating. Among those were family courts mediating for custody and visitation rights, divorce, and small automobile insurance claims. In 1983, Robert Wilentz, chief justice of the New Jersey Supreme Court, appointed a committee to recommend ADR programs for the state courts.

- The Massachusetts Mediation Service was placed in the Executive Office for Administration and Finance. At that time, the state had two other mediation programs, as well as a long-standing labor-management mediation office. One state group consisted of twenty-nine neighborhood mediation programs handling local disputes. The other included six consumer mediation programs scattered through the state. Mediation under the NIDR grant involved disputes on hazardous waste disposal, the clean-up of a Superfund site, and long-term health care insurance regulation.

- Minnesota's Office of Dispute Resolution was placed in the State Planning Agency, guided by an Ad Hoc Advisory Board. One of its early efforts was the development and implementation of a farmer-lender mediation program within the Department of Agriculture Extension.

- The Hawaii ADR Program was located in the Office of Court Administration under the chief judge. The program helped implement a court-ordered arbitration plan in the civil courts and encouraged mediation in public resource allocation disputes.

- In Wisconsin, instead of hiring a staff or creating a separate office, Howard Bellman, the Wisconsin secretary of labor, industry and human resources, chaired an informal screening panel to determine when ADR should be attempted. In 1985, two statewide disputes between the Department of Natural Resources and Indian tribes over fish and game regulation were mediated.

Chapter Fifteen

The Great Expansion

ADR in the 1990s

The 1990s were the go-go years. The economy and the stock market boomed. The Internet became a force. And ADR made its way into virtually every sector of U.S. society from Wall Street to Main Street.

Strong federal government support, the warming of private sector users, and U.S. overseas work in revamping the former Soviet Union's legal systems all demonstrated the wide range of ADR acceptability. Most states replicated what the federal government was doing, with a state office charged with promoting ADR use. ADR matured not just in court reform or as a new specialty practice for lawyers, but in work that many with other backgrounds, even grade school children, could perform. While volunteers were still welcome, ADR become a solid career for many individual and group practitioners.

Evidence of ADR Success

The last decade of the twentieth century demonstrated the remarkable truth of Victor Hugo's statement 150 years ago: "An invasion of armies can be resisted, but not an idea whose time has come." Only a few examples are needed to show the diverse and yet compelling evidence that ADR's time had come. A massive directory, overseas work, and on-line dispute resolution highlight the remarkable growth of ADR.

A Directory Inventorying ADR

In 1995, Martindale-Hubbell, in cooperation with the American Arbitration Association, published the premier edition of the *Dispute Resolution Directory*. Over three and a half inches thick and printed on eight-and-a-half by eleven-inch telephone-directory paper, the book is a comprehensive guide to dispute resolution practitioners, organizations, areas of practice, and rules.

An excellent display of the who and what of 1990s ADR, the book begins with twenty pages of attractive ads by ADR organizations promoting their services. Their number and the services offered were unheard of twenty years earlier. Demonstrating the marketplace that ADR services had become, they argue their superiority on cost (guaranteed hourly charges not to exceed $150), seniority in business (since 1980), experience (80,000 cases handled), and range of services offered (mini-trials to med-arb and everything in between).

The book has four major sections, beginning with 50 pages describing thirteen ADR processes, followed by 36 pages describing ten practice areas. The largest section provides 1,949 pages of directory listings of organizations and individuals providing ADR services by state. A 588-page cross-reference section sorts the directory by location, practice area, and service provided. The final section of 183 pages provides rules and codes, ethical standards, forms, clauses, agreements, policy statements, and a glossary. The directory also comes in an on-line version.

ADR Business for Sale

Other businesses offering professional services have prospered, merged, or failed to survive—in other words, faced and experienced the ups and downs of the free market. In 1999, many ADR practitioners were surprised when they received a letter offering for sale a fifteen-year-old ADR business. A sole practitioner was seeking to sell his practice, described in detail, for "a high six figure amount," including a small office. That letter provided an unmistakable indication that ADR had arrived at a happy level of acceptance and financial success.

Spreading ADR Beyond U.S. Borders

As early as the start of the cold war, the AFL-CIO had begun an overseas program to counter communist influence by supporting local labor movements in South America, Africa, Asia, and Europe. The thrust of these programs was training and technical assistance in the basic ADR of negotiations, but eventually expanded to cover mediation and arbitration. The AFL-CIO efforts also supported any indigenous movement for enhancing human rights and trade union rights. Modest U.S. foreign aid for this work was consistently provided from both Republican and Democratic administrations since Harry Truman. These efforts to build a trade union movement in third world countries, capable of using ADR, had few dramatic successes as they struggled against, in most cases, a nondemocratic government and hostile business interests.

With the demise of the Soviet Union, two dramatic success stories gained worldwide attention for the previously unacclaimed work of the AFL-CIO. The American trade unions' long, and often discouraging, support of foreign trade unions was rewarded by developments in Poland and South Africa: the triumph of the Solidarity union movement over Poland's communist government and the trade union leadership in the African National Congress (ANC), the political party that led the opposition to apartheid, elected Nelson Mandela president of South Africa, and won a majority in parliament. According to press reports in 1989, Lech Walesa, the leader of the Solidarity movement, thanked the AFL-CIO for its support, saying, "You helped us survive the most difficult days, the moments of despair and hopelessness."

After the Berlin Wall came down, U.S. aid shifted to reforming justice and court systems and promoting free enterprise. With

USAID support, the American Bar Association/Central and Eastern European Legal Initiative and other nongovernmental organizations became heavily involved with justice and court reform, and to a lesser extent in promoting ADR. FMCS and nongovernmental organizations became very involved in promoting and training ADR overseas. The movement of China toward free enterprise has recently initiated similar efforts there as well.

In Eastern European countries, an independent judiciary and justice system is being put in place, including rights that were not part of the former communist regimes. Rights typical of democratic nations are achieving government support, including due process, free assembly, and collective bargaining. In addition, an ADR movement is developing concurrently with these government reforms. For example, in the former satellite state of Georgia, recent AID-supported training has prepared mediators to handle disputes in business, employment, and boundaries.

The 2000 *SPIDR Membership Directory* lists members from twenty-eight countries, further demonstrating a rising international interest in ADR. SPIDR members hail from every continent and all Canadian provinces.

ADR On-Line

Like every other business, government, or nonprofit, ADR has relied on and benefited increasingly from computers and the Web. On-line instruction, information sharing, rosters of ADR providers, and even conflict resolution are becoming popular. Most of the ADR organizations referred to in this book have a Web site. A quick scan through the 1995 *Dispute Resolution Directory* makes clear the extensive connection that ADR has to the Web.

Two examples of the Web items that ADR practitioners were exposed to during the 1990s are the Federal ADR Network (FAN) and Natalie J. Armstrong's golden-media e-mails, which offer practical business and marketing advice on how to expand ADR businesses and practices.

The FAN provides on-line information for those involved actively in federal ADR. An average of twenty-five messages per month cover ADR development in the federal sector, a conference calendar, reprints of articles and speeches, and useful information on ADR developments outside the federal establishment. FAN reaches eleven hundred e-mail addresses, including 950 federal sector members, representing over 130 federal entities.

In addition, a number of on-line newsletters provide information, including reprints of journal articles on the latest developments in the ADR field. Several Web sites provide extensive information on numerous aspects of ADR.

Peace Talks

The United States attempted to assert itself as an intermediary for peace in a number of difficult international conflicts in the 1990s, with decidedly mixed results. In this area, as in so many others, it must be emphasized that ADR is a process that requires at least the beginnings of willingness on the part of the parties to establish a peaceful and productive relationship. In long-standing feuds with ethnic, religious, and historical animosities, this remains difficult.

Muscular Diplomacy in Bosnia

In 1995, Special U.S. Representative Richard Holbrooke stepped into such a situation in Bosnia-Herzegovina. From the start, this was clearly not a traditional peace effort. On his first journey to the region, Holbrooke lost several top members of his team when their heavy personnel carrier caused an unstable road to collapse. Moreover, the unsavory nature of the conflict forced Holbrooke to choose carefully whom he would negotiate with. He isolated Bosnian Serb leader Radovan Karadzic, who was indicted by the UN War Crimes Commission, and dealt directly with the Serbian president, Slobodan Milosevic, whose indictment for war crimes came just a few years later.

The unusual nature of the negotiations was highlighted by Holbrooke's particularly muscular version of diplomacy. In order to convince both sides of the U.S. resolve to end the war, he started by engineering a series of U.S. bombing strikes against Serb targets. In a phone call to Washington, Holbrooke grandly incited "Operation Deliberate Force" with the words: "Give us bombs for peace" (Holbrooke, 1998, p. 132).

Once the sides—Milosevic, Croatian President Franjo Tudjman, and Bosnia-Herzegovina President Alija Izetbegovic—had been brought to the conference table at a military base in Dayton, Ohio, U.S. intimidation tactics continued. Much has been made of the use of high-resolution satellite imaging to help the sides visualize the boundaries of prospective agreements (Johnson, 1999). But the images were also put to a more chilling use: all sides were shown images of their own homes—a clear signal that the United States knew where they lived and how to find them if they defied the treaty (Johnson, 1999).

After twenty-one days of talks, they had an agreement that ended the war, although it did not address some of the larger regional issues. That would be resolved later with another round of NATO bombing in Kosovo and the ultimate ouster of Milosevic from power.

The Middle East

President Clinton's long effort in Middle East diplomacy ended in even more frustration. Through back-channel communications, Clinton was able to get Palestinian leader Yasser Arafat and Israeli Premier Ehud Barak to return to the bargaining table in 2000 to resume the peace process that had begun with the 1993 Oslo Accord. In Oslo, the two sides had agreed on a framework that would eventually create two neighboring states. The toughest issues, however, administration of Jerusalem and other areas holy to both sides, were left unresolved. In talks at Camp David, Barak came with concrete concessions and a desire to put a peace agreement in place. But Arafat was in a completely different frame of mind. He wanted to talk minutiae and intermediate steps, not the big picture. With this huge gap in their positions, the talks foundered. Nevertheless, the sides continued to meet secretly for months at the King David Hotel in Jerusalem in hopes of finding a solution for carving up the ancient city in a way that Israelis and Palestinians could support (Sontag, 2001). In the end, the erosion of Barak's political position and the end of Clinton's term effectively ran out the clock on this historic window of opportunity for the two sides to reach a lasting solution.

In the midst of the secret talks, hard-line former General Ariel Sharon, campaigning to replace Barak, paid a visit to what Muslims call the Noble Sanctuary and Jews know as the Temple Mount. This demonstration of Israeli sovereignty over the area, which houses the Al-Aksa Mosque, prompted Palestinian protests. The Israelis put them down with deadly force that led to the current intifada and a resumption of the sense of hopelessness that the two sides can ever live together as equals. In the next decade, unofficial talks would try to achieve what the two sides' leaders could not accomplish.

The Federal Government and ADR

All three branches of the federal government continued to promote ADR through new laws, policies, and practices.

Legislative Branch

In 1990, Congress unanimously enacted two statutes promoting ADR in the federal government. The Administrative Dispute Resolution Act (ADRA) gave federal agencies additional authority to use ADR in most administrative disputes. The act expanded FMCS jurisdiction to offer mediation and training to federal agencies. It also directed federal agencies to place ADR requirements in all their standard contracts for goods and services.

The Negotiated Rulemaking Act (NRA) of 1990 directed regulatory agencies to use negotiation as well as facilitated consensus building to develop administrative rules. This act flowed directly from the work of the Administrative Conference of the United States (ACUS) with Congress and the ABA. The statute resembles the ACUS draft and reports on negotiated rule-making experience in the prior five years. The act named FMCS as a potential facilitator/convener/mediator for federal agencies to engage in regulatory negotiations.

Although both the ADRA and the NRA had sunset provision to expire in five years, both were reenacted in 1996 without sunset provisions and with expanded provisions. The 1996 ADRA added ombuds to the definition of ADR and increased coverage of other protected rights, including prohibited personnel practices, nepotism, political limitations, retirement, and insurance issues. The new act removed the authority of agency heads to vacate arbitration awards and directed agencies to allow nonlawyers to act as representatives in ADR proceedings.

In June 1997, the Individuals with Disabilities Education Act (IDEA) was reauthorized with a new requirement that local school boards offer mediation to resolve disputes with parents. Disputes over identification, evaluation, educational placement, or the provision of a free and appropriate public education for a disabled child must be mediated if the parents so choose.

Disputes over the high cost of special education led New York and other states to create mediation programs in the 1980s. The success of these programs encouraged the IDEA mediation requirement. Although mediation is voluntary for parents, mediated agreements are committed to writing and are binding on both parties. The mediation is in addition to the parents' due process right to a formal, impartial hearing to resolve their dispute. With the increased use of mediation, the use of impartial hearings has declined.

Administrative Branch

President Clinton's attorney general, Janet Reno, pushed hard for ADR use within the Department of Justice. For example, she required all department lawyers to be trained in ADR and to provide a written statement explaining, if they went to trial, why that was necessary. As the keynote speaker at SPIDR's 1996 annual conference, Reno spoke enthusiastically about the progress she had made in advancing the department's use of ADR. Just prior to her speech, she had attended a conference workshop on peer mediation conducted by children for children. She reported in her keynote that the enthusiasm in that workshop gave her great hope for the future.

In 1993 President Clinton signed Executive Order 12871 on labor-management relations in the federal government. The order promoted partnerships between federal agencies and their unionized employees and promoted the use of interest-based bargaining between federal agencies and unions. During the Clinton administration, these methods flourished, resulting in significant savings and in some cases reversing years of hostile relations.

Within weeks after George W. Bush became president, he revoked Clinton's 1993 executive order, offering no explanation for this move against ADR. Although partnerships and interest-based negotiations were not barred by Bush's action, their use declined dramatically as federal managers reverted to their old practices.

During the first half of the 1990s, ACUS continued to provide useful support of ADR throughout the federal government, including two new laws passed in 1990, and the creation and maintenance of a roster of mediators and arbitrators. Since ACUS had authority to accept private-sector funds, three grants—from the Meyer, Culpeper, and Hewlett foundations—greatly increased the capacity of ACUS to promote federal ADR. Unfortunately in 1996, congressional budget cuts of advisory committees forced ACUS to close down.

FMCS increased its ADR work at home and overseas during the 1990s. The two ADR statutes passed in 1990 increased FMCS work in mediation, facilitation, and training in the federal establishment, adding to the FMCS traditional work in federal labor-management relations. In 1999 alone, FMCS conducted 586 ADR cases, including four involving RegNeg. Aiding the growth of ADR work for FMCS were changes in law and regulations allowing FMCS to charge for some services (ADR services for federal agencies, a few exceptional ADR private sector cases, and for arbitration panel costs). In the late 1990s, FMCS created the FMCS Institute, which greatly expanded its training work under its traditional preventive mediation program. The institute's large offering of courses covered a wide spectrum of employment and labor relations topics.

The FMCS ADR work overseas depends solely on funds from other sources, primarily USAID and the U.S. Department of Labor. In 1999 alone, FMCS mediators were working on sixty-one cases in other countries.

The Judiciary

In 1990, Congress enacted the Civil Justice Reform Act (CJRA) initiating an experiment to reform the federal court system. The CJRA required all federal district courts to develop plans implementing procedures for ADR to combat cost and delay in civil litigation. The district courts were authorized to refer cases to mediation, mini-trials, and summary jury trials. The courts were also encouraged to develop neutral-evaluation programs. The resulting court plans greatly expanded court-related ADR in the 1990s.

In one of the marquis cases in the rapidly changing technology sector, mediation was twice called on to try to bring a speedy resolution to a seemingly intractable problem: how to keep Microsoft from dominating the Internet without unduly restraining one of the most successful corporate business models of all time.

The Clinton Justice Department and a group of state attorneys general spent years trying to control Microsoft's monopoly over personal computer operating systems. As the era of on-line commerce dawned, the huge software company used its dominant Windows software—the visual interface and related programs used on 95 percent of PCs—to channel users through to its Internet Explorer search engine and put the company in a dominant position on the World Wide Web.

The highly complex case dragged on for years in court. The first court-appointed mediator, Judge Richard Posner of the U.S. Court of Appeals in Chicago, called off settlement talks in April 2000, saying the sides were too far apart to reach a settlement (Wilke and Blumenthal, 2000). While the negotiations had backed away from a demand that Microsoft be broken up into two companies—one that would retain the Windows monopoly and a second that would become just another player in the world of on-line software—the talks foundered as the states pushed even harder than the Justice Department to restrain the company. Judge Posner later said he thought the states muddied the water and should not have been involved in the dispute (Wilke and Blumenthal, 2000).

On September 11, 2001, the sides were scheduled to meet at 2 P.M. at the Justice Department amid a new round of settlement talks. The terrorist attacks in New York and Washington that morning cancelled those plans. A few weeks after the attacks, Judge Colleen Kollar-Kotelly pushed the sides to work "seven days a week, around the clock" to reach a settlement. She invoked both the uncertainty engendered by the terrorist attacks and the economic slowdown to push the parties to get the matter behind them.

On October 15, after the sides had made little progress, the judge appointed a new mediator, Eric Green, a Boston University law professor. Green had already gained a strong reputation mediating claims over a rash of childhood cancers in a small New Jersey town and an international vitamin price-fixing case.

Green spent hours with the two sides going over the minutiae of the case. The government was pushing Microsoft to let computer users choose more easily among competing software that works with Windows. The company fought any provision that would infringe on what it called its "freedom to innovate."

As the negotiations dragged on, government lawyers later conceded to the *Wall Street Journal*, the seemingly tireless Microsoft team essentially wore out the Justice Department side. "It was a marathon session, and new [settlement] language that had not been there before . . . showed up in new drafts," one government lawyer said. "The provisions were weakened at every turn by qualifying exceptions" (Wilke, 2001, p. A1).

In the end, the agreement did little to restrain Microsoft's drive to dominate the Internet. With the trial judge putting extreme pressure on both sides for a settlement—and with the Bush administration much less inclined to pursue the case than the Clinton team had been—the outcome was perhaps inevitable. Given the pugnacious position of the Microsoft side up to the last minute, arbitration might have been a better form of ADR to use in the dispute. When one side is hardly willing to yield an inch, there is only so much a mediator can do.

Labor-Management Relations

Given the jarring changes to the collective bargaining paradigm in the 1980s, three committees were created in the 1990s to deal with the new labor-management model. Members of each study group consisted of labor, management, and neutral representatives. The groups wrestled with a host of questions. Was cooperation the answer? Should the laws be changed or the rules of the game be adjusted? What about nonunionized workers? Can labor laws be administered better using ADR? What about the employer practice of providing their own processes for employment disputes?

Dunlop Commission

While two of the groups would each have a relatively narrow focus, the third was given a broad mandate. Former Secretary of Labor and long-time Harvard faculty member John Dunlop headed the third group, the Commission on the Future of Worker-Management Relations, which became known as the Dunlop Commission. Its task covered the entire scope of labor-management and employment relations, including making recommendations for the future.

After holding hearings and studying the issues for nearly a year, the commission issued a comprehensive report in 1995. Its most important recommendation for ADR involved labor law and policy reform: the commission sought an increase in the use of ADR in employment disputes and the creation of a national forum on workplace issues for continuing dialogue.

One of the recommendations of the Dunlop Commission was the establishment of statutory due process protections for employment disputes. This was prompted by the commission's finding that dispute resolution processes sponsored by employers often lacked fairness and simple due process. To address this problem, a Task Force on ADR was formed by concerned groups, including AAA, FMCS, SPIDR, ABA, ACLU, and the National Academy of Arbitrators (NAA). The task force met for nine months in 1994–1995 and produced the Due Process Protocol for Mediation and Arbitration of Statutory Disputes Arising Out of the Employment Relationship. The thirteen individuals who signed the protocol all had experience in employment law. The protocol covers items such as the right to representation, access to information, mediator and arbitrator qualifications and impartiality, conflicts of interests, and arbitrator authority (Dunlop and Zack, 1997). Given the individuals involved in developing the protocol and the organization they represent, the protocol had an early impact when AAA and Judicial Arbitration and Mediation Service (JAMS)/Endispute integrated the protocol into their rules (Dunlop and Zack, 1997).

Task Force on Public Employment

Secretary of Labor Robert Reich also appointed the Secretary of Labor's Task Force on Excellence in State and Local Government Through Labor-Management Cooperation. The committee held public hearings featuring expert witnesses, visited fifty labor-management cooperation sites, and conducted extensive surveys of labor and management. The eighteen-month study issued a 186-page report in 1996, finding great value in labor-management cooperation in providing better and less expensive public services. The report recommended more ADR to resolve disputes, suggested ways to get cooperation started, and provided examples of successful cooperation programs.

ADR Membership Organizations

A clear sign of ADR's vitality was the growth and increased activities of ADR membership organizations during the 1990s.

Association of Conflict Resolution

After the merger that joined three conflict resolution membership organizations into the Association of Conflict Resolution (ACR), the new group emerged reinvigorated with the help of funding from the Hewlett Foundation. Taking over the best of all three organizations, ACR put in place a quarterly magazine (*ACResolution*), a joint publishing program with Jossey-Bass Publishers, sixteen conflict area sections, increased public outreach, an expanded annual conference, and a more aggressive fundraising effort.

Conflict Resolution Network Canada

Although many Canadians were SPIDR members, including board members and one president, Canada had its own strong ADR membership organization, the Conflict Resolution Network Canada (CRNC). The group's roots were in restorative justice, but CRNC soon expanded to include practitioners in all types of disputes, becoming Canada's largest ADR group. The group has affiliations with several Canadian universities. In addition to ADR practice, it devotes extensive effort to inform and educate the Canadian public on ADR.

Victim Offender Mediation Association

By the late 1990s, this organization linked restorative justice or victim offender programs in 780 locations in the United States. This growing movement had only 150 such programs in 1990. The group's ADR methods challenge the traditional justice approach that is limited to these narrow questions: Was the law broken? Who did it? What punishment is deserved? Thus, the traditional emphasis is on retribution rather than restoration.

The Victim Offender Mediation Association (VOMA), or restorative justice approach, is to assume that a crime is an injury to the victim, the community, the offender, and their loved ones. The questions with this approach are: Who has been hurt? What are the needs? Who has the obligation for repairs? VOMA members work to create opportunities to address these questions and thereby acknowledge and heal physical, emotional, and spiritual injuries. This work is done through support groups, meetings between offenders and victims, and informing people in the justice system of the need for restorative justice—how and why it works.

National Association for Community Mediation

Community mediation centers began to develop in the 1970s in response to community unrest and impatience with the courts. Some developed as local initiatives, others from university or church outreach efforts, and some from the Justice Department funding of pilot justice centers. By the 1990s, a sufficient number existed to create the National Association for Community Mediation (NAFCM). By 2000, NAFCM was a network of 320 community mediation programs in forty-seven states and seven countries. NAFCM provides a national voice for the local centers. The group's national conferences offer a forum for discussion on pressing issues and information sharing. NAFCM facilitates a sharing of training opportunities, ideas for programs, and sources of funding.

New ADR Processes

The ADR field in the 1990s continued to show creative new ways to resolve disputes. Well-planned and facilitated dialogues, following on the pioneering work of Search for Common Ground, with ever-larger groups became a new ADR process in the 1990s.

Public Conversation Project

The Public Conversation Project (PCP) emerged in 1989 from a brainstorming group that explored whether family therapists could use their professional expertise to develop conflict resolution aimed at improving public discourse related to diversity in America. Originally housed under the Family Institute of Cambridge, the project became a nonprofit organization in 1996. The PCP collaborates with participants to create dialogue sessions to discuss the popular misconception of stereotypes, the importance of diversity, and how to promote better relationships.

Prior to each dialogue, the facilitators meet with participants to exchange their hopes, concerns, and experiences. Participants then review a draft of ground rules intended to prepare them to deal with issues in a manner that promotes dialogue rather than debate. Group discussions begin with a series of questions that each person must answer. The dialogue generally ends with participants sharing their reflections on the process and exploring the implications of the process and any next steps that might be taken. Participants are also asked to fill out evaluation forms and, in some cases, to participate in follow-up conversations with the facilitators. The length of each dialogue session varies with the interest of the group.

In 1997, the PCP received the Mary Parker Follett Award for innovative contributions to the field of conflict resolution from SPIDR. Since its inception, PCP has sponsored over sixty dialogue groups of up to two hundred people.

One creative PCP project brought together quilt makers and faith communities to collaboratively create works of art that express the richness of each faith community's religious and cultural heritage. In the Boston area, PCP's bridge building between Muslim and non-Muslim communities emphasized interfaith exchange and greater appreciation of pluralism. PCP's long-term conversations between antiabortion and abortion rights activities began in 1989. Other efforts have included a dialogue on sexuality within the Anglican community and dialogues among foundations and nongovernmental organization leaders concerned with population, the environment, and women's health. PCP publishes reports on the outcomes of its dialogue groups.

Consensus Councils

In the late 1980s, North Dakota governor George Sinner faced difficult budget issues requiring tax increases. Following the passage of these increases, the state's voters rejected the legislation under state procedures allowing such citizen initiative. At a loss as to how to fund needed state services, the governor began thinking about a consensus process that would help align the views of political leaders and citizens. He initially thought that a consensus process could be housed within state government, but the legislature refused to fund it. Private funding from the Northwest Area Foundation in Minnesota was possible, but only if the function was independent of state government. With that help, the North Dakota Consensus Council began in 1990. After meeting with success at home in North Dakota, the organization changed its name to the Consensus Council Inc. (CCI) in 1998 and expanded its work beyond the state's borders (Gross, 2002).

CCI's purpose remains bringing citizens and public officials together in a consensus-building and conflict-resolving environment to seek agreement on important public and community issues.

CCI helped launch the Policy Consensus Initiative (PCI) with a two-year $775,000 grant from the Hewlett Foundation. PCI works nationally to strengthen state offices of dispute resolution and to expand ADR and consensus-building services to other states and Canadian provinces. The Consensus Council deputy director, Dick Gross, codirects PCI with Chris Carlson, former director of the Ohio Commission on Dispute Resolution.

In 2001, the Consensus Council partnered with Search for Common Ground to organize the U.S. Consensus Council to provide consensus services to leaders of Congress and the White House on difficult issues of national public policy. Legislative hearings were held in 2003 on a bill that would create a sixteen-member United States Consensus Council charged with bringing together diverse stakeholders to build consensus solutions on a wide range of critical legislative issues. The council would be an independent, nonprofit, quasi-governmental entity, on the model of the U.S. Institute of Peace.

The consensus council concept is based on the Danish Board of Technology, formed in 1986, and institutionalized by the Danish Parliament in 1995.

Convenor: Bringing It All Together

ADR has become so diverse in its processes and dispute arenas that professionals are endeavoring to coordinate and make sense of these various efforts. Christopher Honeyman, a practicing mediator-arbitrator until a few years ago, now focuses on helping the broad ADR field itself, using an entity he formed called Convenor, with Hewlett Foundation funding.

Convenor operates as its name suggests—bringing together ad hoc team efforts to better integrate scholarship and practice across the ADR field. For example, the Convenor is currently working with a team of three U.S. law schools and three European universities to integrate strategies and tactics of teaching ADR to enhance understanding of ADR among U.S. and European lawyers and business executives. The Convenor Web site (www.convenor.com) offers papers and published articles sharing Honeyman's and others' work with the ADR world.

What's in a Name?

As ADR developed and expanded, practitioners began to change how they looked at it, even questioning its name. For some practitioners, the courts are really the alternative dispute settlement process, suggesting that "ADR" represents the usual conflict resolution processes. Others have suggested that the "A" in ADR should stand for *appropriate*, since in ADR the parties choose the process they feel is most appropriate for their needs and interests. Still others say *conflict resolution* (CR) should replace ADR. Others offer *collaborative problem solving* (CPR) as the better term.

Chapter Sixteen

ADR and the Twenty-First Century

Threats and Hopes

The twenty-first century began with a series of dramatic events that seemed to bode ill for the future of ADR. The long economic expansion and stock market boom of the 1990s—whose ever-growing pie did much to foster the notion that the win-lose formula of traditional bargaining was outdated—came screeching to a halt amid a wave of corporate scandals. The presidential election of 2000, which hung on a few slips of punctured paper in south Florida, ended in the most bitter and confrontational manner possible before the Supreme Court. And the Pax Americana that began with the fall of the Berlin Wall was shattered by the terrorist attacks of September 11, 2001. America was presented with a foe that appeared to be beyond dialogue or negotiation: terrorist assassins willing to give up their own lives in pursuit of the deaths of thousands of ordinary people.

But as we have seen many times in this book, ADR is most valuable at the darkest moments. It was used by the ancient Greeks to avert war over land disputes on numerous occasions. It turned back Attila before he marched on Rome. It was used creatively by Muhammad to bring peace among his people. It was used repeatedly in an attempt to stave off the Civil War. It helped resolve the urban tensions threatening to rip cities apart in the 1960s. And it expanded its scope in the 1970s, 1980s, and 1990s to embrace conflict at schools, in the home, and in hugely complex environmental and legal cases.

ADR is prepared to face these challenges because confronting and managing conflict is what it does best. ADR is a maturing institution in a world badly in need of its services.

Positive Signs for ADR

There are many positive signs for an expanding future for ADR. While ADR's use is far from universal, there is broad acceptance of ADR in many quarters, from children on playgrounds to the business world, from helpful computers and Web sites to formalized efforts at forgiveness and to a wiser peace movement.

Good News Headlines

The American Arbitration Association (AAA), as a long-time leader in ADR, is well connected to what is happening in the field. Its quarterly newspaper, *Dispute Resolution Times*, overflows with the latest news on ADR happenings. Here is a sampling of the headlines from the September-November 2003 issue:

> "AAA's Large, Complex Case Program: Reviewed, Reinvigorated, Ready for Growth"
>
> "Blasting Claims Go to AAA for Discharge"
>
> "Revised Code of Ethics for Arbitrators Approved"
>
> "AAA Establishes Supplementary Rules for Class Arbitration"
>
> "Justice Department to Fund Criminal Mediation Program"
>
> "ADR Pilot Program Begins for FTC"
>
> "EEOC Implements New ADR Program"

These headlines and many others go a long way to pointing up the vibrancy of the ADR movement.

Counting on ADR

The people charged with the mundane business of keeping the federal government supplied with paper clips, computers, and everything in between have discovered the merits of ADR. They have even begun to give an annual award for innovations in ADR in their field. The award is called the Office of Federal Procurement Policy (OFPP) Award on Alternative Dispute Resolution. The press release announced: "The Executive Office of the President, Office of Management and Budget, Office of Procurement Policy (OFPP) presented the second annual Federal Acquisition ADR Awards in December 2003 recognizing innovative conflict resolution practices that provide an effective and expedited process for resolving contract disputes."

OFPP was not alone in giving the award. Cosponsors included the Federal Acquisition Council and the Interagency ADR Working Group, with the U.S. attorney general serving as chairman. The affiliations of award judges illustrate the wide support for ADR: Department of Justice senior counsel, president of CPR Institute for ADR, and U.S. Court of Claims Judge.

ADR On-Line

Today's twenty-year-olds were born the year the personal computer was introduced, making them very comfortable with—or even dependent on—computers and the Internet. Using the computer to resolve disputes is quite natural to them and the next generation or two their senior. So the logic of linking computers and ADR was unavoidable. In the late 1990s, ADR on-line got a name: on-line dispute resolution (ODR). At a minimum, ODR can overcome time and geography by applying ADR on-line among disputants and a neutral dispersed throughout the world, with parties participating at times most convenient to their schedule. Disputes with large amounts of data are particularly good candidates for ODR, as well as disputes where several languages are spoken. A group of ACR members with an interest in using ODR for environmental disputes has created a Web site where members can learn and share resources (www.adrforums.com).

ACResolution, the quarterly magazine of the Association for Conflict Resolution, has a regular on-line feature, Online CR Update, by Colin Rule, professor at the Center for Information

Technology and Dispute Resolution at the University of Massachusetts-Amherst and ACR cochairman of the ADR Online Dispute Resolution Section. In a recent issue, Rule reported on ACR's new Web site's enhanced capacity to inform and communicate with a discussion forum, e-newsletters, and section sites. In an earlier report, Rule discussed how the entire record in a mediation center case might be hand-written notes scrawled illegibly on two legal pad sheets and might be as brief as the names and phone numbers of two parties with a date and time. Rule then explains that today's case record might use eXtensible Markup Language to seamlessly transfer lengthy and complex records between individuals and offices.

In 2000, FMCS introduced its Technology Assisted Group Solutions system (TAGS), a network of mobile computers and customized software to help parties resolve disputes. TAGS can help groups brainstorm, gather and organize information, prioritize, evaluate, and build consensus. It also can connect groups and individuals from several locations, thus saving travel expenses and reducing meeting time by enabling quicker decisions. It has been used to conduct a large union election in Florida.

After a year of very positive reaction to TAGS, FMCS added seven electronic conference centers to the mobile portions of TAGS. The centers are located in Newark, New Jersey, Washington, Atlanta, Cleveland, Minneapolis, and Oakland, California. FMCS can now offer dispute resolution on the Web.

Mediation and Children

A middle school student today can explain to a grandparent everything about computers. When all children can explain conflict resolution and ADR, peace and civility will blossom. There are hopeful signs that we are moving in that direction.

The Southern Law Center (SLC), well known for its successful legal pursuit of extremist organizations, has an energetic and creative program to help teach children to be tolerant and avoid bullying.

SLCs *Teaching Tolerance Magazine*, distributed free to school systems, offers an array of teacher strategies and ideas for promoting tolerance. The magazine's stories, cartoons, videos, teaching tools, reports, book reviews, and articles help move the message along. One of the ideas promoted by SLC is called "Mix It Up at Lunch Day." In 2003, three thousand schools had their students sit with someone they ordinarily would not have. The idea is to bridge social barriers by sharing a meal with someone new. The barriers include grade, clothing style, race, nationality, gender, and athletic interest. Many students reported discovering how much they had in common with the new person or group they shared lunch with.

The SLC magazine frequently offers challenging quotes, such as this one by Wendell Berry:

> It is useless to try to adjudicate a long-standing animosity by asking who started it or who is the most wrong. The only sufficient answer is to give up the animosity and try forgiveness, to try to love our enemies and to talk to them and (if we pray) to pray for them. If we can't do any of that, then we must begin again by trying to imagine our enemies' children who, like our children, are in mortal danger because of enmity that they did not cause [Berry, 2003, p. 5].

Cool Kids Mediation Newsletter, published by elementary school students in Perth, Western Australia, can be found on-line. It features simple stories about using mediation on the playground, understanding the mediation process and how it got started in the writers' school. The newsletter offers prizes for suggestions on improving mediation and requests stories, poems, and pictures about mediation. The charming four-page newsletter credits its young editors simply: "This newsletter is created by Naome B., Naome C., Hannah and Michelle."

In 2000, Congress funded an FMCS effort using its TAGS technology to address youth violence issues. This technology allows youth to seek help or voice their concerns anonymously, thus eliminating barriers such as differences in gender, class, education level, and age. The technology encourages greater participation, including community participants who can share information and experiences and engage in problem solving.

FMCS conducted pilot programs in six diverse communities using TAGS technology and the problem-solving skills of their mediator staff to address a variety of issues. After this initial success, the program expanded to other communities.

Uniform ADR Act

The National Conference of Commissioners on Uniform State Law adapted a Uniform Mediation Act (UMA), which won the endorsement of the American Bar Association in 2002. The idea of UMA was to standardize the way mediation is practiced throughout the fifty states with respect to issues of confidentiality, neutrality, fairness, qualifications, and training. Currently some state mediation laws are not based on an adequate understanding of the mediation process, and other states have no mediation statute. UMA is under consideration in several states. Having UMA in effect in most states enhances users' comfort, assuring them of the quality of mediation.

Truth and Reconciliation Commission

Following South Africa's first multiracial elections in 1994 that placed Nelson Mandela in the presidency and a black majority in parliament, President Mandela appointed Archbishop Desmond Tutu to serve as chairman of the Truth and Reconciliation Commission (TRC), charged with investigating the human rights violations of the previous thirty-four years. Archbishop Tutu counseled forgiveness and cooperation rather than revenge for past injustices. Restorative justice was Tutu's goal, in keeping with the National Unity Act that created the TRC.

Based on investigations, individuals were called to appear before the TRC or could appear voluntarily to publicly admit their crimes and seek amnesty. Those who appeared included public officials, police and army officers, as well as individuals from the other side of apartheid, such as blacks who retaliated against black informers and blacks who engaged in violence against whites. Those who admitted their crimes were granted amnesty and forgiven without any punishment. Unlike what happened in the Congo, Rhodesia, and elsewhere, there were no incidents of mass slaughter or violence.

When the TRC approach was initially announced, many believed it would not succeed because of the strong feelings on both sides and the long history of violence under apartheid. Certainly social problems remain in South Africa; however, this humane approach has proved very successful, providing a model for others. Countries as diverse as Sierra Leone, East Timor, and Peru have attempted to follow South Africa's lead.

Moving Toward Peace

In much of the world, ADR is an underdog to violence, hatred, and war. Certainly the human race has learned more about peacefully resolving disputes since the disputing cavemen deferred to a deciding stone, as depicted at the start of Chapter One. But in the competition between ADR and violence, ADR and its precursors have most often been overwhelmed by our more base nature, allowing war heroes to cast their long shadow.

Two recent books offer encouragement. *Cultures of Peace: The Hidden Side of History* (2000), by Elise Boulding, traces the long history of peace seekers who persisted in spite of war's popularity. Boulding points to the many roots of the peace movement and its vibrancy yet today. *War Is a Force That Gives Us Meaning* (2002), by Chris Hedges, a foreign correspondent for fifteen years covering violence and war, describes the horror of war and the empty reasoning used to justify it. But more telling, he shows the seductiveness of war for those on the front lines and those supporters comfortably safe at home. Hedges presents the frightening truth that ordinary young men experience exhilaration and addiction in the warrior role, and for them and others at home, it provides meaning for their lives.

The combined messages of these two books have the potential of a sea change in attitude with ADR the big winner.

Shadow Negotiations

For an extended period, neither Israeli nor Palestinian officials could make any move toward peace. They were caught in a tangle of paralyzing political and social demands that restricted any movement.

In the fall of 2003, two former officials from each side of the divide chose to negotiate a peace accord covering all the issues dividing the parties, including the most intractable ones. When they reached an agreement, they publicly announced and celebrated it, hoping to pressure both governments to break the deadlock and begin talks for peace. The accord was criticized as impracticable and a distraction by authorities on both sides. But in a world dominated by guerrilla war efforts, perhaps it was time for some guerrilla peace initiatives.

ADR and the Law

This history has carefully traced the growing acceptance and indeed the necessity for the use of ADR as an adjunct to the court system. Former Chief Justice Warren Burger was a long-time supporter of these efforts. His successor, William Rehnquist, has taken up the ADR banner. Speaking at ABA conferences and many other meetings, the chief justice has suggested that ADR is becoming the usual and customary method for dispute resolution.

Recent research indicates that that day may have already arrived. Although the number of civil and criminal court cases continues to rise, the number that go to trial have been falling for forty years. In 1962, for example, 11.5 percent of federal criminal cases went to trial. In 2002, that number tumbled to just 1.8 percent, according to an American Bar Association study by Marc Galanter, who teaches law at the University of Wisconsin and the London School of Economics. The number of federal criminal trials also fell to 5 percent in 2002 from 15 percent in 1962 (Liptak, 2003).

At an ABA forum on the "disappearing trial" in December 2003, some lawyers bemoaned the trend. Paul Butler, a law professor at George Washington University, calls the dwindling number of trials a real loss. "Nobody does trials like Americans," Butler said. "We made it an art form. It's almost as fundamental a part of our culture as jazz or rock 'n' roll." Others recognize the high cost in lost time and money of this "art form." "If a trial occurs," said Samuel R. Gross, a law professor at the University of Michigan, "it usually means a whole lot of efforts by a whole lot of people have failed."

How ADR Can Prosper

Benjamin Franklin created the first fire department on December 7, 1736, "which made Philadelphia, so far as fire was concerned, one of the safest cities in the world." At the time, people resisted Franklin's idea because they felt it would make people careless in handling fire; others felt it should be available only to those who paid a fee (Van Doren, 1938, p. 130).

Today, the idea of living without a fire department is unthinkable, a risk we do not face because fire departments are universal. ADR will have arrived when its availability and acceptance are that universal. At that point, information on ADR will surround citizens like this example. At the supper table, the ten-year-old daughter describes her experience that day mediating between two other girls on the playground. Her parents compliment her on her responsible work. Then her dad tells her their next-door neighbor recently reached an agreement with the school system on their son's special education needs with the help of a mediator. Her mother reminds her that her uncle used arbitration to resolve an employment grievance.

For this family, ADR is like oxygen or stereo music: they are surrounded by it and would not want to be without it. At that point ADR will have won the struggle with hitting, pushing, and other aggressive ways of dealing with each other.

Persistent ADR practitioners are needed as in the biblical story of Abraham negotiating with God. Abraham's efforts to save the inhabitants of Sodom and Gomorrah show a negotiator persistently questioning the Almighty for a better deal. After God announces his intention to destroy the town because of the inhabitants' evil behavior, Abraham asked if there were fifty innocent people in the cities, would God save everyone so as not to harm the innocent. God agrees. Persistent Abraham asks God five more times, each time lowering the number, finally reaching ten.

To get to that day, ADR professionals can draw on the examples presented in this book, such as the story of management and labor in the railroad industry described in Chapter Seven. Unhappy with the legal arrangements that controlled their relationship, they negotiated a better legal arrangement and jointly persuaded Congress to enact it into law. The result is the statute they have used for nearly eighty years. At the time the negotiators reached their agreement, there was no precedent for such negotiations.

The history presented in this book is replete with ADR heroes who challenged tradition and popular beliefs to attempt ADR processes seeking peaceful resolution: Woodrow Wilson and Colonel House following World War I. John Steelman in the late 1930s to the 1950s popularizing mediation in major labor disputes. Lee and Grant at Appomattox fashioning a respectful resolution to civil war. General Howard during Reconstruction in the South introducing a form of arbitration to resolve disputes between former slaves and former owners. An office-bound Bureau of Labor Statistics economist acting as the first conciliator in a labor dispute for the month-old Department of Labor. Jimmy Carter devoting thirteen days of his presidency to fashion a breakthrough accord at Camp David. Lech Walesa and Nelson Mandela using the model of the U.S. labor movement to bring revolution to their countries and advancing ADR to bring a just peace afterward. And the schoolchildren who are bringing ADR to the playground in hopes of fostering a better world.

Readers should find encouragement in this story, confident that the long history of ADR will continue and improve during their lifetime and that their efforts can help write the next chapter.

Bibliography

Adams, W. 1997. *The Paris years of Thomas Jefferson*. New Haven, Conn.: Yale University Press.

Administrative Conference of the United States. 1987. *Sourcebook: Federal agency use of alternative means of dispute resolution*. Washington, D.C.: Administrative Conference of the United States.

AFL-CIO Executive Council. 1985. Report of the AFL-CIO Executive Council 30th Anniversary. Anaheim: AFL-CIO.

Ager, S. L. 1996. *Interstate arbitrations in the Greek world, 337–90* B.C. Berkeley: University of California Press.

Albert, I. E., T. Awe, G. Herault, and W. Omitoogun. 1995. *Informal channels of conflict resolution in Ibadan, Nigeria*. Ibadan: Institut Français de Recherche en Afrique.

Ambrose, S. E. 1996. *Undaunted courage: Meriwether Lewis, Thomas Jefferson, and the opening of the American West*. New York: Simon & Schuster.

Appleby, J. 2003. *Thomas Jefferson*. New York: Times Books.

Aristotle. *Rhetoric*. 1:13, 1373b.

Aubet, M. E. 1993. *The Phoenicians and the West: Politics, colonies and trade*. Cambridge, Eng.: Cambridge University Press.

Auerbach, J. S. 1983. *Justice without law? Resolving disputes without lawyers*. New York: Oxford Press.

Babson, R. W. 1919. *W. B. Wilson and the Department of Labor*. New York: Brentanos.

Baer, H. 2002. History, process, and a role for judges in mediating their own cases. In *New York University annual survey of American law*. New York: NYU Law School.

Bakke, E. W., and C. Kerr. 1948. *Unions, management and the public*. New York: Harcourt, Brace.

Barrett, J. T. 1967. Mediation in civil rights. *Monthly Labor Review*, 90(7): 44–46.

Barrett, J. T. 1969–1970. Mediation: An alternative to violence. *Journal of Urban Law*, 47(1): 157–163.

Barrett, J. T. 1971. Governmental response to public unionism and the recognition of employee rights. *Oregon Law Review*, 51(1): 113–133.

Barrett, J. T. 1985. FMCS contributions to nonlabor dispute resolution. *Monthly Labor Review,* 108(8): 31–34.

Barrett, J. T. 1989. Partners in change: Jointly confronting change and planning a joint future. In *Association for Quality and Participation Spring Conference.* Kansas City, Mo.: Association for Quality and Participation.

Barrett, J. T. 1990. A win-win approach to collective bargaining: The P.A.S.T. model. *Labor Law Journal,* 41(1): 41–44.

Barrett, J. T. 1995. *The origin of mediation: The United States Conciliation Service in the U.S. Department of Labor.* Falls Church, Va.: Friends of FMCS History Foundation.

Barrett, J. T. 1996. *The First Director of FMCS: An interview of Cyrus Ching.* Falls Church, Va.: Friends of FMCS History Foundation.

Barrett, J. T. 1997. A brief history of SPIDR on its twenty-fifth anniversary. *Negotiation Journal,* Jan., pp. 5–11.

Barrett, J. T. 1999. In search of the Rosetta stone of the mediation profession. *Negotiation Journal,* 15(3): 219–227.

Barrett, J. T. 2000. Labor management dispute settlement is not as Neanderthal as you've heard. *Journal of Alternative Dispute Resolution in Employment,* 2(2): 40–51.

Barrett, J. T. 2002. *The history of joint labor-management training: The FMCS story.* Falls Church, Va.: Friends of FMCS History Foundation.

Barrett, J. T., and H. D. Jascourt. 2003. ADR in the federal government. *AD Resolution,* 2(2): 26–27.

Barrett, J. T., and I. B. Lobel. 1974. Public sector strikes: Legislative and court treatment. *Monthly Labor Review,* 97(9): 19–22.

Barrett, J. T., and L. D. Tanner. 1981. The FMCS role in age discrimination complaints: New uses of mediation. *Labor Law Journal,* 32(11): 745–754.

Bartlett, R. 1986. *Trial by fire and water: The medieval judicial ordeal.* Oxford, Eng.: Clarendon Press.

Bergstrom, R. 1985. Interview with the author, Mar. 19.

Bernhardt, J. 1923. *The division of conciliation: Its history, activities and organization.* Baltimore, Md.: Johns Hopkins Press.

Bernstein, I. 1948. Recent legislative developments affecting mediation and arbitration. *Industrial and Labor Relations Review,* Vol. 1, April, pp. 406–420.

Bernstein, I. 1995. The historic context: A short history of arbitration. In C. H. Friedman, ed., *Between management and labor: Oral histories of arbitration,* pp. 165–179. New York: Twayne Publishers.

Berry, W. 2003. A citizen's response to the national security strategy of the United States of America. *Teaching Tolerance Magazine,* Fall, p. 5.

Blechman, F. 2004. E-mail message to author from former GMU faculty member.

Boggs, S. T., and M. N. Chun. 1990. "Ho'oponopono: A Hawaiian method of solving interpersonal problems." In K. Watson-Geogeo and G. M. White, eds., *Disentangling: Conflict discourses in Pacific societies.* Palo Alto, Calif.: Stanford University Press.

Borman, F. 1986. Interview with the author. May 20.

Boulding, E. 2000. *Cultures of Peace: The hidden side of history.* Syracuse, N.Y.: Syracuse University Press.

Bowen, C. 1974. *The most dangerous man in America: Scenes from the life of Benjamin Franklin.* New York: Little, Brown.

Bowers, C. G. 1929. *The tragic era: The revolution after Lincoln.* New York: Little, Brown.

Braun, K. 1944. *Settlement of industrial disputes.* Richmond, Va.: Johns Hopkins Press.

Breen, V. I. 1943. *The United States Conciliation Service: Doctoral dissertation.* Catholic University: Washington, D.C.

Brommer, C., G. Buckingham, and S. Loeffler. 2002. Cooperative bargaining styles at FMCS: A movement toward choice. *Pepperdine Dispute Resolution Law Journal,* 2(3): 465–490.

Brooks, T. R. 1971. *Toil and trouble: A history of American labor.* New York: Delacorte.

Burner, D. 1979. *Herbert Hoover: The public life.* New York: Knopf.

Castel, A. 1979. *The presidency of Andrew Johnson.* Lawrence: Regents Press of Kansas.

Chalmers, W. E. 1948. The conciliation process. *Industrial and Labor Relations Review,* 3(3): 337–350.

Chamber of Commerce of the State of New York. 1913. *Earliest arbitration records: Committee minutes, 1779–1792.* New York: Press of the Chamber.

Ching, C. 1953. *Review and reflections: A half century of labor relations.* New York: B. C. Forbes & Sons.

Cicero, *Pro quinto roscio comoedo,* IV, 6–11.

Clifford, C. 1991. *Counsel to the president.* New York: Random House.

Cohen, R., and R. Westbrook. 2000. *Amarna diplomacy: The beginnings of international relations.* Baltimore: Johns Hopkins University Press.

Commager, H. 1982. *The blue and the gray.* New York: Fairfax Press.

Corbin, D. A. 1990. *The West Virginia mine wars.* Martinsburg, W. Va.: Appalachian Editions.

Costantino, C., and C. Merchant. 1996. *Designing conflict management systems: A guide to creating productive and healthy organizations.* San Francisco, Calif.: Jossey-Bass.

CRS Oral History. 2000 [http://www.colorado.edu/conflict/civil_rights/topics/0800.html].

Current, R. 1988. *Those terrible carpetbaggers: A reinterpretation.* New York: Oxford University Press.

Davies, N. 1997. *Europe: A history.* London: Pimlico.

Davies, W., and P. Fouracre, eds. 1986. *The settlement of disputes in early medieval Europe.* Cambridge, Eng.: Cambridge University Press.

Davis, A., and K. Porter. 1985. Dispute resolution: The Fourth "R." *Missouri Journal of Dispute Resolution,* 1985: 121–139.

Davis, H. 1984. Interview with the author, June 14.

Debax, H. 2001. Médiations et arbitrages dans l'aristocratie languedocienne aux XIe et XIIe siècles. In *Le règlement des conflits au moyen âge*. Paris: Sorbonne.

Dembart, L., and R. Kwartler. 1980. The Snoqualmie River conflict: Bringing mediation into environmental disputes. In R. Goldman, ed., *Roundtable justice*. Boulder, Colo.: Westview Press.

Deutsch, M. 1973. *The resolution of conflict: Constructive and destructive processes*. New Haven, Conn.: Yale University Press.

Dispute Resolution Journal. 1996. 70th Anniversary of the American Arbitration Association, *51*(2–3): 108–139.

Donahoo, R. 1973. Interview with M. Ross.

Dotson, D. 1980. Letter to the editor. *American Bar Association Journal*, July, p. 3.

Dublin International Arbitration Centre. 2004. History of arbitration in Ireland. [http://www.dublinarbitration.com].

Dunlop, J. T., and A. M. Zack. 1997. *Mediation and arbitration of employment disputes*. San Francisco: Jossey-Bass.

Ellis, J. 2000. *Founding brothers: The revolutionary generation*. New York: Vintage Books.

Esthus, R. A. 1988. *Double Eagle and Rising Sun: The Russians and the Japanese at Portsmouth in 1905*. Durham, N.C., and London: Duke University Press.

Fausold, M. L. 1985. *The presidency of Herbert C. Hoover*. Lawrence: University Press of Kansas.

Ferrell, R. H. 1988. *The presidency of Calvin Coolidge*. Lawrence: University Press of Kansas.

Fine, E. S., and E. S. Plapinger (eds). 1987. *ADR and the courts: A manual for judges and lawyers*. New York: Butterworth Legal Publishers.

Fisher, R., and W. Ury. 1981. *Getting to yes: Negotiating agreement without giving in*. Boston: Houghton Mifflin.

Folger, J., and J. Shubert. 1986. *Resolving student-initiated grievances in higher education: Dispute resolution procedures in a non-adversarial setting*. Washington, D.C.: National Institute for Dispute Resolution.

Follett, M. P. 1918. *The new state: Group organization the solution of popular government*. White Plains, N.Y.: Longman.

Follett, M. P. 1924. *Creative experience*. White Plains, N.Y.: Longman.

Follett, M. P. 1935. *Dynamic administration: The collected papers of Mary Parker Follett*. New York: HarperCollins.

Foner, E. 1988. *Reconstruction: America's unfinished revolution, 1863-1877*. New York: HarperCollins.

Franklin, B. 1964. *The autobiography of Benjamin Franklin*. New Haven, Conn.: Yale University Press.

Friedman, C. H. 1995. *Between management and labor: An oral history of arbitration*. New York: Twayne Publishers.

Friedman, L. 1988. *American law*. New York: Norton.

Furniss, E. S., and L. R. Guid. 1925. *Labor problems: A book of materials for their study*. New York: Houghton Mifflin.

Gaddis, J. L. 1997. *We now know: Rethinking Cold War history*. New York: Oxford Press.

Garb, P. 1996. Mediation in the Caucasus. In A. W. Wolfe and H. Yang, eds., *Anthropological contributions to conflict resolution*. Athens, Ga.: University of Georgia Press.

Gellhorn, W. 1967. *Ombudsmen and others*. Cambridge, Mass.: Harvard University Press.

Gibbs, J. L. 1963. The Kpelle moot. *Africa, 33*(1).

Gilbert, H. K. 1942. *The United States Department of Labor in the New Deal period: A doctoral dissertation*. Madison, Wis.: University of Wisconsin Press.

Girard, K., J. Rifkin, and A. Townley. 1985. *Peaceful persuasion: A guide to creating mediation dispute resolution programs on college campuses*. Amherst, Mass.: The Mediation Project, University of Massachusetts at Amherst.

Goldberg, A. 1995. Remarks by Goldberg's son at his father's posthumous admission to the U.S. Department of Labor Hall of Fame.

Goldberg, S., E. Green, and F. Sander. 1985. *Dispute resolution*. New York: Little, Brown.

Goldmann, R. 1980. *Roundtable justice*. Boulder, Colo.: Westview Press.

Goldstein, I. 1981. *Jewish justice and conciliation: History of the Jewish Conciliation Board of America, 1930–1968*. New York: KTAV Publishing.

Green, E. D. 1982. *Corporate dispute management: A manual of innovative corporate strategies for the avoidance of and resolution of legal disputes*. New York: Matthew Bender.

Greenwood, J. W. 1985. Interview with the author, Nov. 3.

Gregory, C. O. 1961. *Labor and the law*. New York: Norton.

Gross, D. 2002. A U.S. consensus council: State initiatives provide a model for building public consensus on national issues. *Dispute Resolution Magazine, 8*(2): 15–18.

Gross, J. A. 1981. *The reshaping of the National Labor Relations Board: National labor policy in transition, 1937–1947*. Albany: State University of New York Press.

Grossman, J. 1973. *The Department of Labor*. New York: Praeger.

Hall, H. (ed.). 1930. *Select cases concerning the law merchant*, A.D. *1239–1633*. London: Bernard Quaritch.

Harden, D. 1963. *The Phoenicians*. London: Thames and Hudson.

Harrell, H. C. 1936. Public arbitration in Athenian law. *University of Missouri Studies, 11*: 1–42.

Hartfield, E. 1984. Interview with the author, Apr. 25.

Haughton, R. 1983. Analyzing the explosion. In *Ethical issues in dispute resolution: Proceedings of the SPIDR Eleventh Annual Conference.* Washington, D.C.: SPIDR.

Haynes, J. 1981. *Divorce mediation: A practical guide for therapists and counselors.* New York: Springer.

Haynes, J. 1997. *The fundamentals of family mediation.* Albany: State University of New York Press.

Hechler, E. 1982. *Working with Truman: A personal memoir of the White House Years.* New York: Putnam.

Hedges, C. 2002. War is a force that gives us meaning. New York: Anchor Books.

Helsby, R. 1973. History of Society of Professionals in Dispute Resolution: Beginning Concepts and Formulation. Unpublished.

Helsby, R. 1991. Interview with the author, October 18.

Hezel, F. X. 1995. *Strangers in their own land: A century of colonial rule in the Caroline and Marshall Islands.* Honolulu: University of Hawai'i Press.

Hobbs, R. W. 1979. *The myth of victory: What is victory in war?* Boulder, Colo.: Westview Press.

Holbrooke, R. 1998. *To end a war.* New York: Random House.

Horvitz, W. 1986. Interview with the author, Jan. 30, Feb. 21 and 25, June 30, and July 3.

Howarth, P. 2001. *Attila, king of the Huns: Man and myth.* New York: Carroll & Graf.

Independent Chronicle. 1804. *Letter to the Legislature of Massachusetts: Remarks on the Judiciary.* Boston: Jan. 30, 1804.

Jackson, E. 1953. *Meeting of the minds: A way to peace through mediation.* New York: McGraw-Hill.

Jia, W. 2002. Chinese mediation and its cultural foundation. In G. Chen and R. Ma, eds., *Chinese conflict management and resolution.* Norwood, N.J.: Ablex Publishing.

Johnson, R. G. 1999. *Negotiating the Dayton Peace Accords through digital maps.* [http://www.usip.org/virtualdiplomacy/publications/reports/rjohnson-ISA99.html].

Kaltenborn, H. S. 1943. *Governmental adjustment of labor disputes.* Chicago: Foundation Press.

Kellor, F. 1948. *American arbitration: Its history, function and achievements.* New York: HarperCollins.

Kelly, A. 1955. *The American Constitution: Its origins and development.* New York: Norton.

Kheel, T. W. 1999. *The keys to conflict resolution: Proven methods of resolving disputes voluntarily.* New York: Four Walls Eight Windows.

Kheel, T. W. 2001. Interview with the author, May 4.

Kirkham, J. 1984. Interview with the author, Aug. 11.

Kirkham, J. 1985. Interview with the author, Nov. 12.

Klein, P. 1962. *President James Buchanan: A biography.* University Park: Pennsylvania University Press.

Knight, A. 1996. *The life of the law*. New York: Crown.

Kohn, A. 1986. *No contest: The case against competition*. Boston: Houghton Mifflin.

Kolb, D. M. 1983. *The mediators*. Cambridge, Mass.: MIT Press.

Kressel, K., and D. G. Pruitt, eds. 1989. *Mediation research: The process and effectiveness of third-party intervention*. San Francisco: Jossey-Bass.

Kubey, C. 1991. *You don't always need a lawyer: How to resolve your legal disputes without costly litigation*. New York: Consumer Reports Books.

Laue, J. H. 1970. Interview with the author, July 9.

Laue, J. H., and G. W. Cormick. 1973. *Third party intervention in community conflict: Definitions, perspectives and experience*. St. Louis, Mo.: Social Science Institute, Washington University.

LaValley, C. 1985. Interview with the author, July 5.

Lee, N. 1987. Interview with the author, Mar. 7.

Lee, N. 1995. Interview with the author, Dec. 13.

Levy, J. E. 1975. *Cesar Chavez: Autobiography of la Causa*. New York: Norton.

Lichtenstein, N. 1997. *Walter Reuther: The most dangerous man in Detroit*. Chicago: University of Illinois Press.

Link, A. S. 1963. *Woodrow Wilson: A brief biography*. Cleveland, Ohio: World Publishing Co.

Liptak, A. 2003. U.S. suits multiply, but fewer ever get to trial, study says. *New York Times*, Dec. 14.

Lombardi, J. 1942. *Labor's voice in the cabinet: A history of the Department of Labor from its origin to 1921*. New York: Columbia University Press.

Lounsbury, T. 1883. *James Fenimore Cooper*. Boston: Houghton Mifflin.

Lukas, J. A. 1997. *Big trouble: A murder in a small western town sets off a struggle for the soul of America*. New York: Simon & Schuster.

MacMillan, M. 2001. *Paris 1919: Six months that changed the world*. New York: Random House.

Maggiolo, W. 1971. *Techniques of mediation in labor disputes*. New York: Oceana Publications.

Maggiolo, W., with J. T. Barrett. 1985. *Techniques of mediation*. New York: Oceana Publications.

Marks, J. B., E. J. Johnson, and P. L. Szanton. 1984. *Dispute resolution in America: Processes in evolution*. Washington, D.C.: National Institute for Dispute Resolution.

Martin, G. W. 1976. *Madam secretary: Frances Perkins*. Boston: Houghton Mifflin.

Matthews, C. 1996. *Kennedy and Nixon: The rivalry that shaped postwar America*. New York: Simon & Schuster.

McCoy, D. R. 1967. *Calvin Coolidge: The quiet president*. New York: Macmillan.

McCullough, D. 2001. *John Adams*. New York: Simon & Schuster.

McCutchen, G. 1986. Interview with the author, Jan. 30 and Feb. 26.

Menkel-Meadow, C. 2003. *Dispute processing and conflict resolution*. Burlington, Vt.: Ashgate Publishing.

Moffett, K. 1986. Interview with the author, July 11.

Mohr, L. H. 1979. *Frances Perkins: That woman in FDR's cabinet*. Boston: North River Press.

Moore, C. 1986. *The mediation process: Practical strategies for resolving conflict*. San Francisco: Jossey-Bass.

Moran, W. L. 1992. *The Amarna letters*. Baltimore, Md.: Johns Hopkins University Press.

Moussalli, A. 1997. An Islamic model for political conflict resolution: Tahkim (arbitration). In P. Salem (ed.), *Conflict resolution in the Arab world: Selected essays*. Beirut: American University of Beirut.

Munn-Rankin, J. M. 1956. Diplomacy in western Asia in the early second millennium, B.C. *Iraq*, 38: 68–110.

Murray, J. S., A. S. Rau, and E. F. Sherman. 1996. *Mediation and other non-binding ADR processes*. Westbury, NY.: Foundation Press.

National Academy of Arbitrators Oral History Project. 1982. The early days of labor, as recalled by G. Allan Dash, Sylvester Garrett, John Day Larkin, Harry Platt, Ralph T. Seward, and William Simkin. Ann Arbor, Mich.: National Academy of Arbitrators Office of Secretary, Fall.

Nelson, J. L. 1986. Dispute settlement in Carolingian West Francia. In W. Davies and P. Fouracre, eds., *The settlement of disputes in early medieval Europe*. Cambridge, Eng.: Cambridge University Press.

Nelson, W. E. 1981. *Dispute and conflict resolution in Plymouth County, Massachusetts, 1725–1825*. Chapel Hill: University of North Carolina Press.

Nolan, D. R., and R. I. Abrams. 1983. American arbitration: The early years. *University of Florida Law Review*, Vol. xxxv, No. 3, Summer, pp. 373–421.

Norris, G. W. 1945. *Fighting liberal: The autobiography of George W. Norris*. New York: McMillan.

Northrupt, H. R. 1966. *Compulsory arbitration and government intervention in labor disputes*. Washington, D.C.: Labor Policy Association.

O'Connell, M. J. 1986. Interview with the author, July 5.

Popular, J. 1976. Labor-management relations: U.S. mediators try to build common objectives. In *World of Work*, Vol. 1, Sept., pp. 1–3.

Popular, J. 1985. Interview with the author, Nov. 11 and 12.

Power, J. 1986. Interview with the author, Feb. 24.

President's National Labor-Management Conference. 1945. Bulletin No. 77. Washington, D.C.: U.S. Department of Labor, Division of Labor Standards.

Pringle, H. F. 1956. *Theodore Roosevelt*. Old Saybrook, Conn.: Konecky and Konecky.

Raskin, A. H. 1989. Cyrus S. Ching: Pioneer in industrial peacemaking. *Monthly Labor Review*, Aug., pp. 22–35.

Rayback, J. G. 1959. *A history of American labor*. Old Tappan, N.J.: Macmillan.

Rehmus, C. 1976. *The Railway Labor Act at fifty: Collective bargaining in the railroad and airline industries*. Washington, D.C.: Government Printing Office.

Rehmus, C. 1984. *The National Mediation Board at fifty: Its impact on railroad and airline labor disputes*. Washington, D.C.: National Mediation Board.

Rehmus, C. 1986. Interview with the author, Apr. 18.

Reilly, R. 1988. Interview with the author, May 9.

Remini, R. V. 1991. *Henry Clay: Statesman for the union*. New York: Norton.

Rhodes, J. 1895. *History of the United States from the compromise of 1850*. New York: HarperCollins.

Russell, F. 1968. *The shadow of Blooming Grove: Warren G. Harding in his times*. New York: McGraw-Hill.

Salem, P. 1997. *Conflict resolution in the Arab world: Selected essays*. Beirut, Lebanon: American University Beirut.

Salrach, J. M. 2001. Les modalités du règlement des conflits en Catalogne aux XIe et XIIe siècles. In *Le règlement des conflits au moyen âge*. Paris: Sorbonne.

Scearce, J. F. 1976. Report on the 1976 Primary and General Election of the Oglala Sioux Tribe, Pine Ridge Indian Reservation, South Dakota. Federal Mediation and Conciliation, Feb.

Schlesinger, A. M. 1979. Hoover makes a comeback. *New York Review of Books*, Mar. 8, p. 11.

Schlesinger, A. M., and F. L. Israel. 1971. *History of presidential elections: 1789–1968*. New York: McGraw-Hill.

Schultz, L. 1985. Interview with the author, May 2.

Scott, G. 1992. *Ties of common blood: A history of Maine's boundary dispute with Great Britain*. Bowie, Md.: Heritage Books.

Seldon, G. 1974. Interview with Martha Ross.

Shils, E. B., W. J. Gershenfeld, B. Ingster, and W. M. Weinburg. 1979. *Industrial peacemaker: George W. Taylor's contributions to collective bargaining*. Philadelphia: University of Pennsylvania.

Simkin, W. E. 1971. *Mediation and the dynamics of collective bargaining*. Washington, D.C.: Bureau of National Affairs.

Simkin, W. E. 1974. Interview with M. Ross, Oct. 8.

Simmons, M. 1968. *Spanish government in New Mexico*. Albuquerque: University of New Mexico Press.

Simpson, B. 1998. *The Reconstruction presidents*. Lawrence: University Press of Kansas.

Singer, L. R. 1990. *Settling disputes: Conflict resolution in business, families, and the legal system*. San Francisco: Westview Press.

Smith, C. D., ed. 1985. *The hundred percent challenge: Building a national institute of peace*. Washington, D.C.: Seven Lock Press.

Smith, P. 1985. *A people's history of the progressive era and World War I: America enters the world*. New York: McGraw-Hill.

Smith, P. 1987. *A people's history of the 1920s and the New Deal: Redeeming the time*. New York: McGraw-Hill.

Sontag, D. 2001. And yet so far: Quest for Mideast peace: How and why it failed. *New York Times,* July 26.

Srodes, J. 2002. *Franklin: The essential founding father.* Washington, D.C.: Regnery.

Steelman, J. R. 1975. Interview with M. Ross.

Stepp, J., and J. T. Barrett. 1990. New theories on negotiations and dispute resolution, and the changing role of mediation. In *Alternative Dispute Resolution Report.* Washington, D.C.: Bureau of National Affairs.

Susskind, L., and J. Cruikshank. 1987. *Breaking the impasse: Consensual approaches to resolving public disputes.* New York: Basic Books.

Tanner, L. D., and J. T. Barrett. 1986. Bargaining in the health care industry: A study revisited. In *IRRA 39th Annual Proceedings.* Madison, Wis.: University of Wisconsin.

Tanzman, D. S. 1986. Interview with the author, Nov. 23.

Taylor, G. W. 1948. *Government regulation of industrial relations.* New York: Prentice-Hall.

Thernstrom, M. 2003. Untying the knot. *New York Times,* Nov. 24.

Tower, L. 1988. Interview with the author, Sept. 23.

Trani, E. P. 1977. *The presidency of Warren Harding.* Lawrence: University Press of Kansas.

Tuleja, T. 1992. *American history in one hundred nutshells.* New York: Fawcett, 1992.

Updegraff, C., and W. McCoy. 1946. *Arbitration of labor disputes.* Washington, D.C.: Bureau of National Affairs.

Updike, J. 1992. *Memories of the Ford administration.* New York: Knopf.

Ury, W. L. 2002. The power of the "third side": Community roles in conflict resolution. In W. L. Ury, ed., *Must we fight? From the battlefield to the schoolyard—A new perspective on violent conflict and its prevention.* San Francisco: Jossey-Bass.

Ury, W. L., J. Brett, and S. Goldberg. 1988. *Getting disputes resolved: Designing systems to cut the cost of conflict.* San Francisco: Jossey-Bass.

U.S. Department of Labor. 1914. Annual Report of the Secretary of Labor. Washington, D.C.: U.S. Department of Labor.

Usery, W. J. 1974. Interview with S. C. Shannon and J. Grossman.

Usery, W. J. 1975. Interview with M. Ross.

Van Deusen, G. G. 1937. *The life of Henry Clay.* New York: Little, Brown.

Van Doren, C. 1938. *Benjamin Franklin.* New York: Viking Press.

Walton, R. E., and R. B. McKersie. 1965. *A behavioral theory of labor negotiations: An analysis of a social interaction system.* New York: McGraw-Hill.

Walton, R. E., R. B. McKersie, and J. E. Cutcher-Gershenfeld. 1994. *Strategic negotiations: A theory of change in labor-management relations.* Boston: Harvard Business School Press.

Warren, E. L. 1948. The conciliation service: V-J Day to Taft-Hartley. *Industrial and Labor Relations Review,* 1(3): 351–362.

Washington, G. 1799. Last Will and Testmont. The Claremont Institute [www.pbs.org/georgewashington/milestone/free_slaves_read.html].

Washington, G. 1800. *The Washingtoniana: Containing a sketch of the life and death of the late Gen. George Washington, with a collection of elegant eulogies, orations, poems, etc.* Petersburg, Va.: Blandford Press.

Watson-Geogeo, K. A., and G. M. White. 1990. *Disentangling: Conflict discourses in Pacific societies.* Palo Alto, Calif.: Stanford University Press.

Wheeler, H. N. 1985. *Industrial conflict: An integrative theory.* Columbia, S.C.: University of South Carolina Press.

Wilke, J. R. 2000. Microsoft suit mediator rues state antitrust role. *Wall Street Journal*, Sept. 19.

Wilke, J. R. 2001. Hard drive: Negotiating all night, tenacious Microsoft won many loopholes. *Wall Street Journal*, Nov. 9, p. A1.

Wilke, J. R., and R. Blumenthal. 2000. Microsoft settlement efforts collapse: Software firm has time to solidify its position on Internet. *Wall Street Journal*, Apr. 3.

Wills, G. 2002. *James Madison.* New York: Holt.

Wilson, J. 1984. Interview with the author, Aug. 12.

Winik, J. 2001. *Apr. 1865: The month that saved America.* New York: HarperCollins.

Wise, H. 1881. *Seven decades of the Union: A memoir of John Tyler.* Richmond, Va.: J. W. Randolph and English.

Witte, E. E. 1952. *Historical survey of labor arbitration.* Philadelphia: University of Pennsylvania Press.

Wolfe, A. W., and H. Yang. 1996. *Anthropological contributions to conflict resolution.* Athens, Ga.: University of Georgia Press.

Young, H. A. 1982. The causes of industrial peace revisited: The case of RBO. *Human Resources Management*, 21(2–3): 50–57.

Zubrod, D. 2001. The history of maritime arbitration in New York. *The Arbitrator*, 32(2): 2.

About the Authors

Jerome T. Barrett began his mediation career in the early 1960s as a Minnesota State labor conciliator in St. Paul, following several years with the National Labor Relations Board in Detroit. He continued his mediation career with the Federal Mediation and Conciliation Service (FMCS) in Washington, D.C., Chicago, and Milwaukee. By the late 1960s, as campus and community violence gained everyone's attention, he published several articles explaining how civil rights and antiwar disputants could use the labor-management model to resolve their disputes peacefully.

In 1969, after five years as a federal mediator, he joined the newly created National Center for Dispute Settlement to mediate civil rights, campus, and community disputes.

As union organizing of public employees increased in the early 1970s, Barrett joined the Department of Labor to head a new office providing advice to state and local governments and their unions on establishing procedures for resolving disputes. During that period, he wrote extensively about that rapidly developing field. In 1973, he returned to FMCS to head the newly created Office of Technical Assistance to manage mediator training, preventive mediation, and the start of FMCS work outside the labor-management field.

In the early 1980s, he left FMCS to teach labor relations at Northern Kentucky University and complete his doctoral degree in human resource development with a dissertation on the history of joint labor-management training with a focus on FMCS and its predecessor, the U.S. Conciliation Service. While teaching, Barrett began an arbitration practice and did overseas consulting on labor relations and ADR. He would eventually work in twenty-four countries. His other education includes a B.A. from the College of St. Thomas and an M.A. from the University of Minnesota.

In the mid-1980s, he returned to the Department of Labor's Bureau of Labor Management and Cooperative Programs, where he developed the Partners in Change program with an FMCS colleague. He also created an interest-based bargaining program called P.A.S.T. and an accompanying training program, which he has since used hundreds of times. He introduced FMCS mediators to interest-based negotiations (IBN) with his P.A.S.T. training model, helping to start what is now an extensive FMCS program.

Since leaving the government in 1988, Barrett has written, arbitrated, trained, and facilitated. He has written two books on IBN and produced an IBN video with the University of Wisconsin. He served as historian of the Society of Professionals in Dispute Resolution and FMCS. For the past three years, he has written a history column for the *ACResolution* quarterly magazine. For the past six years, he has been an elected school board member in Falls Church, Virginia, where he lives with his wife, Rose. They have five sons and five grandchildren.

Joseph P. Barrett is a senior special writer for Page One at the *Wall Street Journal*. In seventeen years as a reporter and editor, he has worked in New York City, Brussels, Detroit, and Hampton, Virginia, covering everything from a session of the Virginia General Assembly to noisy toilets and the men who love them. He received a B.A. in English literature from the College of William and Mary and a master's of philosophy in American studies from New York University. He lives in Brooklyn with his wife, Lori; their children, Henry and Stella; and a big dog named Mucho.

Index